A 52-Week Experiment

Project 2 Craigs

Craig Cutler | Craig Frazier

goff BOOKS

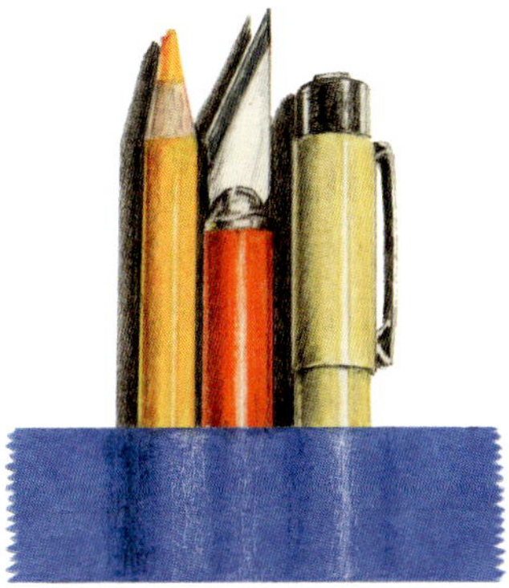

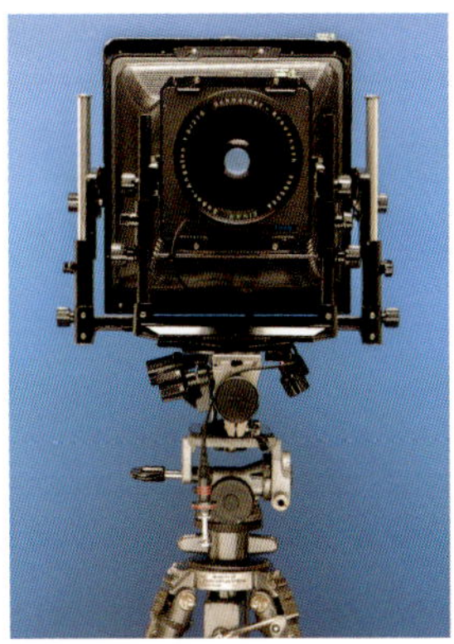

Contents

Foreword by Joe Morse

Illustrator, Professor, Faculty of Animation, Arts & Design, Sheridan College, Ontario

"This project is rooted in the hand, the eye, and lived experience. It is not a return to some long-lost craft, it is an affirmation of the essential need for process, where discovery is well-fed curiosity, and meaning emerges through making."

—Joe Morse

This book is a compilation of a collaborative project that offered two distinct visions—one armed with pencil, pen, brush, and paper, the other with lens, light, and the physical world. Over the course of 52 weeks, the efforts of Craig Cutler and Craig Frazier converged into something more than just shared images—a celebration of the art of visual dialogue.

In a world saturated with fleeting imagery—where content is consumed in seconds and forgotten just as quickly—these weekly visual pairings offered a pause in the endless scroll. They called out for attention, welcomed interpretation, and rewarded reflection. The concept behind this visual conversation had strict rules: one word per week chosen at random, and no talking. Let the dialogue speak in the images. The result is a masterclass in creative problem-solving, where discipline and exploration inspire invention.

At the outset, I don't think the two Craigs fully knew what they were getting themselves into. The early weeks feel like two prizefighters circling, cautiously measuring the terrain of the posted results. The images are stunning, but both of them know how formidable the other's work is, and finding your footing in a new landscape can take time. But by week four, something shifts. They're given a noun with a diverse visual quality, and it acts as a key that unlocks the vault of their ideas. From that point forward, the project begins to speak with a collective chemistry.

In this book, you will see brilliant examples of two fertile imaginations honed by decades of practice and informed by the rich history of visual art and graphic communication. But more than that, you'll see process. The discarded sketches, the failed experiments, the mistakes, and the paths abandoned are the critical underpinnings that have built the final image. The finished pieces are hard-earned through experienced eyes looking for visual opportunities, an iterative discipline, and a weekly deadline that never wavered.

One of this book's most brilliant decisions is the omission of the weekly prompt on the image pages. The curious can read the word in the Artists' Notes pages. Without it, the viewer is free to enter without direction, to discover their own stories in the collision of the images. When two nouns collide, they result in a synthesis. Each week, new combinations emerge, narratives are created, and connections are made. One of my early favorites is week 12. Craig Frazier—a master of visual economy—offers an image with the utmost simplicity, which he guesses will sharpen the contrast between their contributions. Craig Cutler, with his unerring eye for the design of form and figure/ground, offers a glass construct of clarity and elegance. The resulting image is a perfect melding of their singular way of seeing. Amidst so many standout pairings, week 31 is another highlight—both artists distill their ideas to the essential. Cutler's flower, a study in silhouette and absence, and Frazier's portrait pared to its expressive detail.

Project 2 Craigs rewards repeat viewing, as each time I explore this archive, it conjures new insights.

This project is not just a record of a year of shared images; it's a sustained conversation between mediums, thinking, and the unique approach each Craig brings to their work. It reminds us that making images is not just about output, but about intention, attention, and response. At a time when image-making is increasingly effortless, when a prompt typed in seconds can yield a dozen authorless results in minutes, *Project 2 Craigs* is a powerful statement of visual thinking and embodied engagement with materials. This project is rooted in the hand, the eye, and lived experience. It is not a return to some long-lost craft; it is an affirmation of the essential need for process, where discovery is well-fed curiosity, and meaning emerges through making. It is a potent reminder of what human creativity does best, transforming limitations into the limitless.

This book is both an inspiration and an invitation to look more closely, to make with purpose, and to celebrate the irreplaceable voice of the eye and human hand.

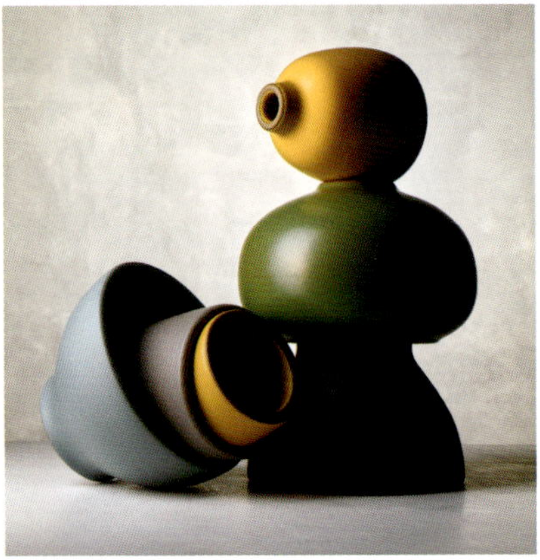

The Story

Introduction by Craig Frazier

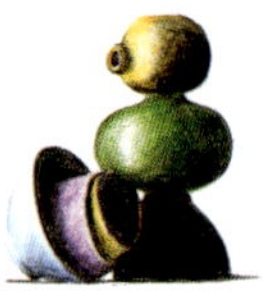
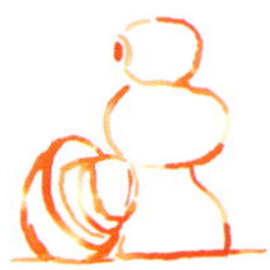
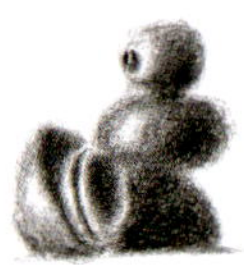
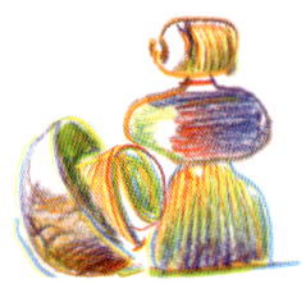
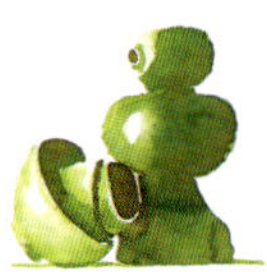
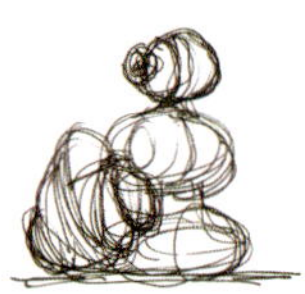
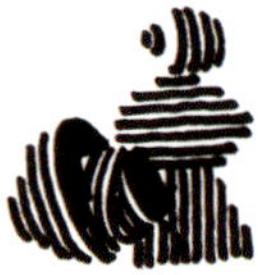
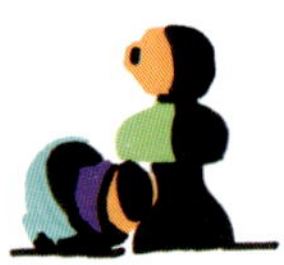
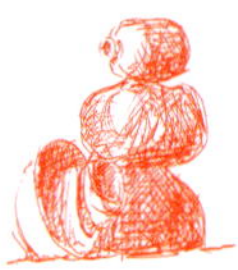
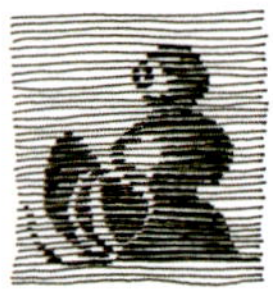

In March 2024, I hired Craig Cutler for a product shoot for a winery client. We had never met or worked together before.

Rather than producing the expected lifestyle shots with flowers, cheese, and half-full glasses of wine, I wanted simplicity—compositions of single bottles amidst Heath Ceramics' renowned colorful bowls and vases. I envisioned classic still lifes, like the photographs of Irving Penn or paintings by Giorgio Morandi—a perfect Craig Cutler assignment. We spoke over the phone about my loose vision. He was enthusiastic about the project despite my scant budget. It wouldn't afford me to travel from San Francisco to Los Angeles to art direct the shoot—something I customarily do. My absence would turn out to be a gift.

I shipped Craig a dozen vases, bowls, and a case of wine. Days later, he emailed me eight stunning photographs with ceramics playfully composed adjacent to each bottle—bowls inside bowls, supporting an upside-down vase, leaning on the bottle—each staged in sublime chiaroscuro.

Craig also created a series of still lifes featuring only the ceramics. These photographs were the product of a man with an eye and a lifetime of chops behind a camera. He didn't need direction; he needed to be left alone.

I believe in that same solitude. I have spent the last thirty years illustrating for clients all over the world—every drawing out of my own vision, not the concept of an art director. I want to own the ideas I execute—so does Craig Cutler.

Intrigued by one of Craig's "stacked bowls" images, I started sketching one morning while eating my breakfast. I tested myself to see how many styles I could employ to reimagine his composition. When I reached thirty, I sent them to Craig. He called the next day and said, "We've got to do a project together."

The experiment.

We conceived an experiment to test our mutual penchant for ideas during that phone call. How would we perform without art direction and the obligatory trappings of commercial work? Our premise was simple: we would receive the same assignment and deadline and execute it without conference. To give our experiment breadth, we decided on 52* one-week assignments. Adding a one-year time frame would allow us to get some practice and rhythm—and maybe break some new ground. The pace would force quick decisions. Our only constraints would be self-imposed. As we said from the beginning, "We have no idea what we are doing."

We made the weekly assignments simple: one word, a prompt to illustrate and photograph it in any way we wanted. Craig and I each came up with a list of 52 words and sent them to my son's girlfriend. Every week, she randomly drew a word from a Pyrex cup and emailed us our assignment. At the end of the week, we placed our images side-by-side, posted them to our website, and received a new word: no conversation allowed.

Craig and I spoke few words, except for the occasional text. You see, we have never met in person. Months into the project, we were both smitten with the unfolding creative alchemy—we knew we couldn't meet and risk jinxing the magic. In keeping with that theme, we wrote everything in this book independently, without conference or reading the other's words.

After the project had officially ended, we continued to suspend our first meeting. In fact, Craig staged and directed my portrait for this book and left the click of the shutter in his wife's able hands. We intend to finally meet when we present our story at the AIGA National Design Conference in October 2025. We also plan to toast our grand experiment—and a new comradeship.

**We continued the project for an additional four weeks for a total of 56—all included in this book.*

1

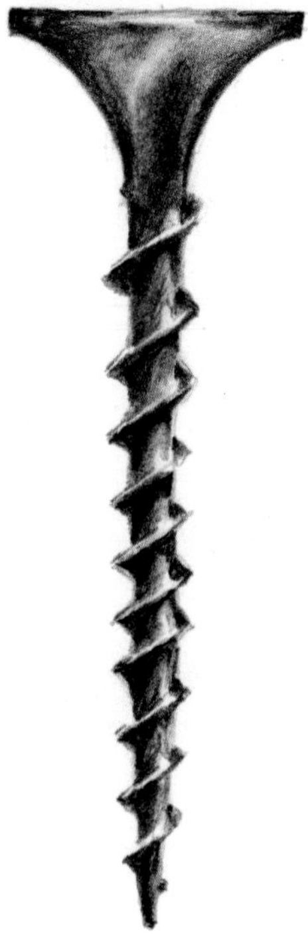

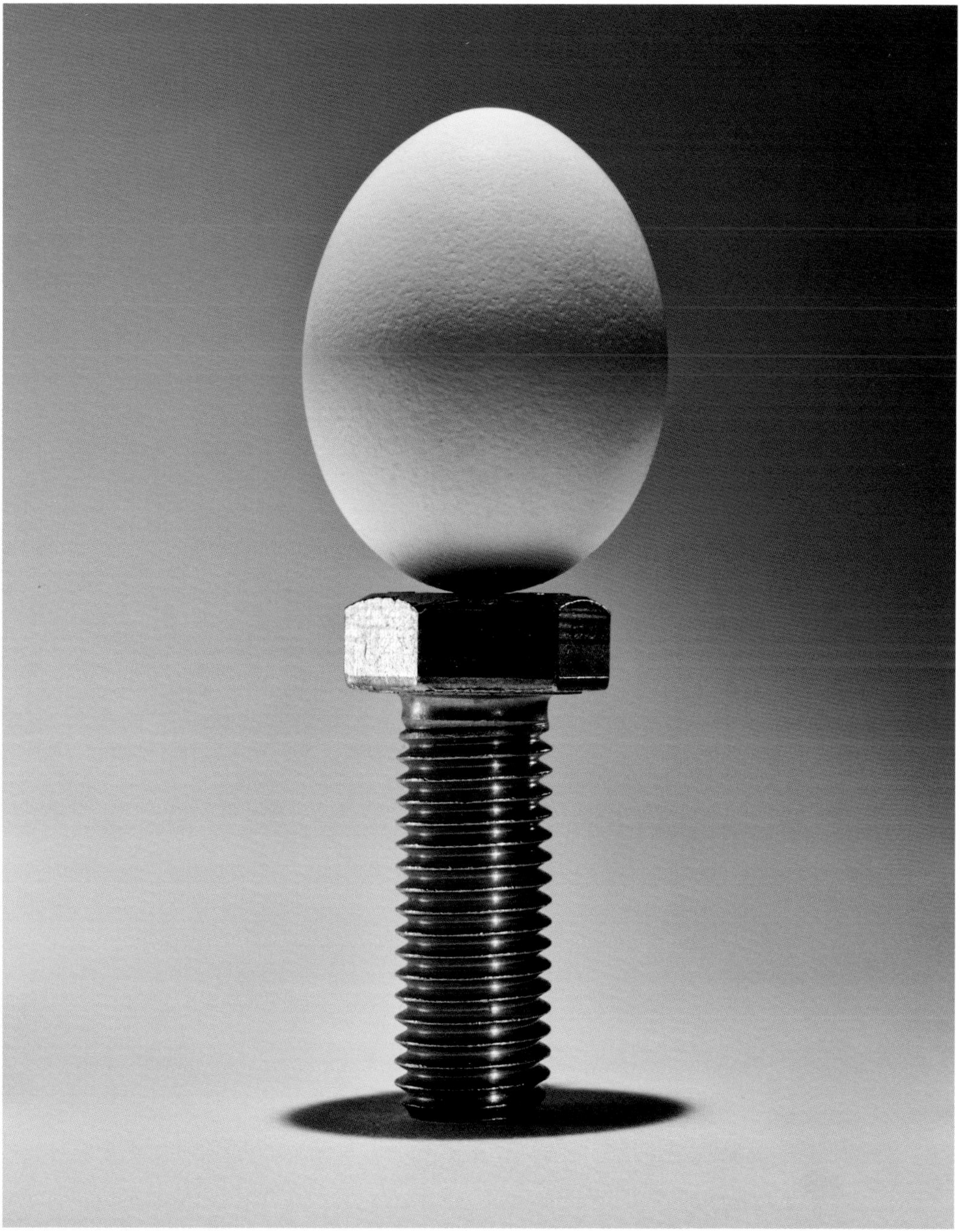

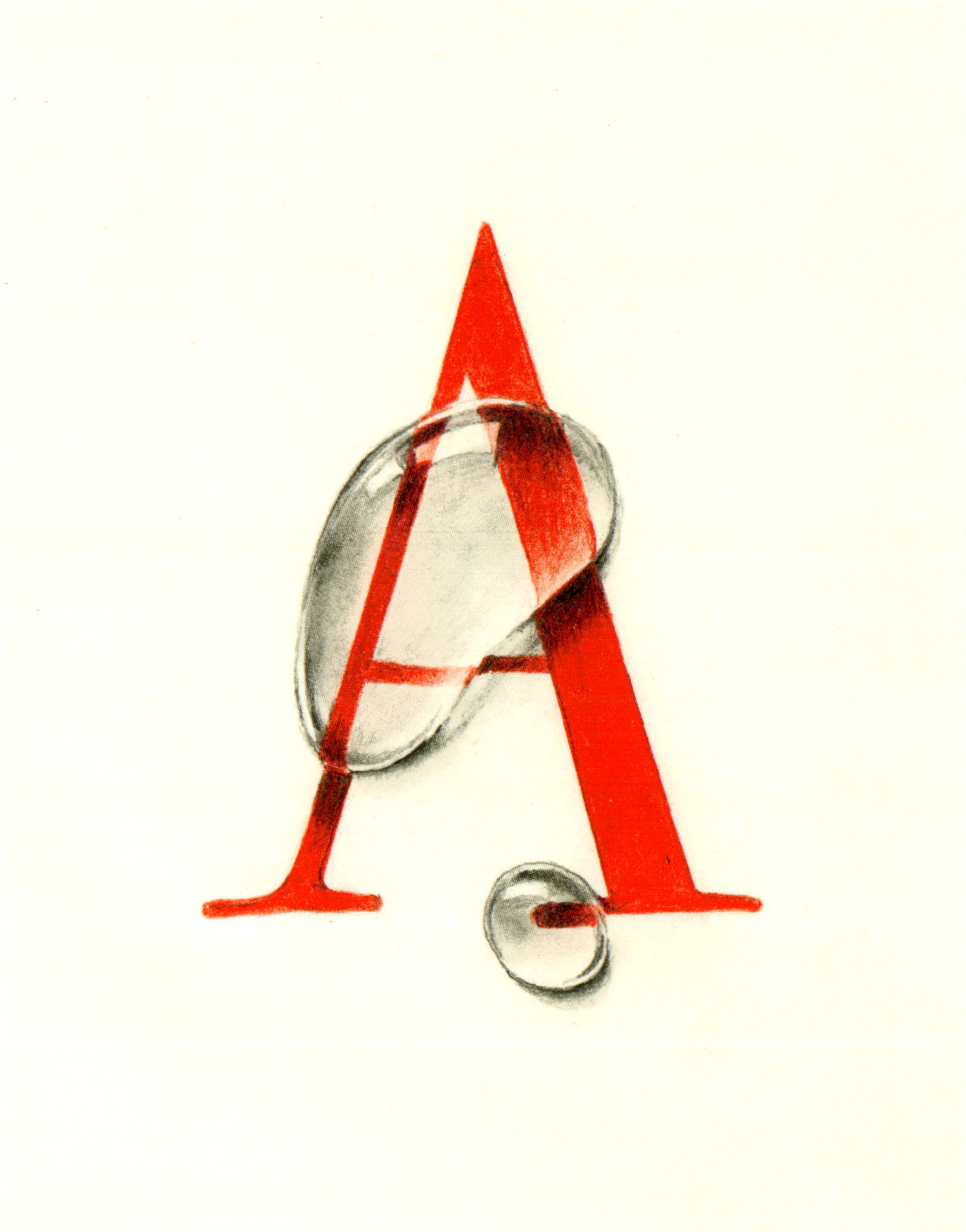

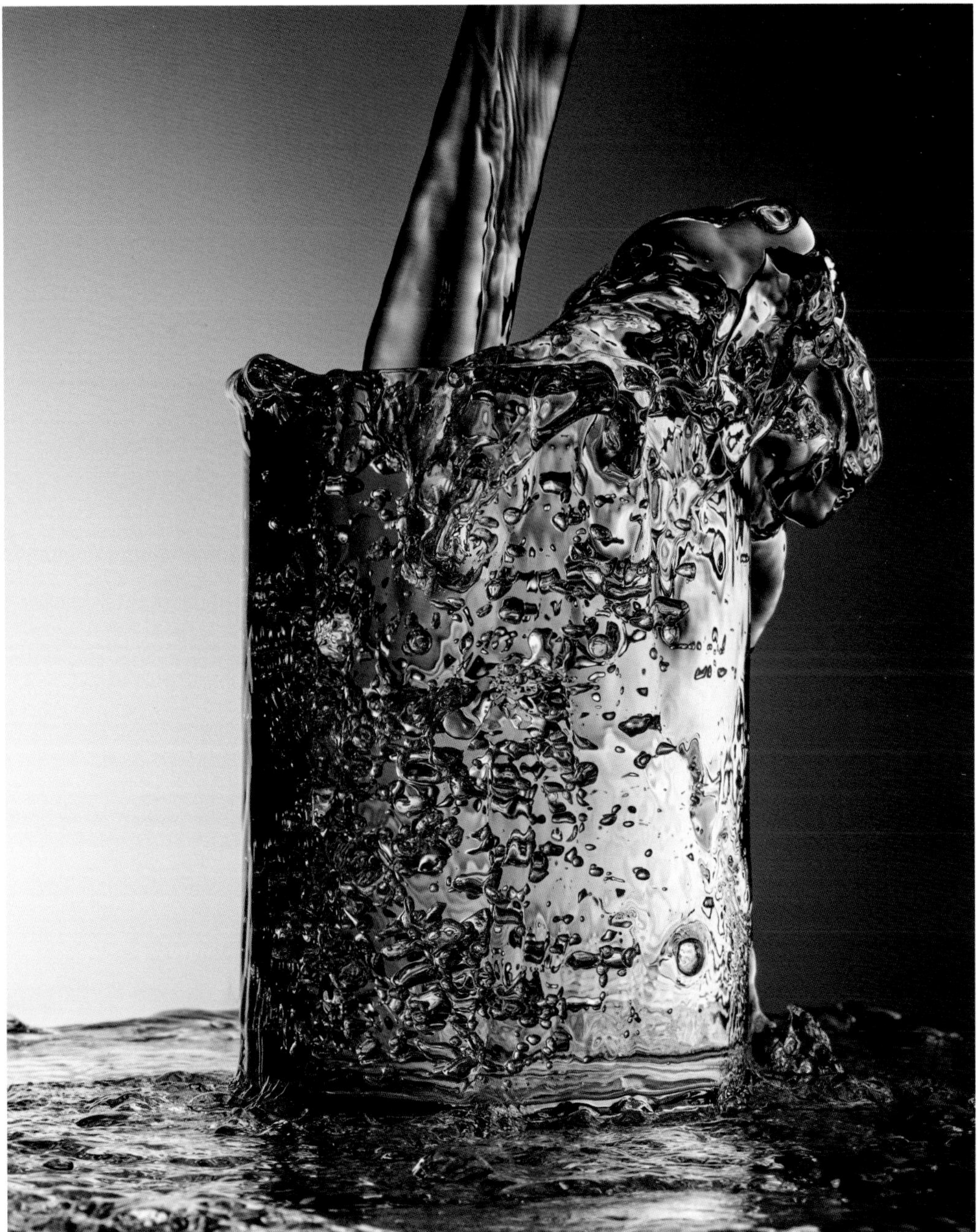

3

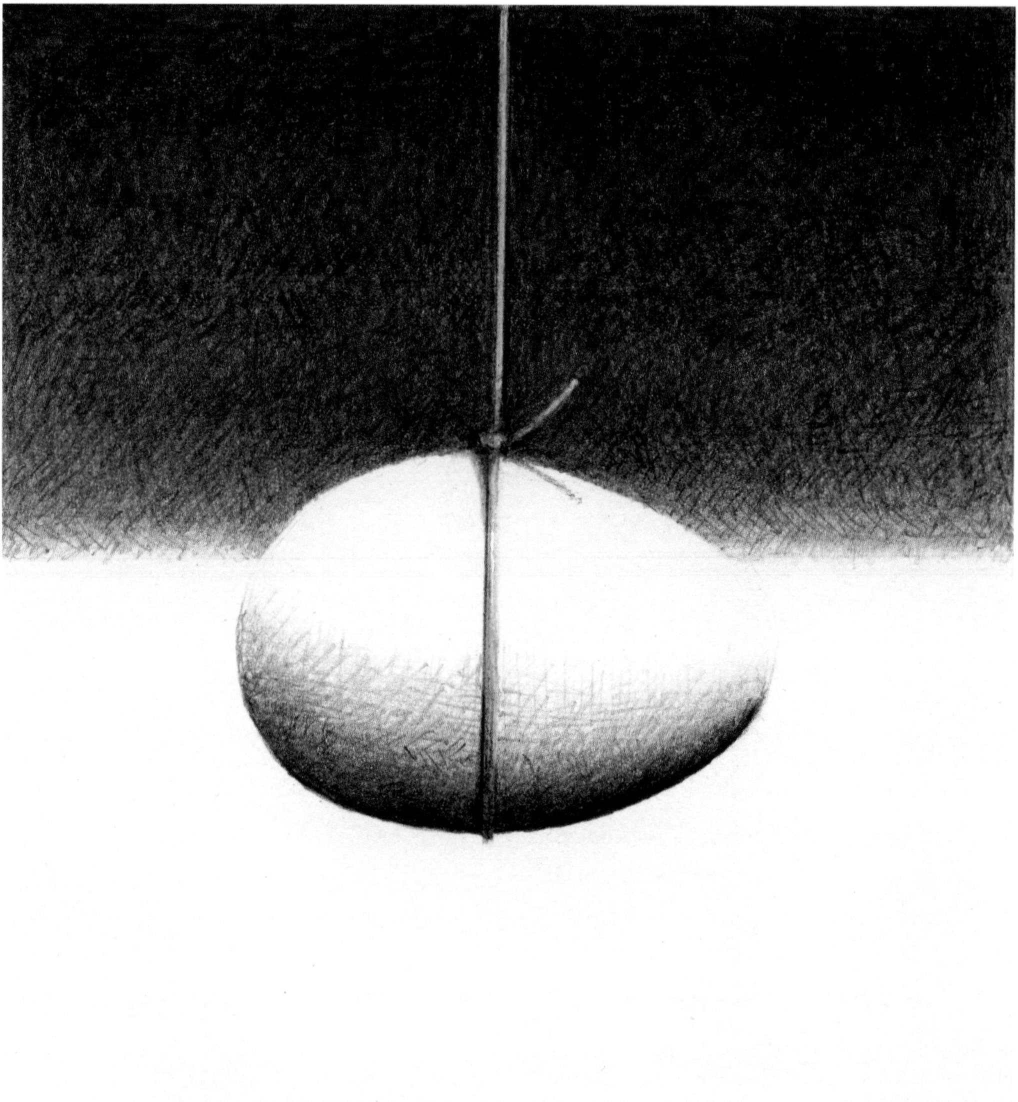

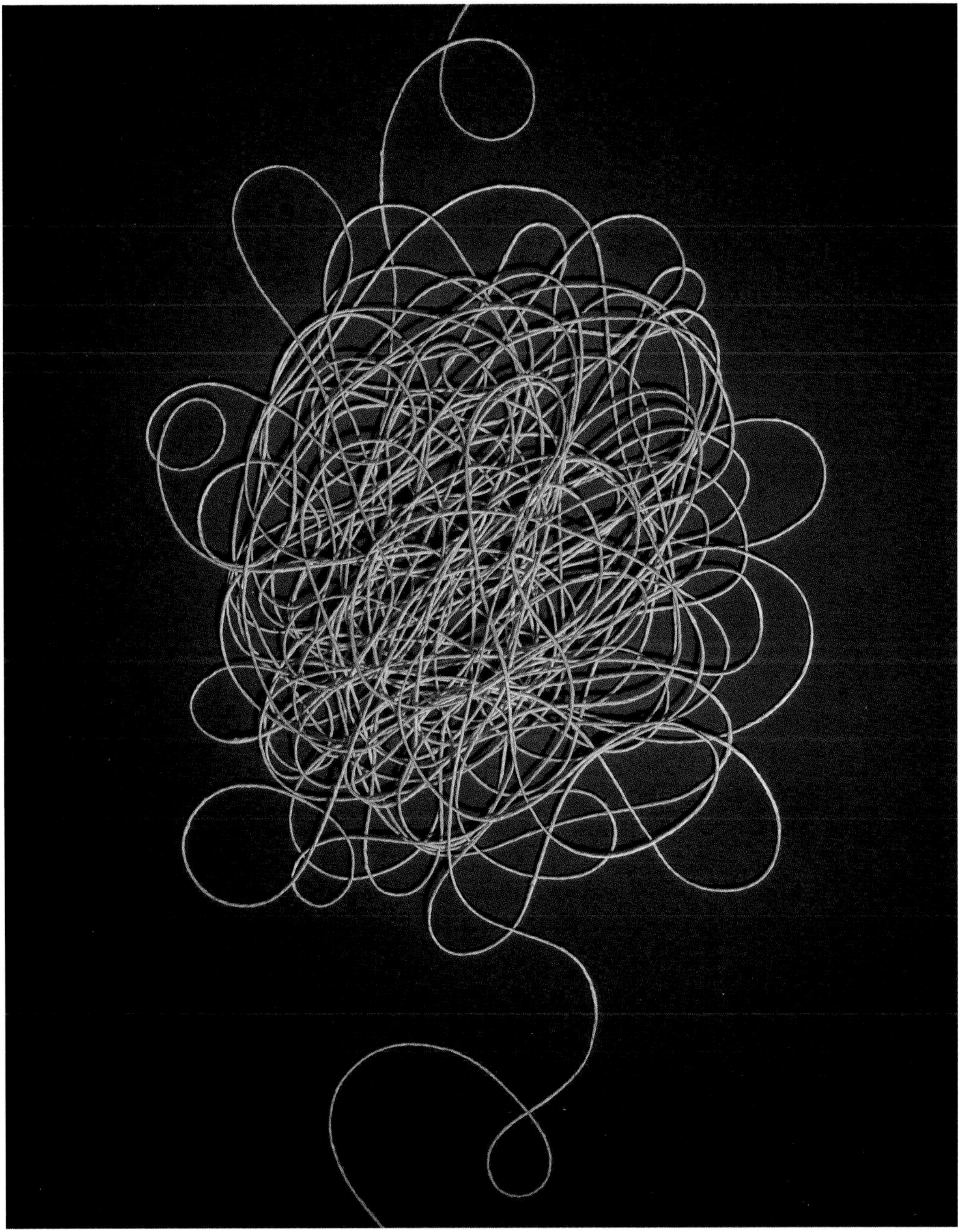

4

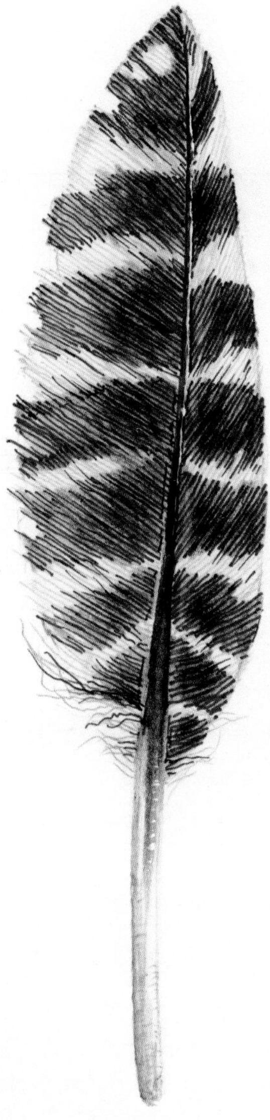

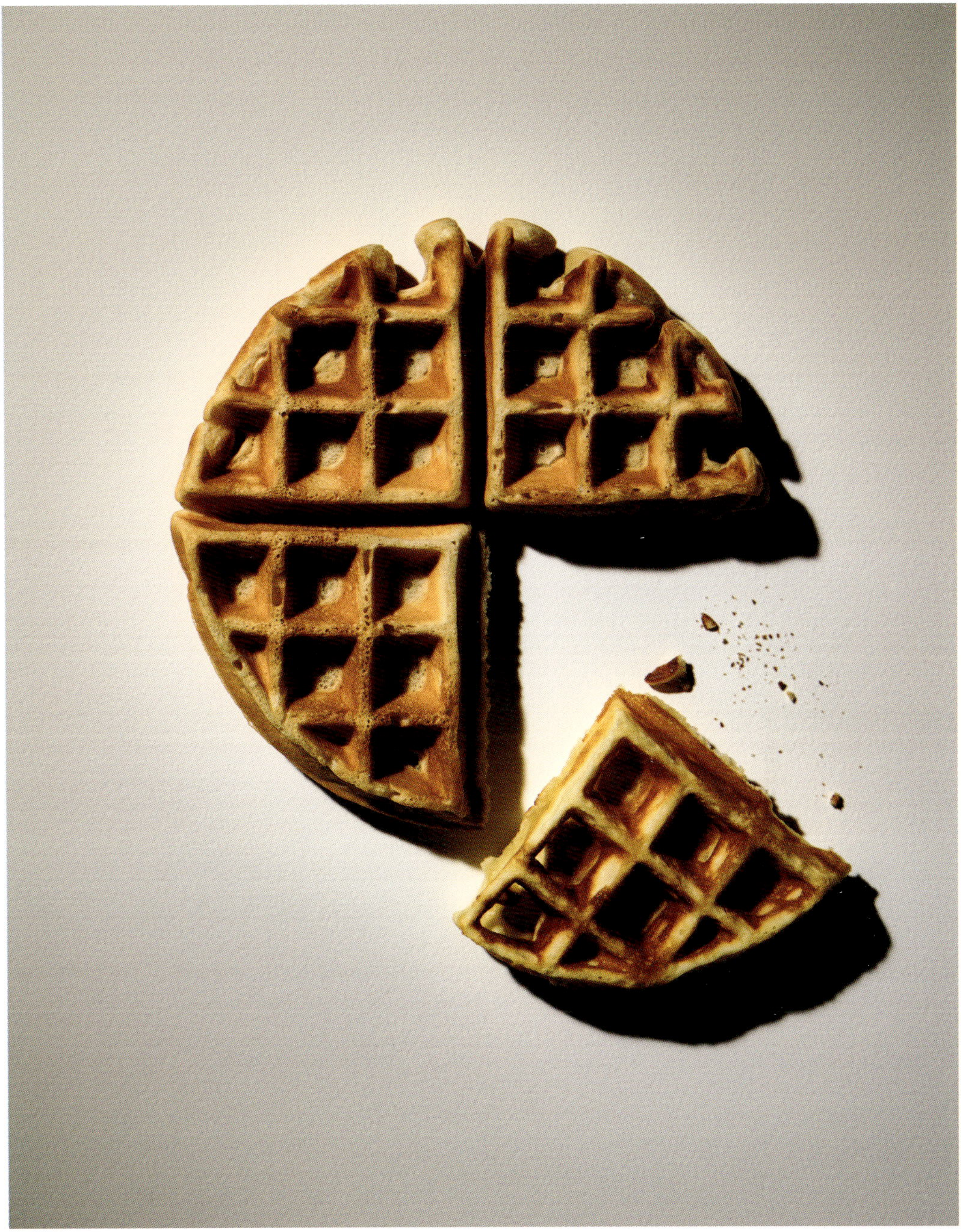

5

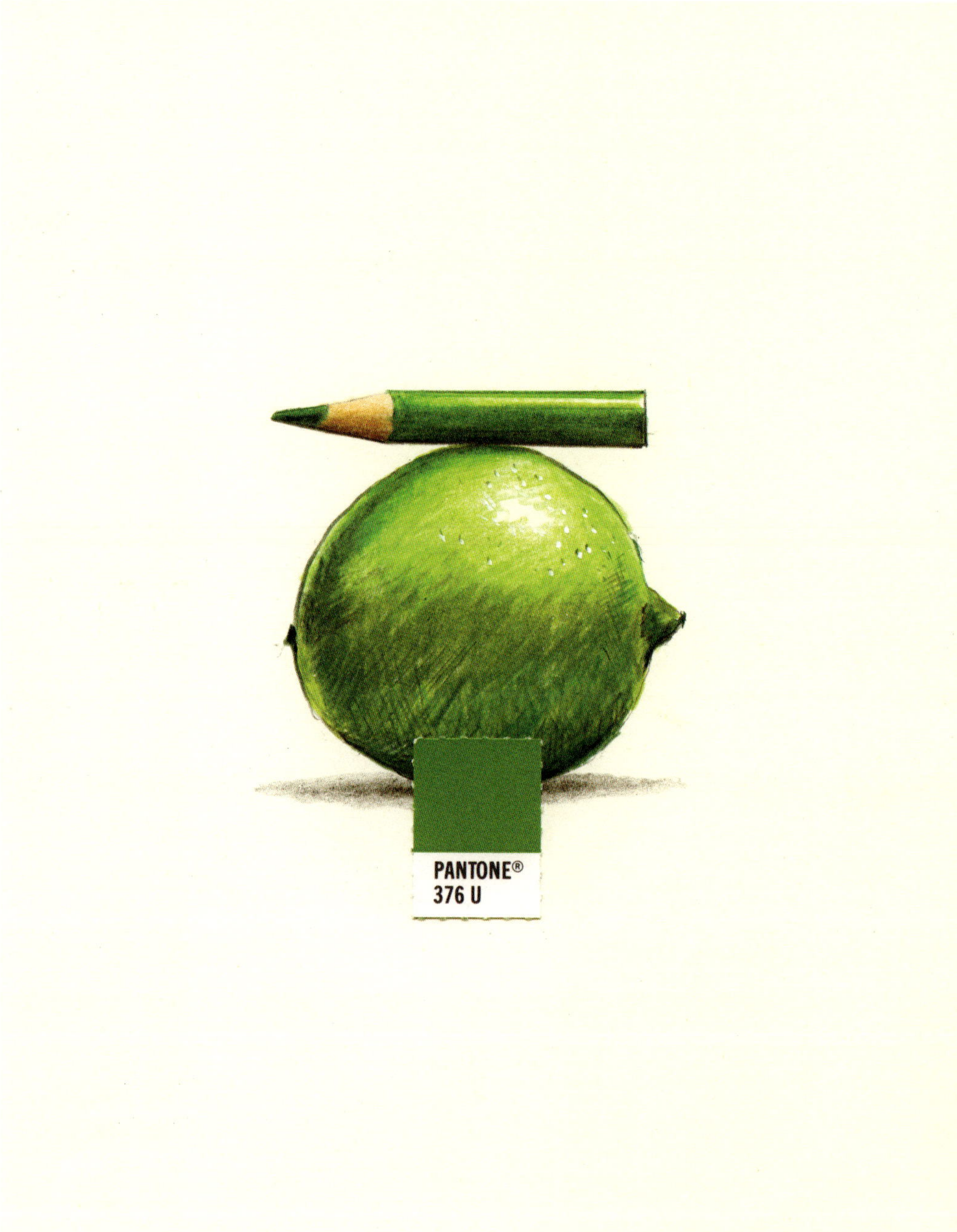

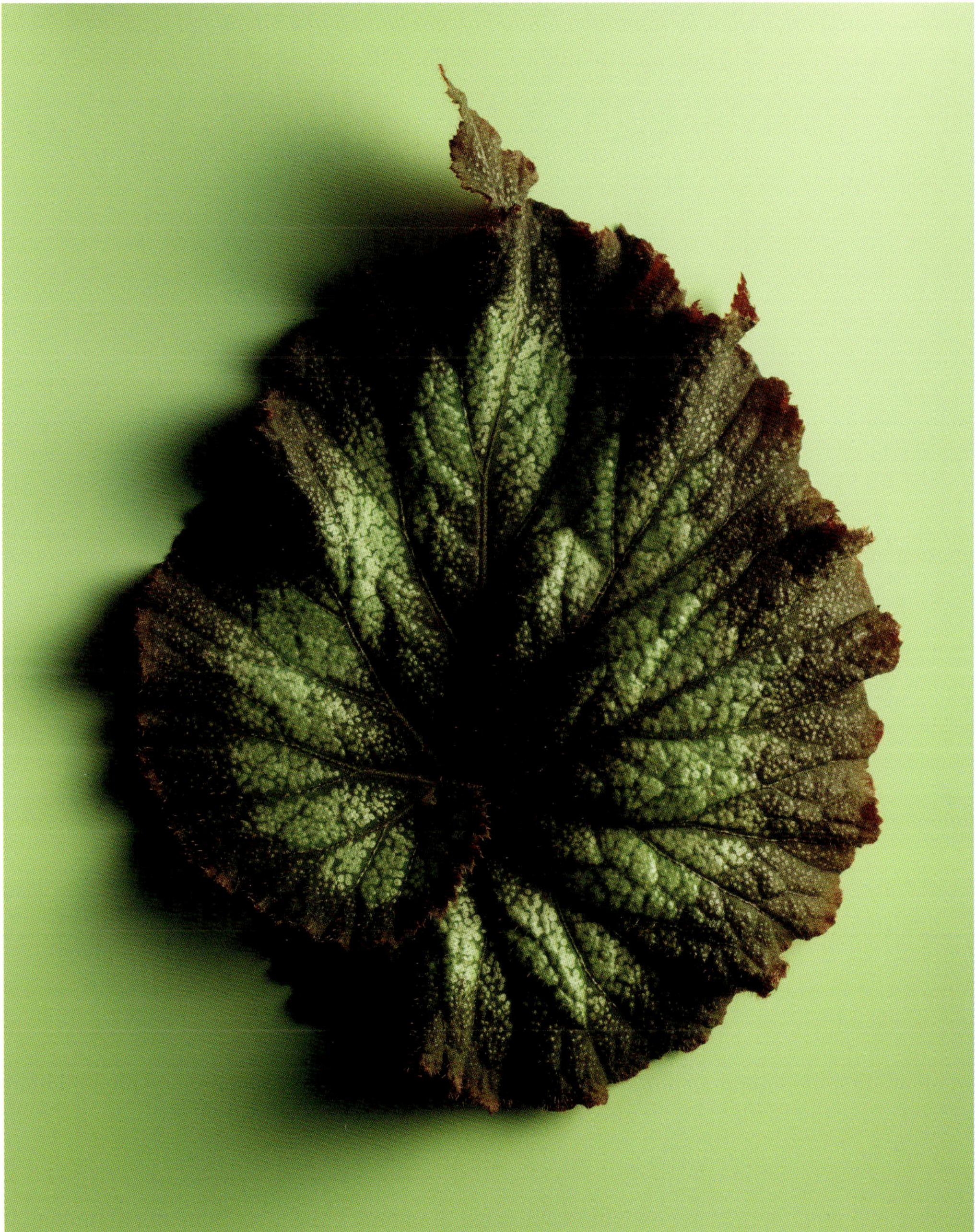

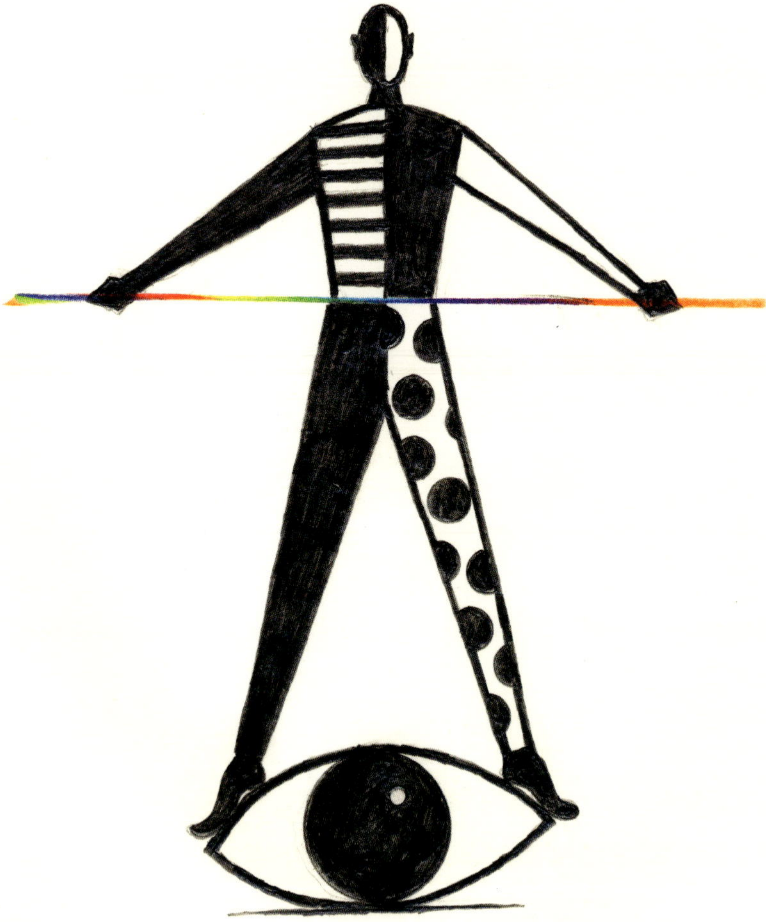

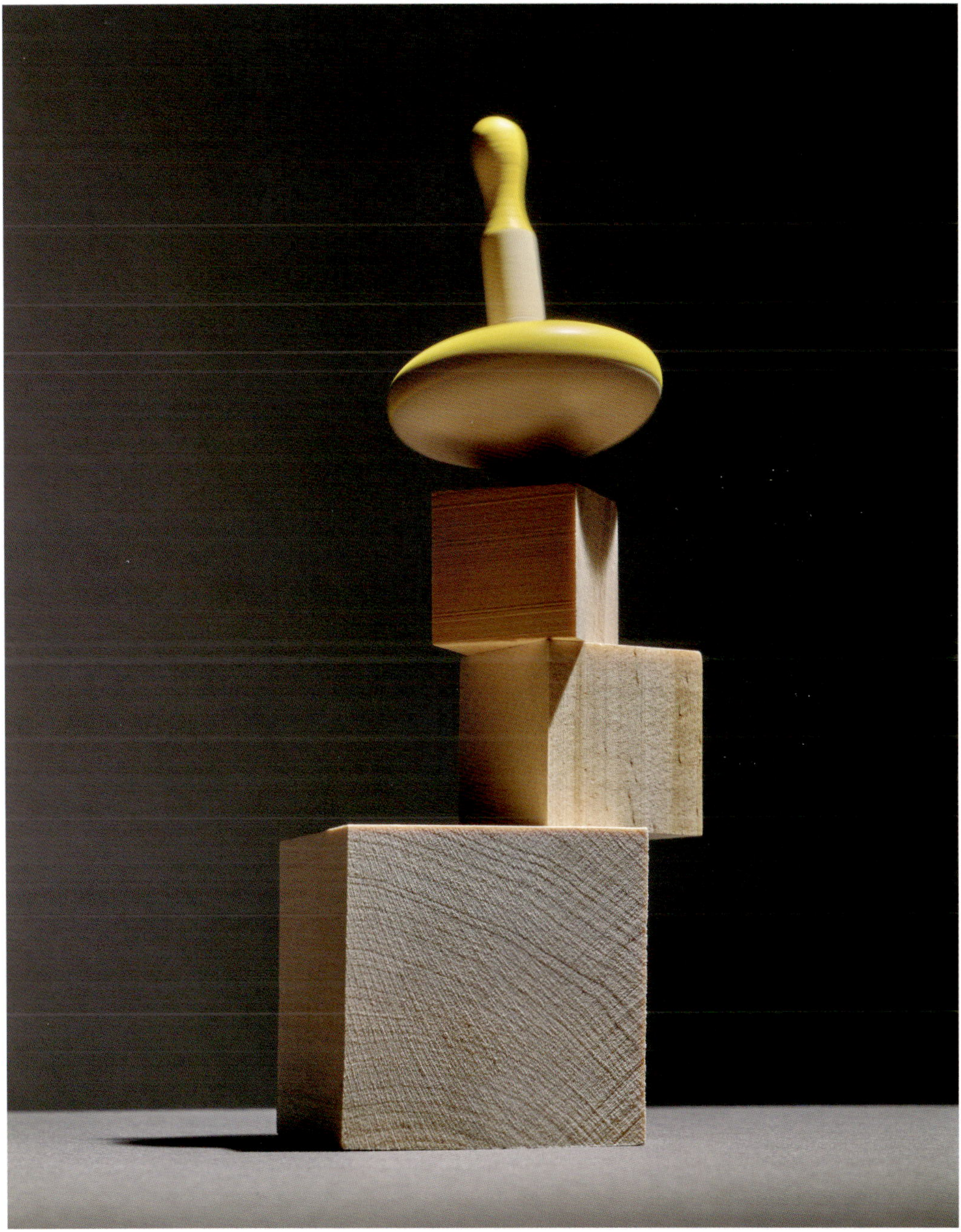

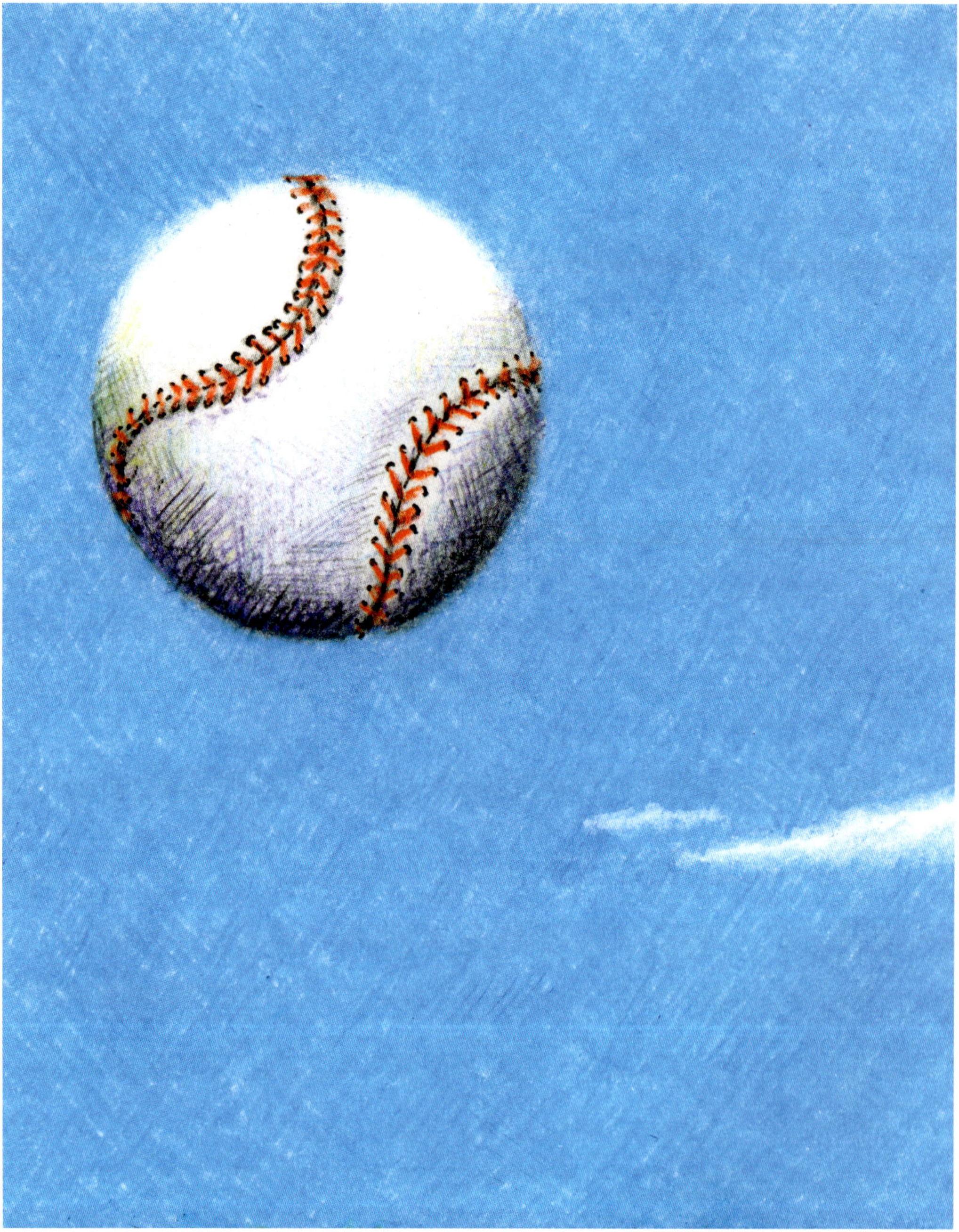

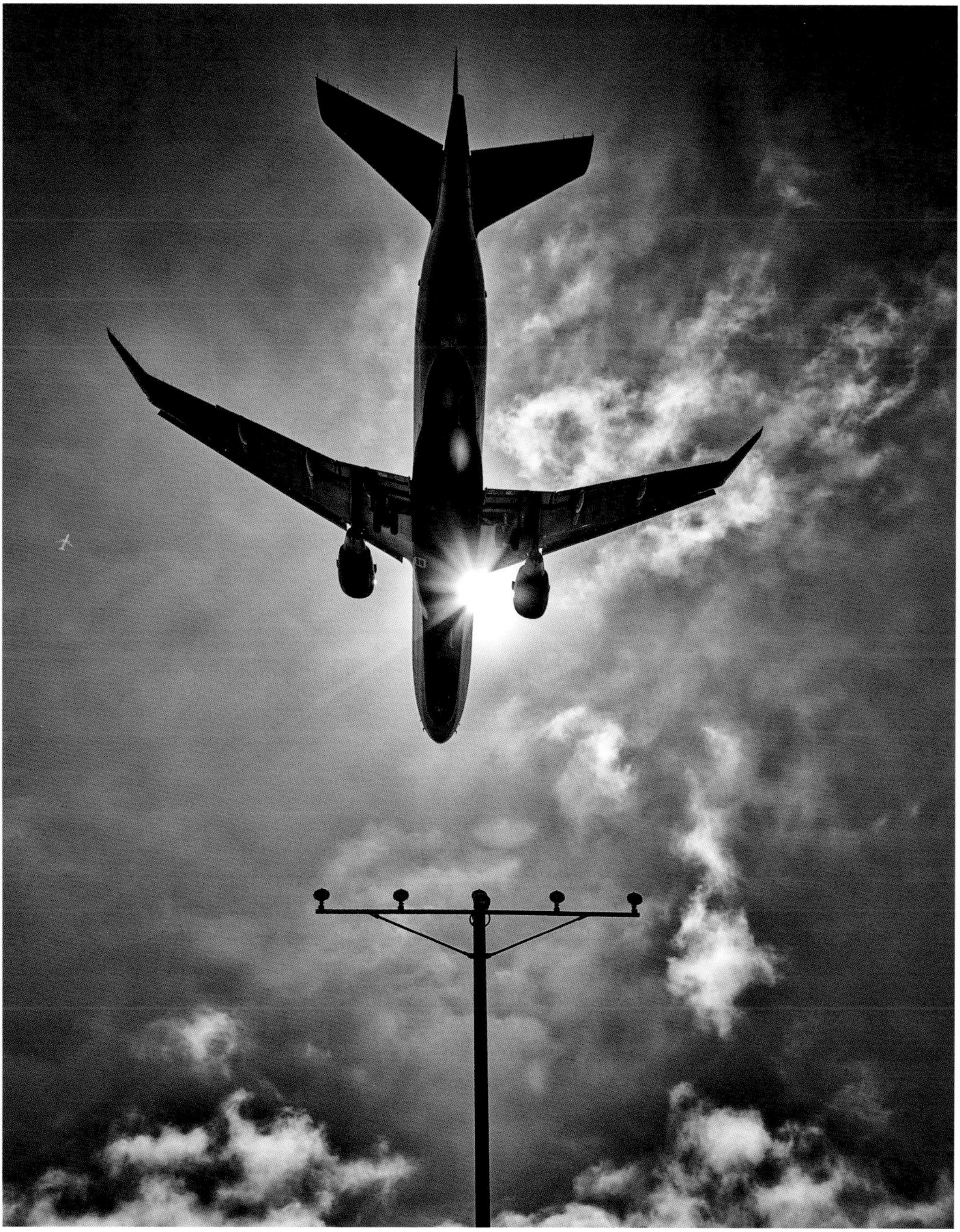

8

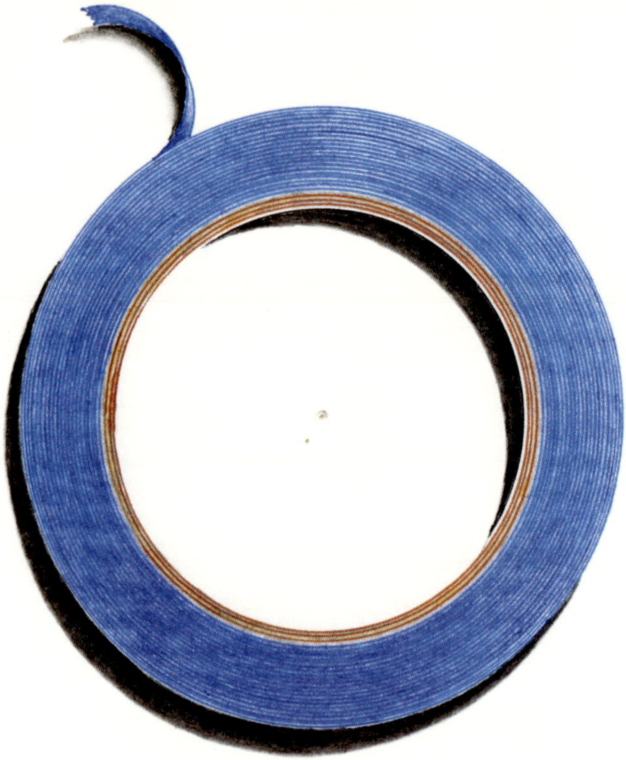

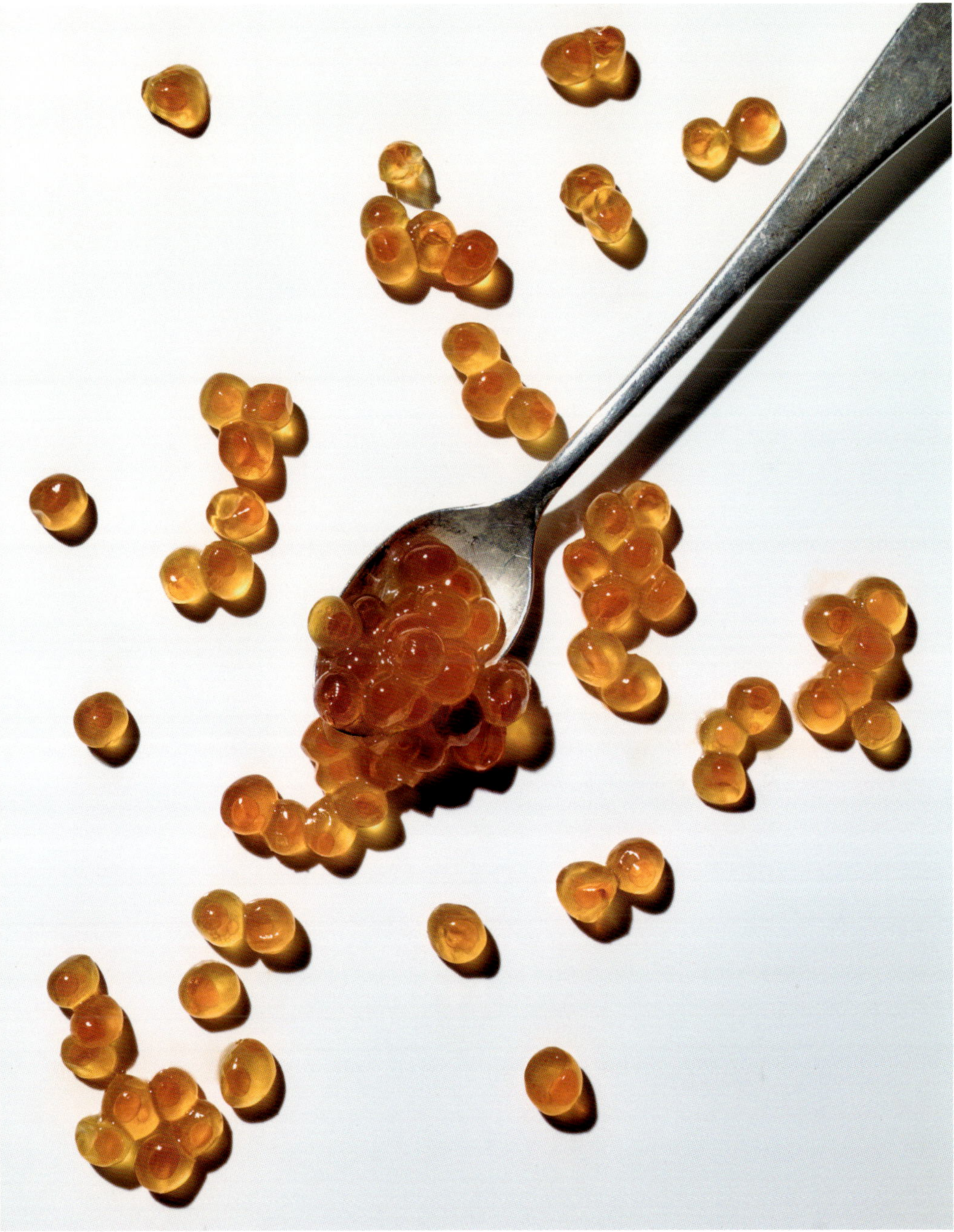

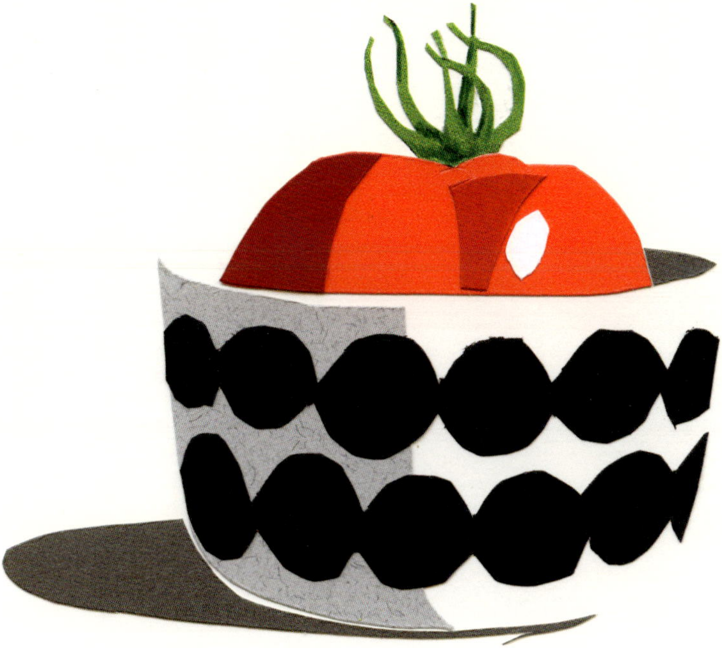

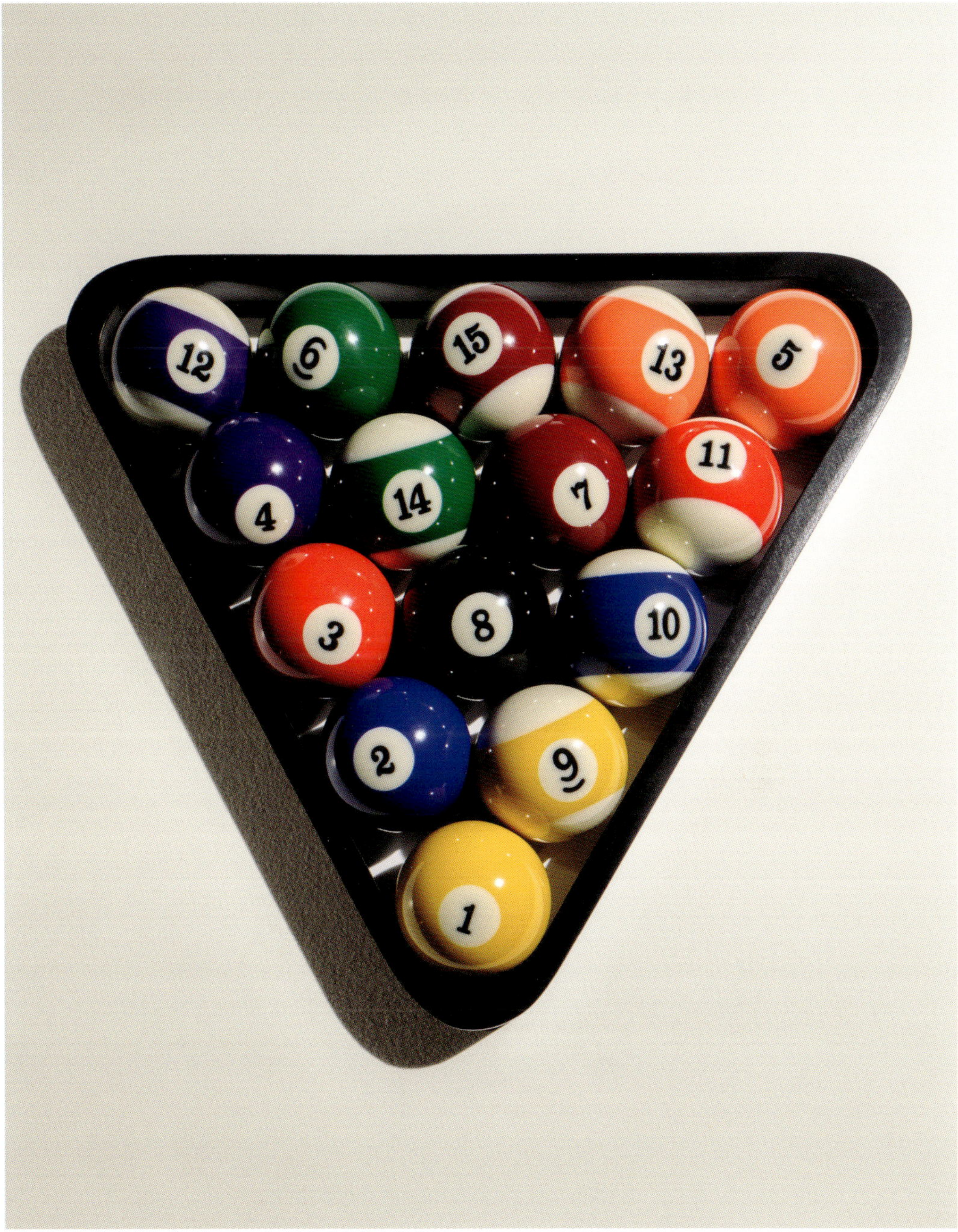

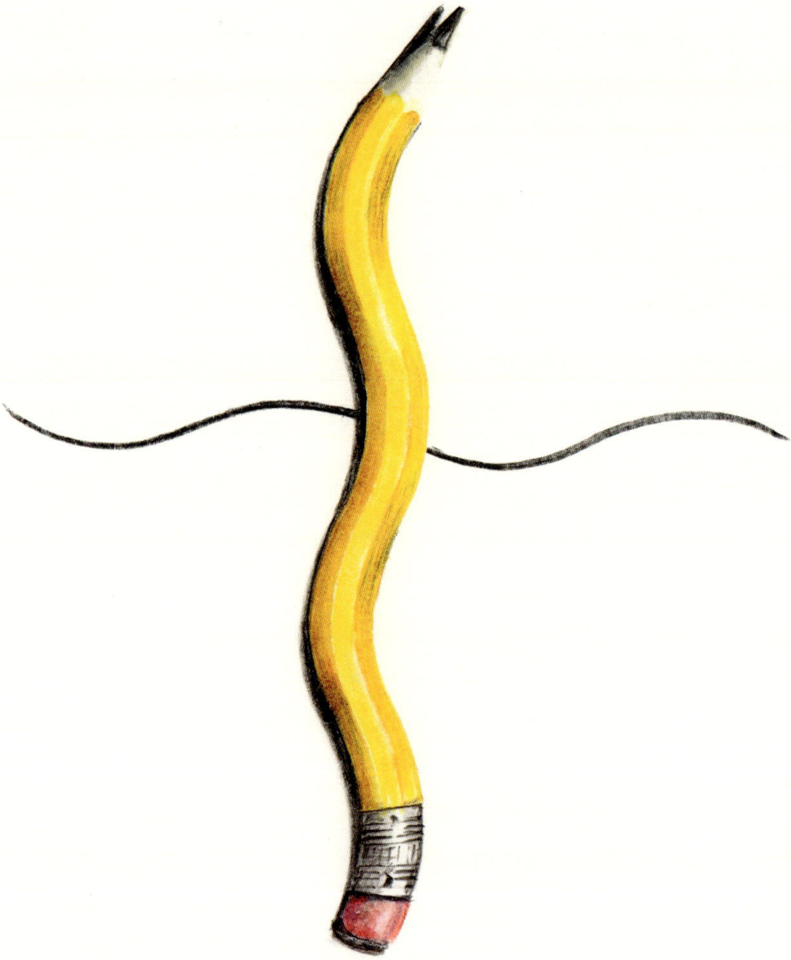

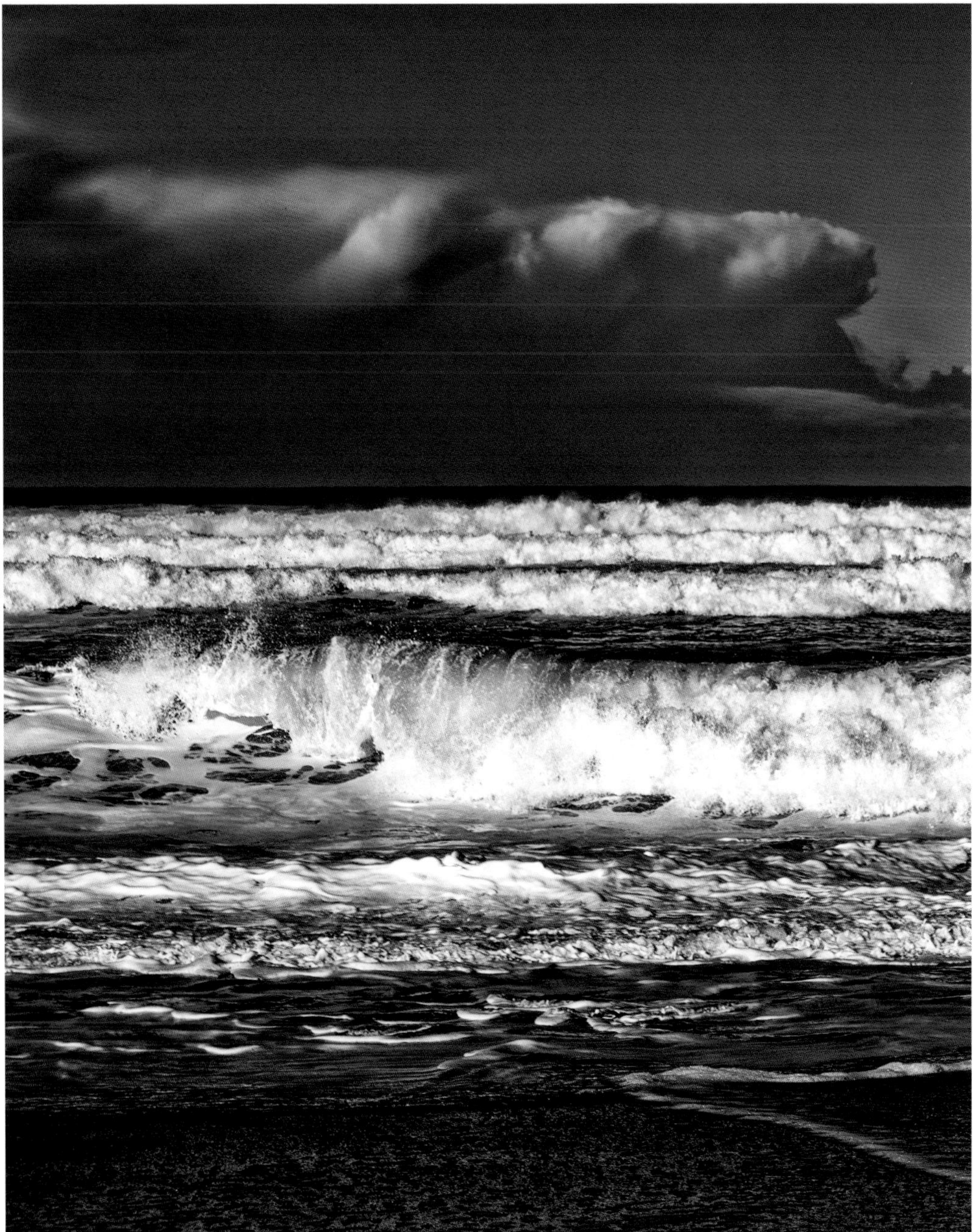

11

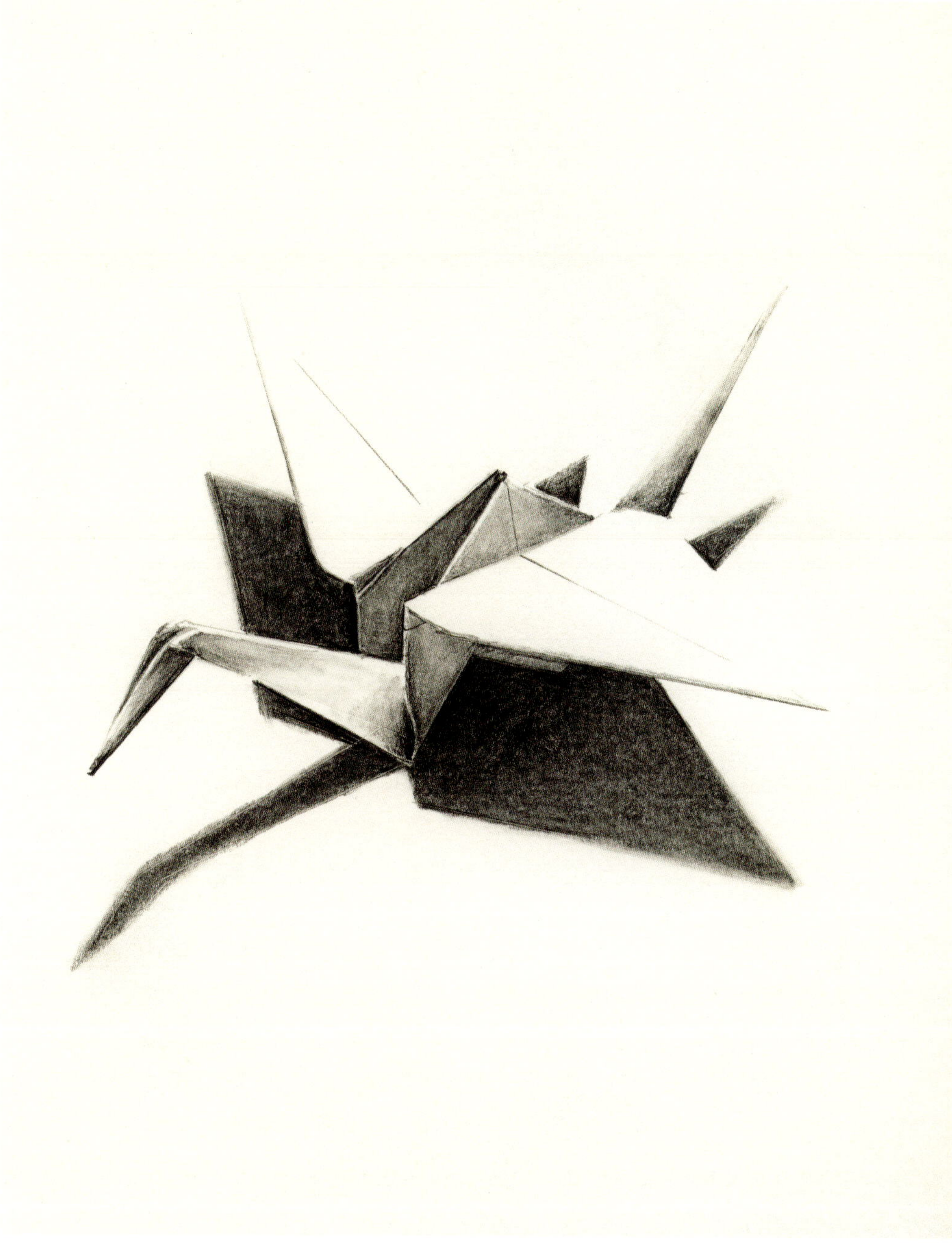

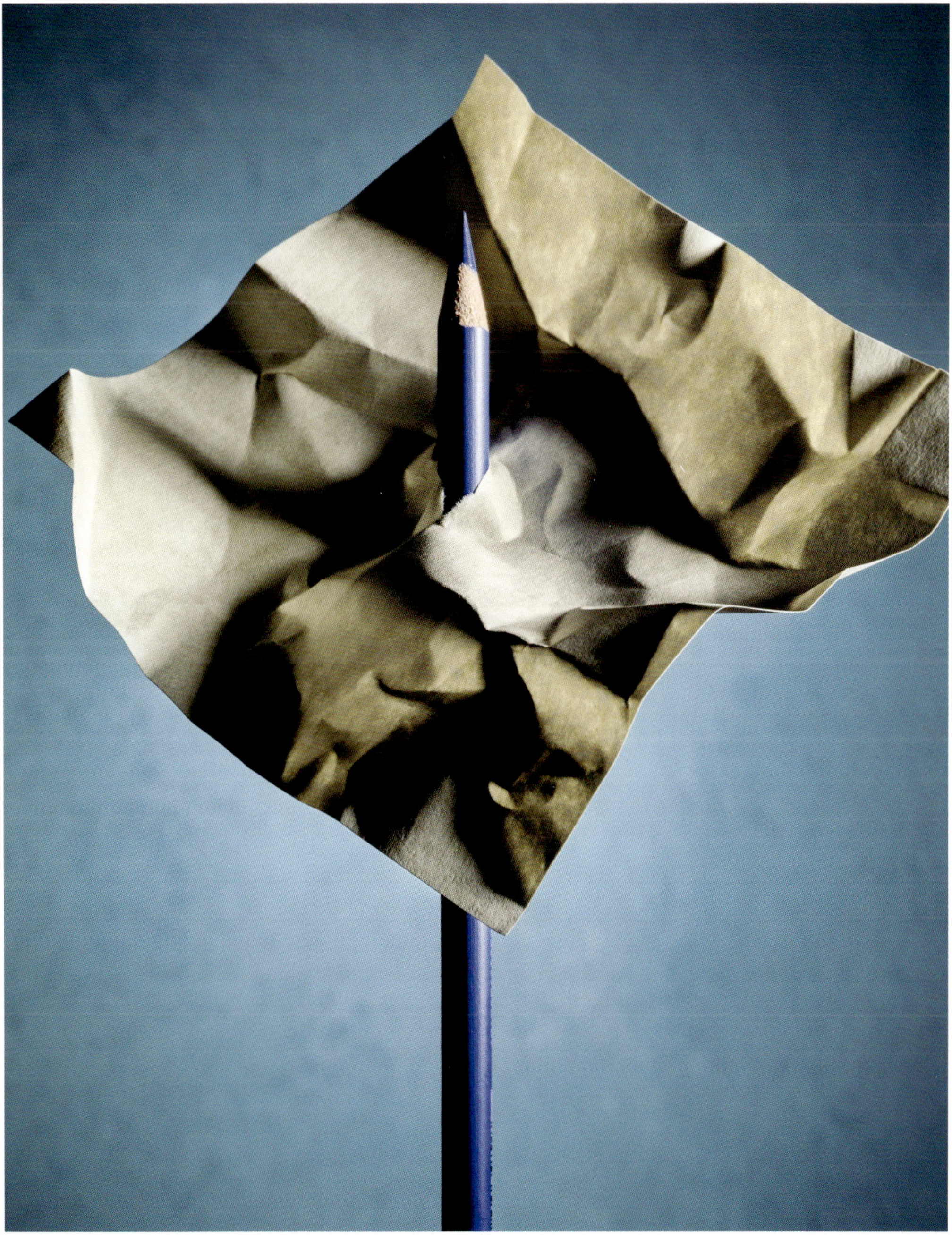

12

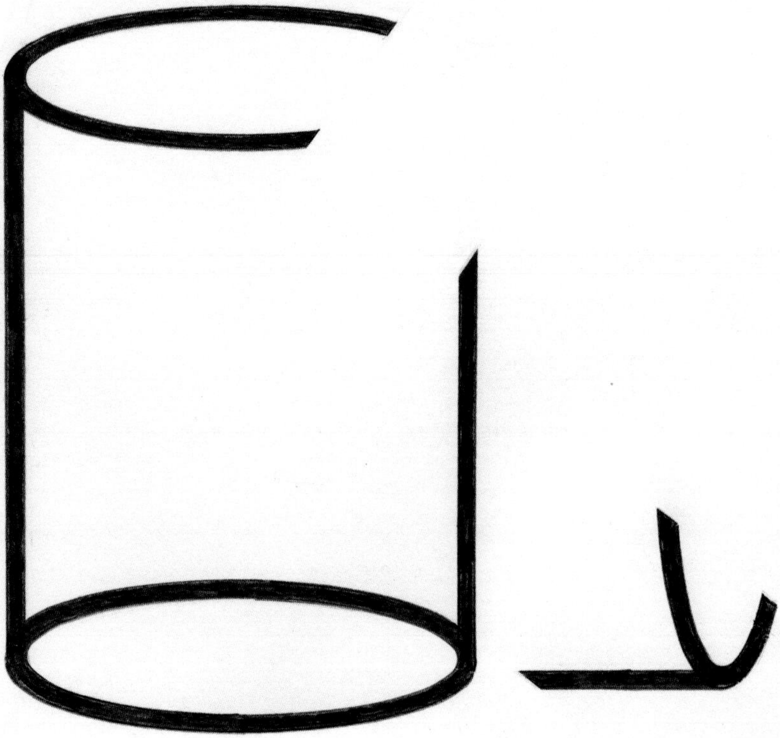

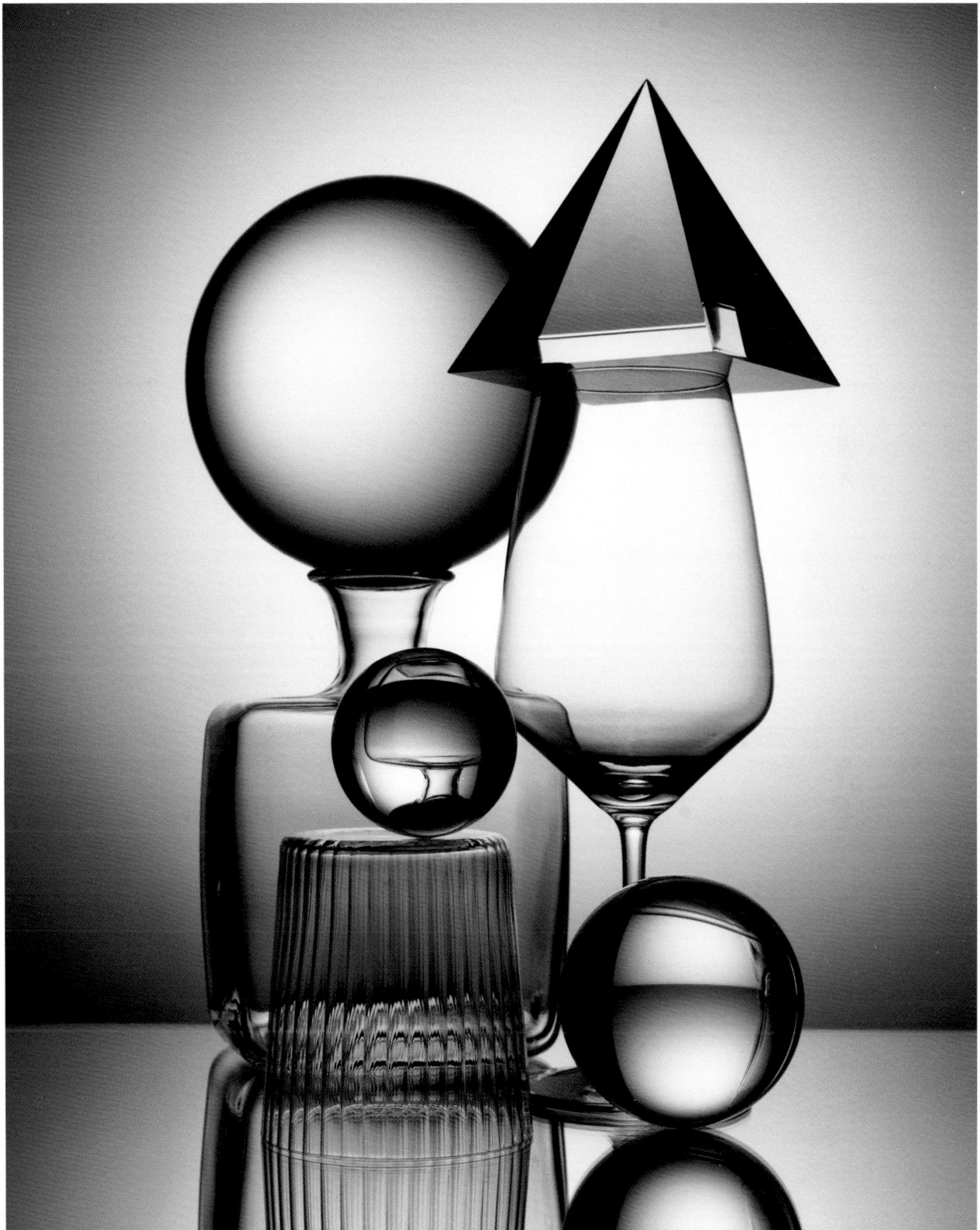

13

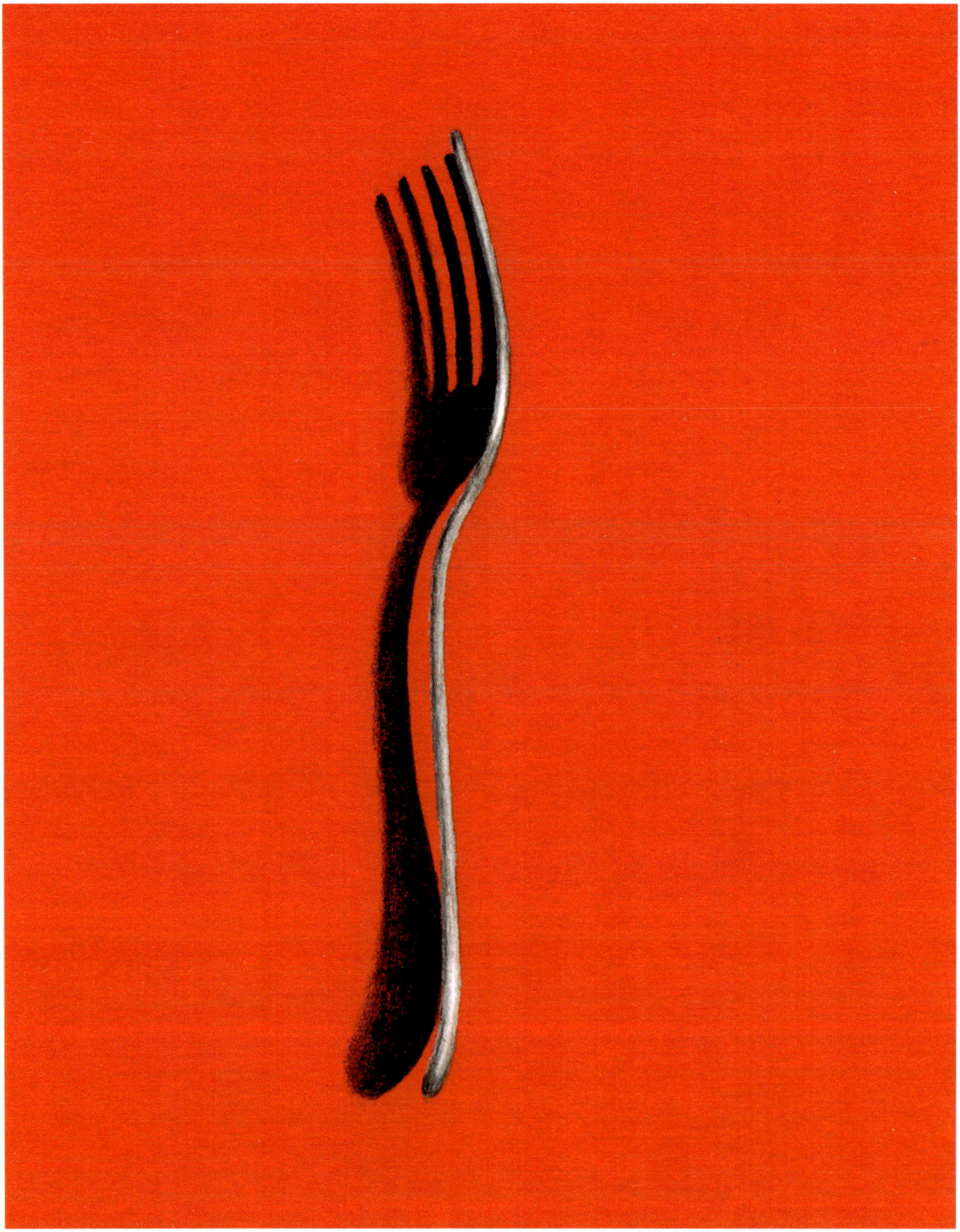

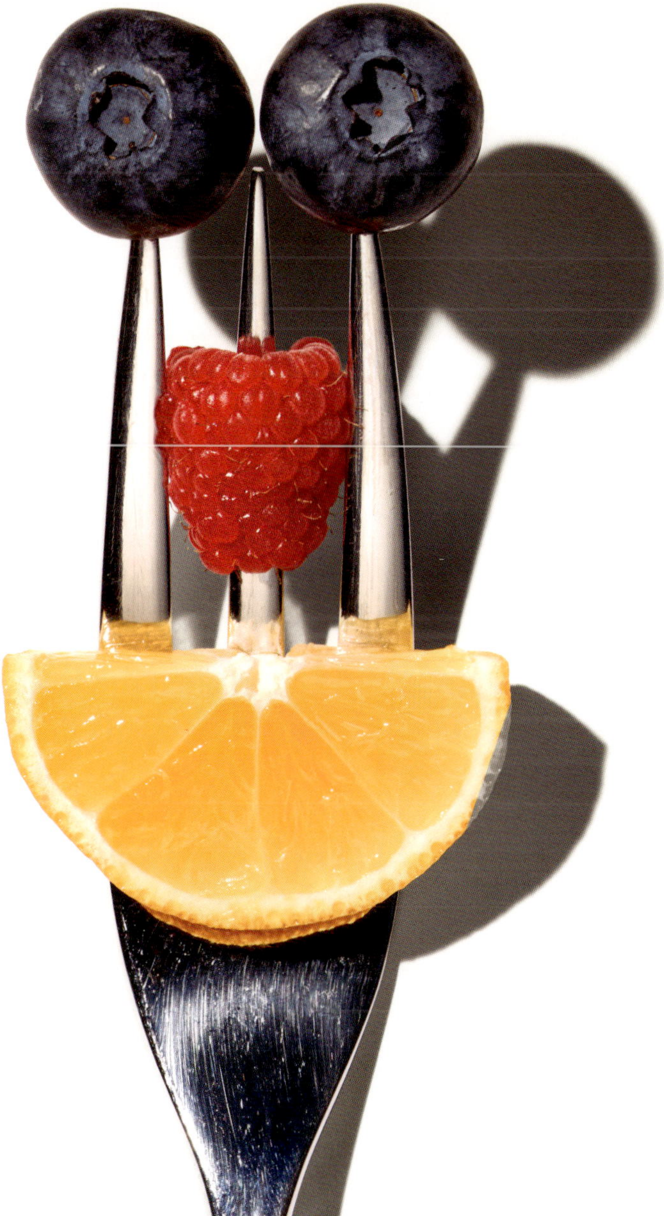

14

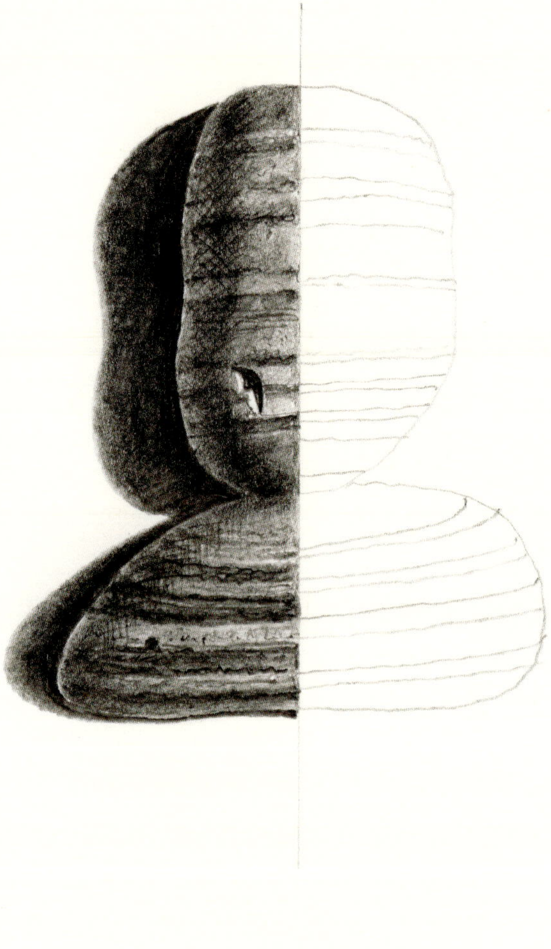

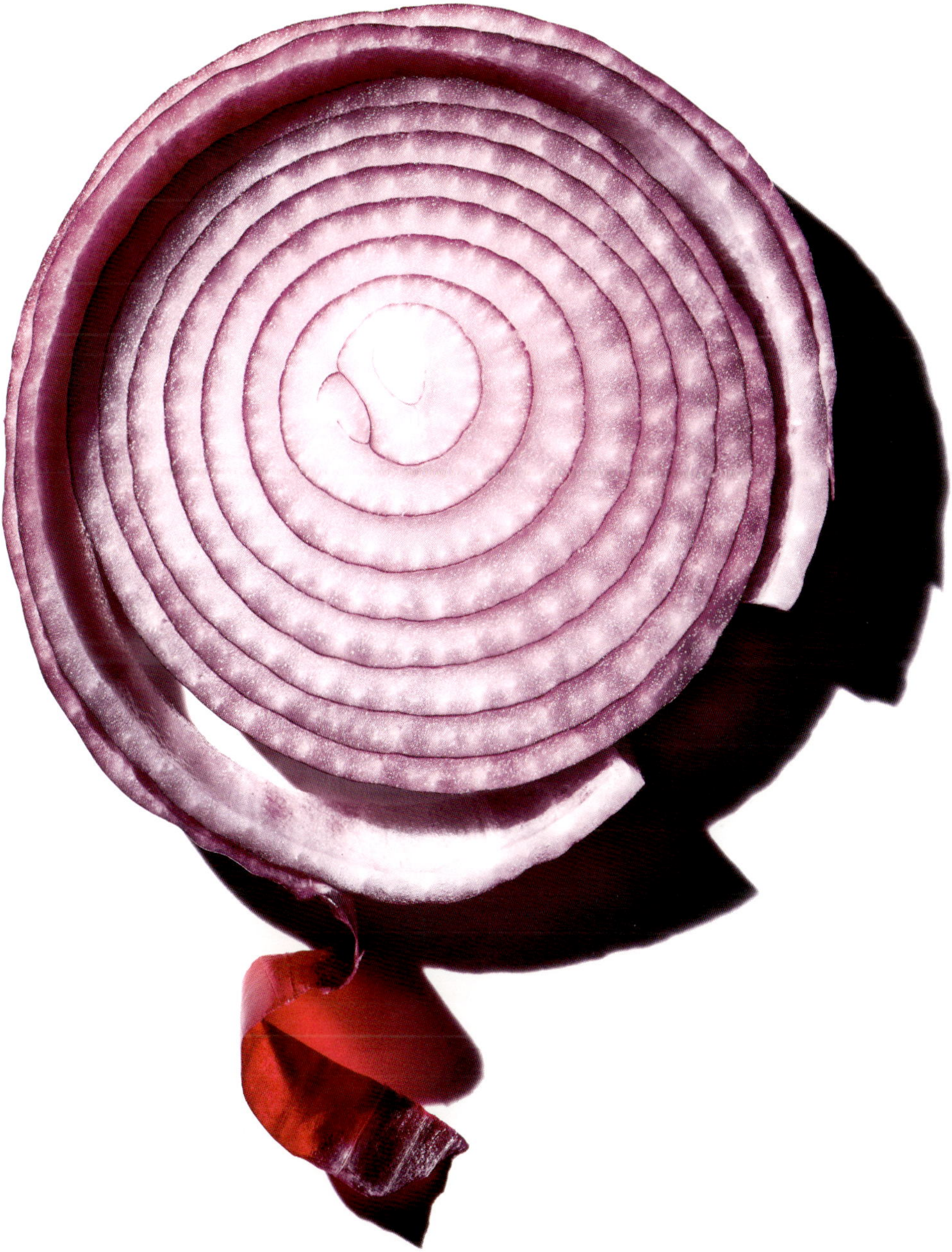

15

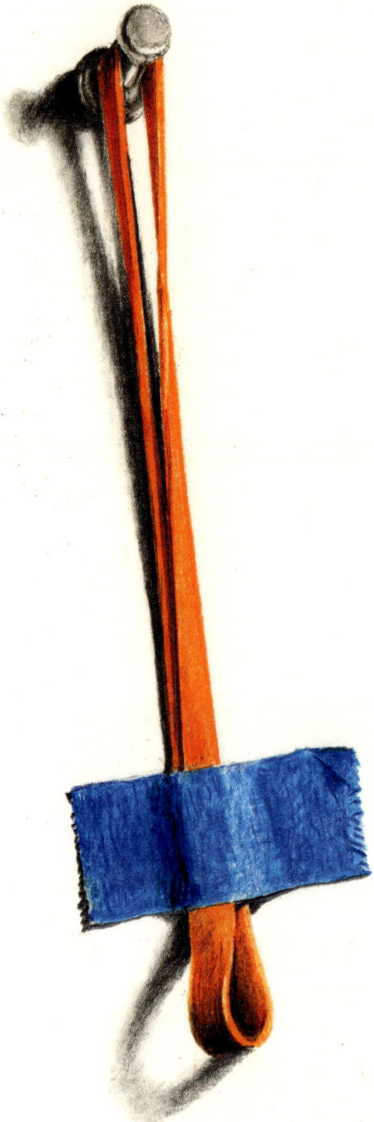

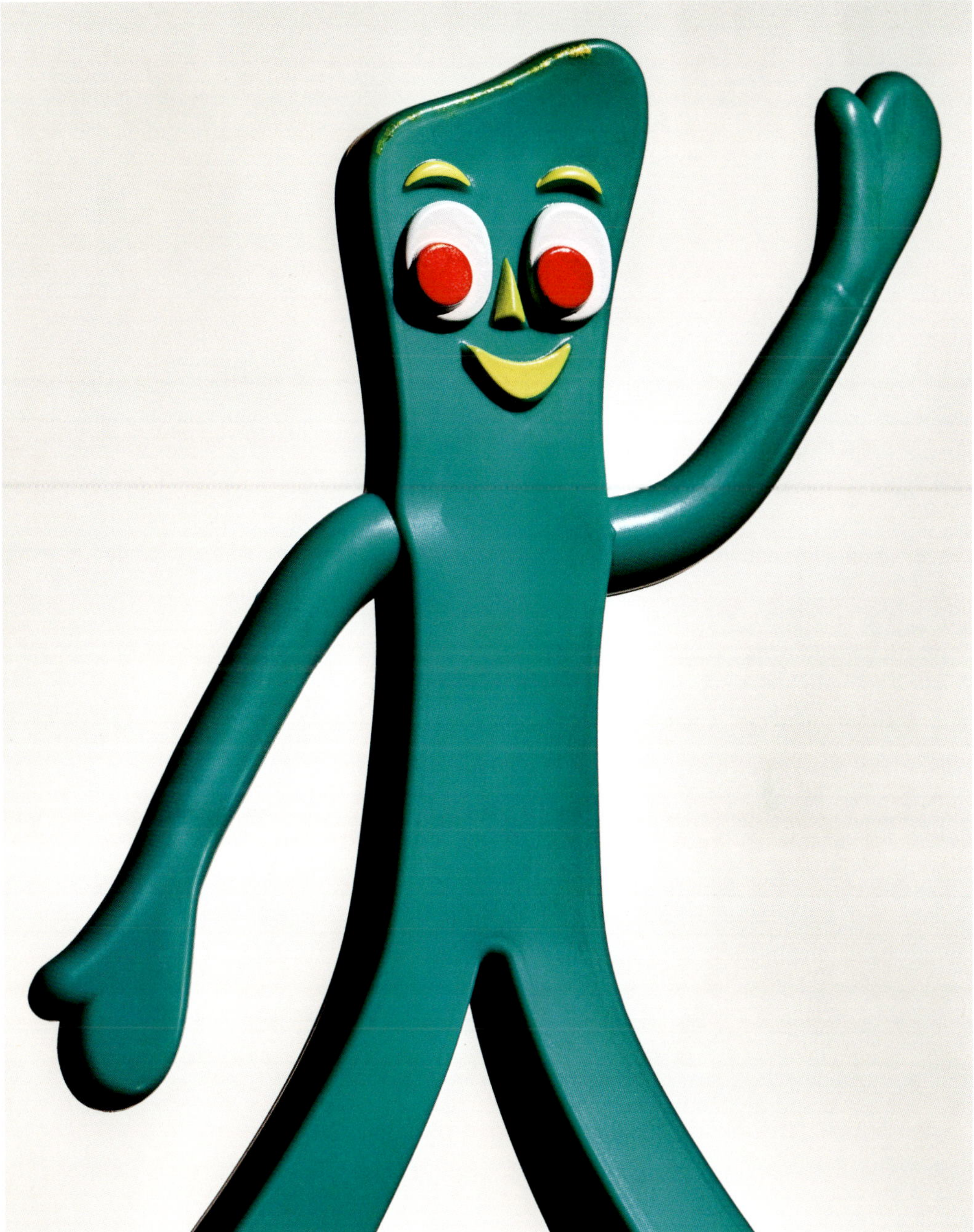

16

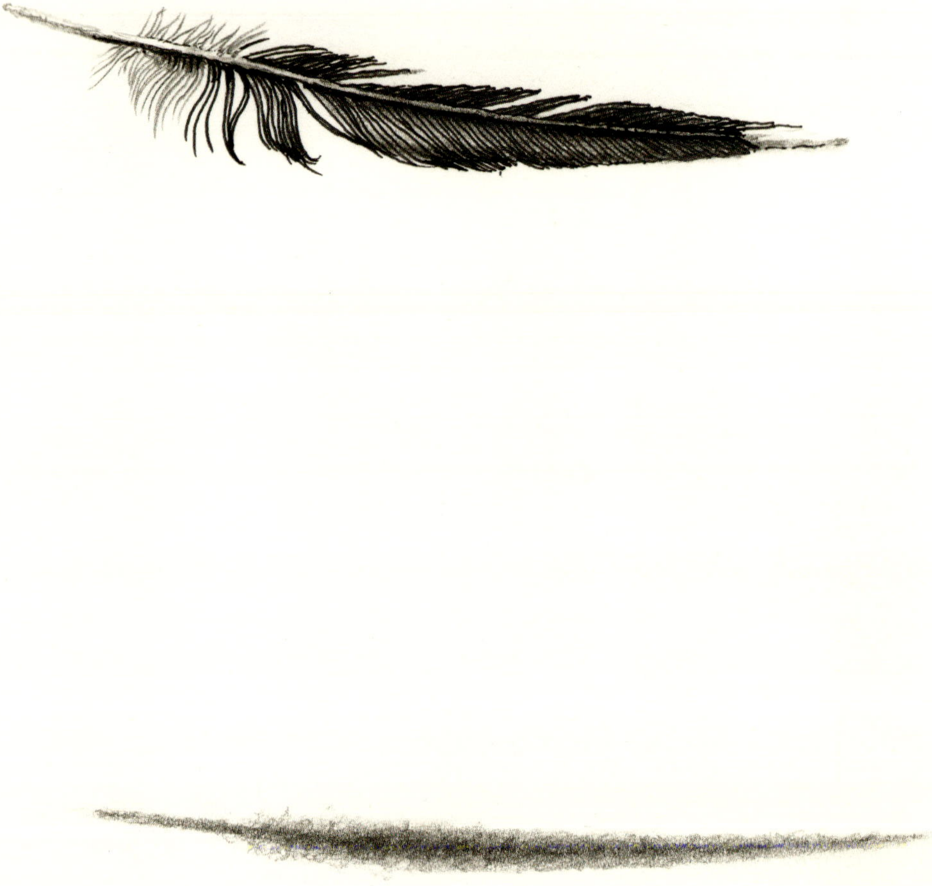

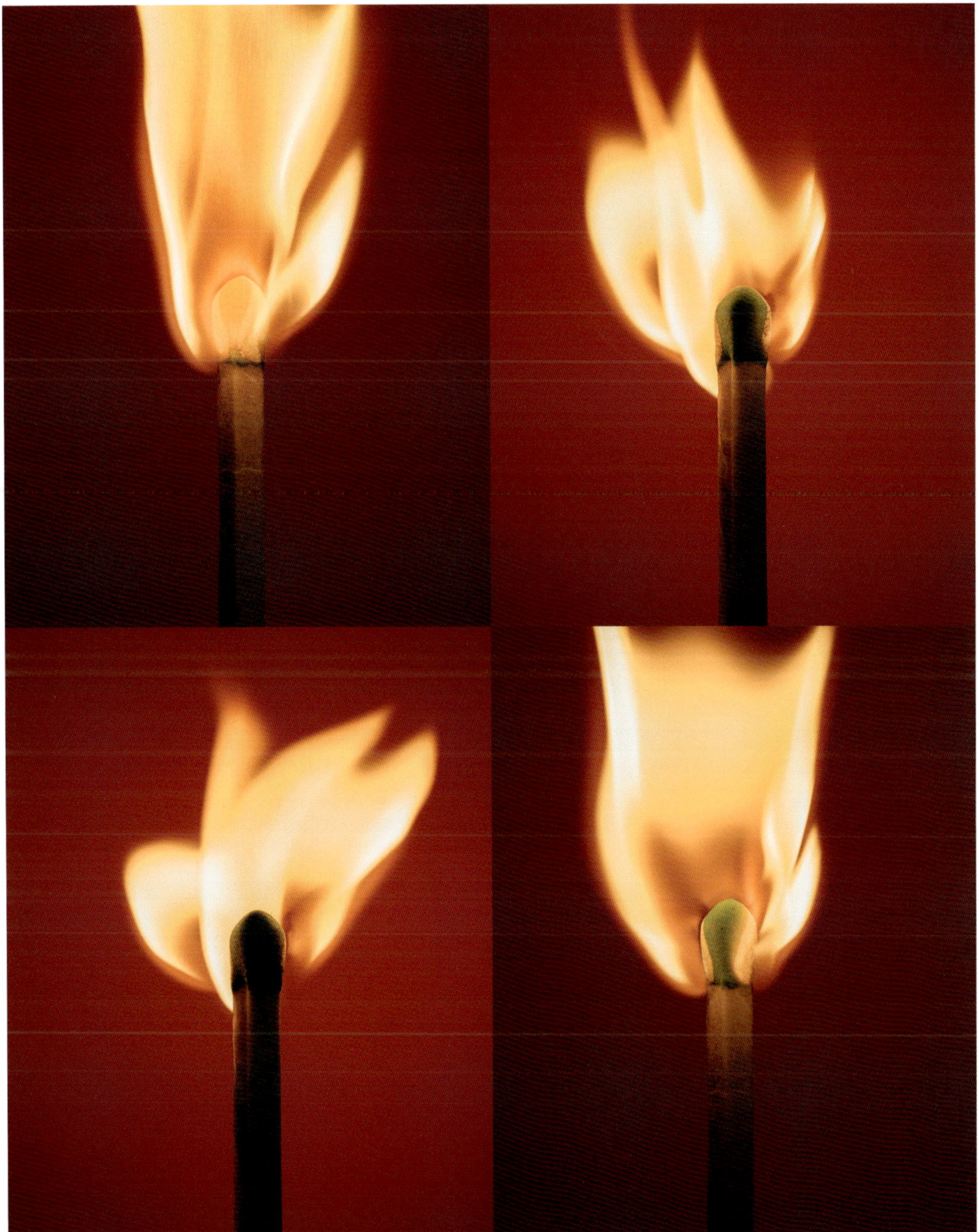

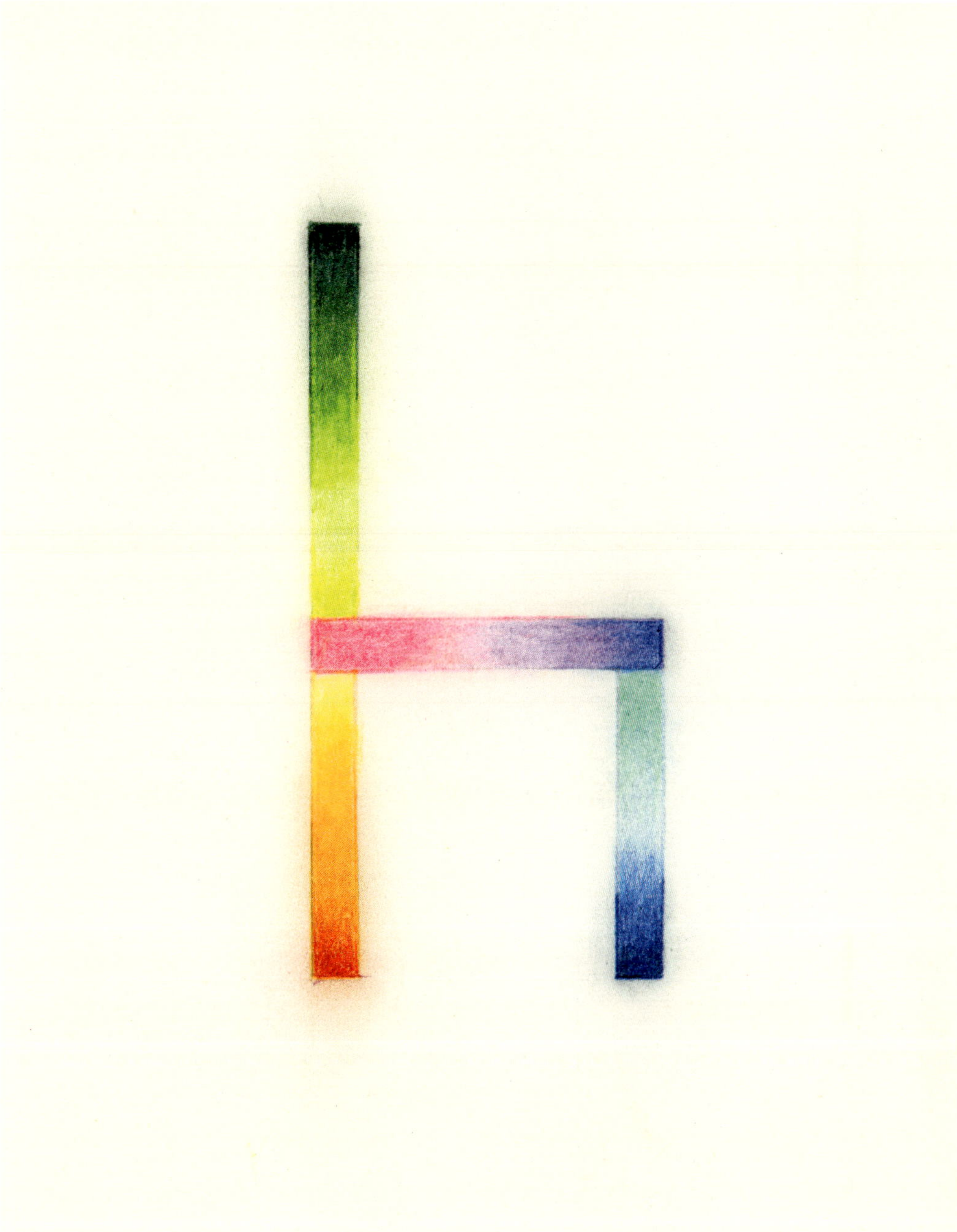

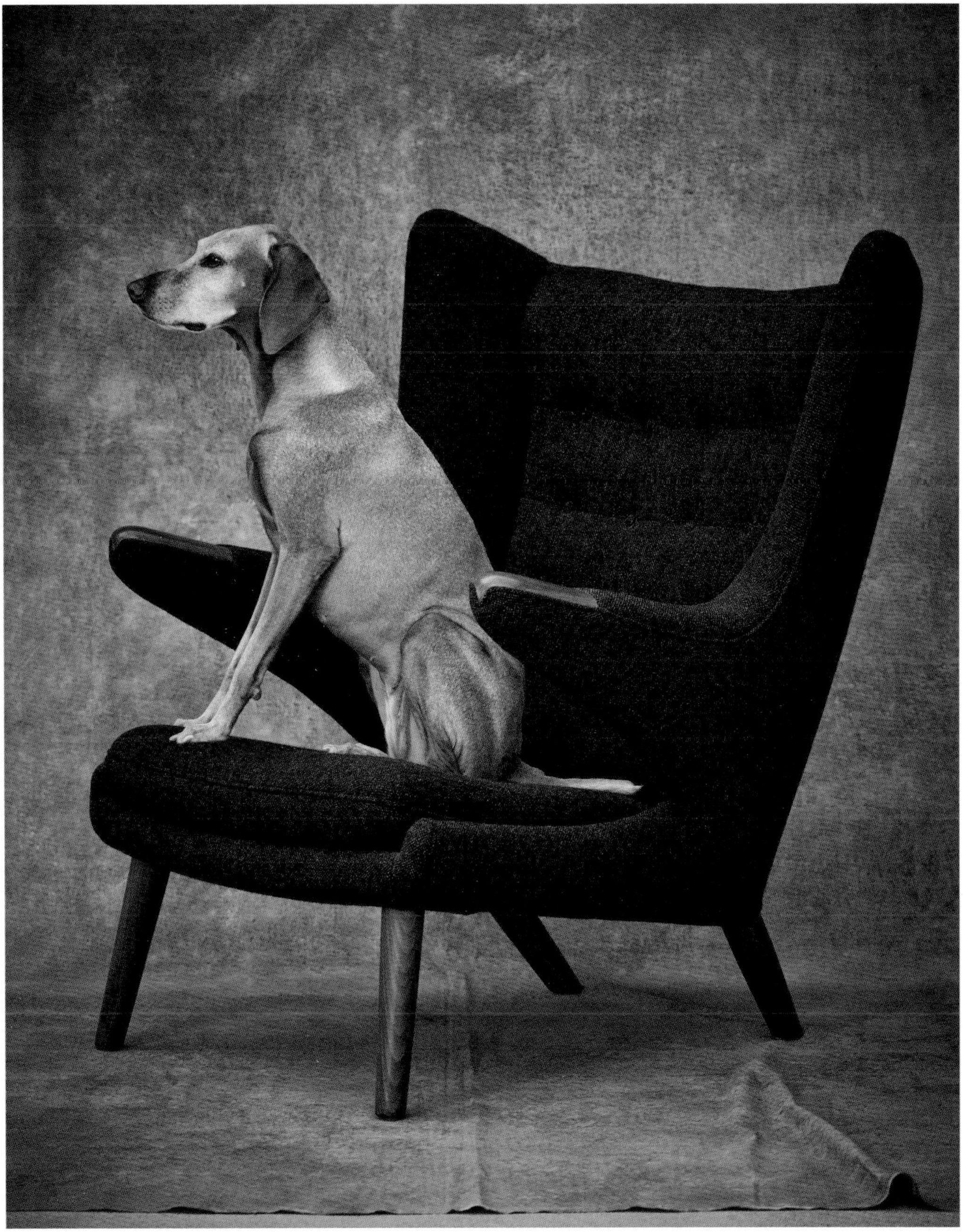

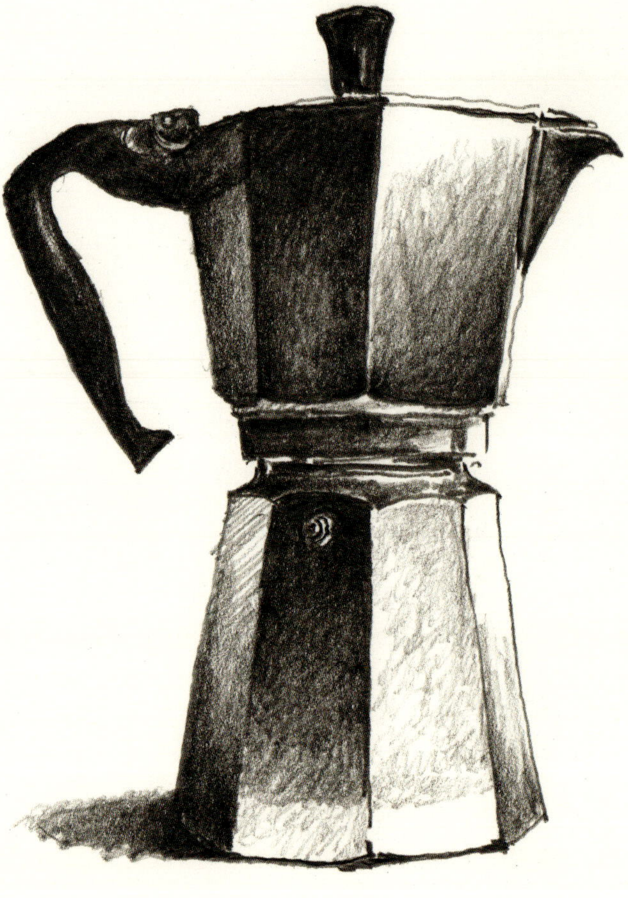

19

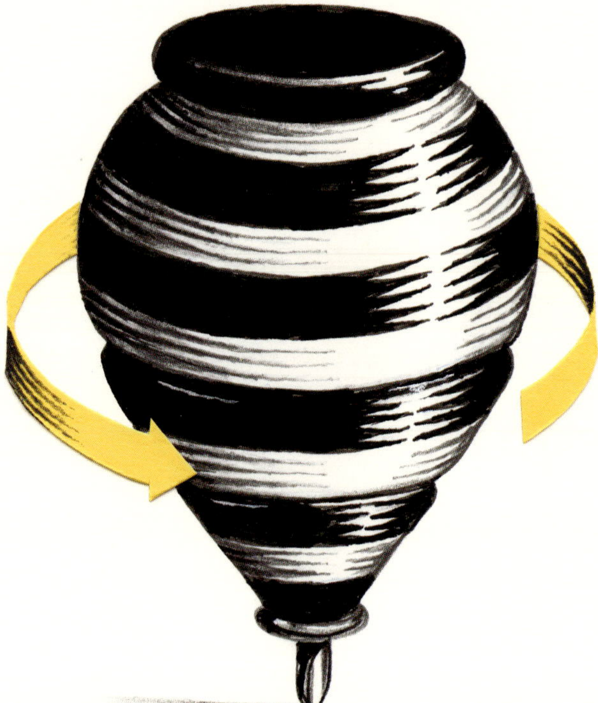

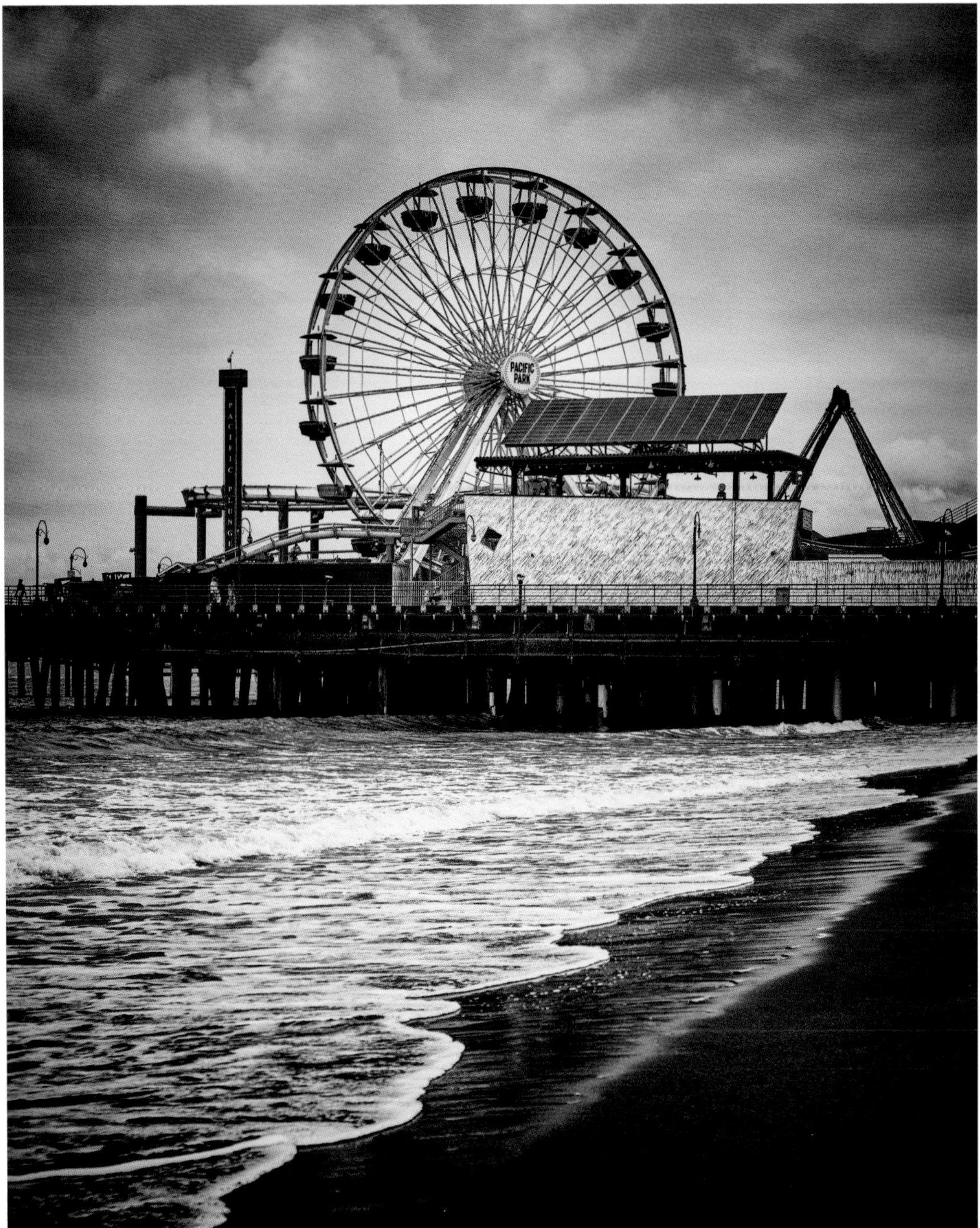
PACIFIC
PARK

20

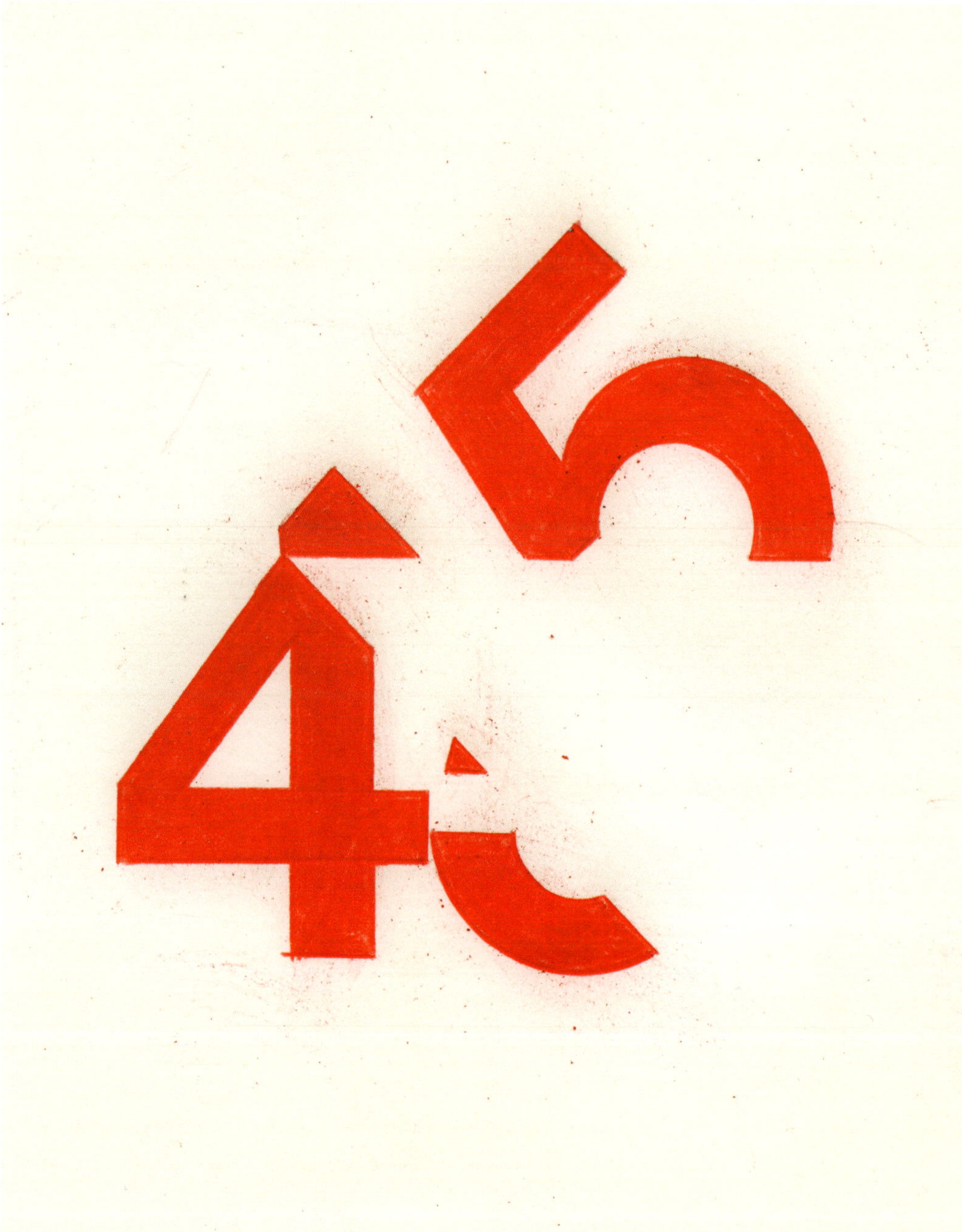

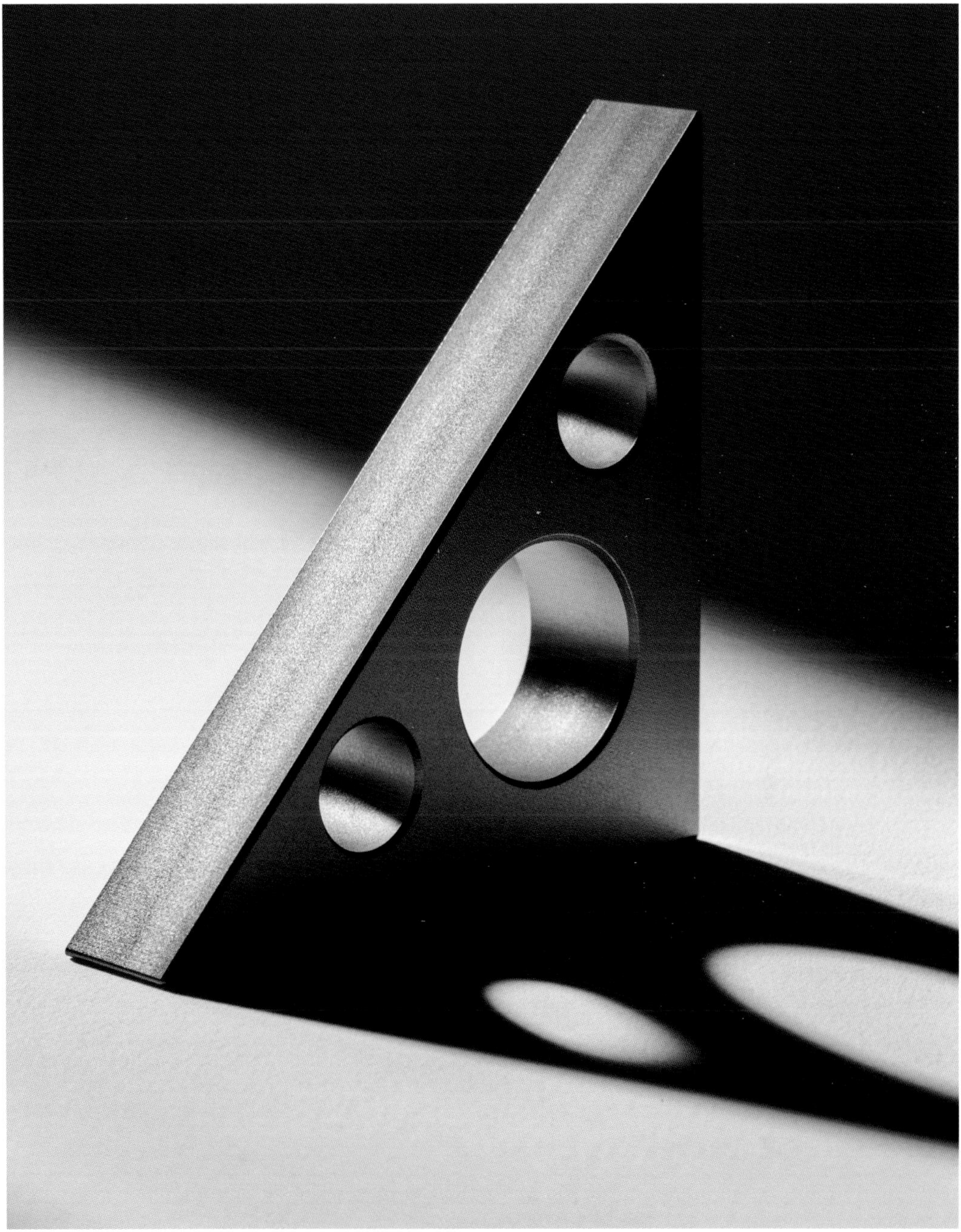

21

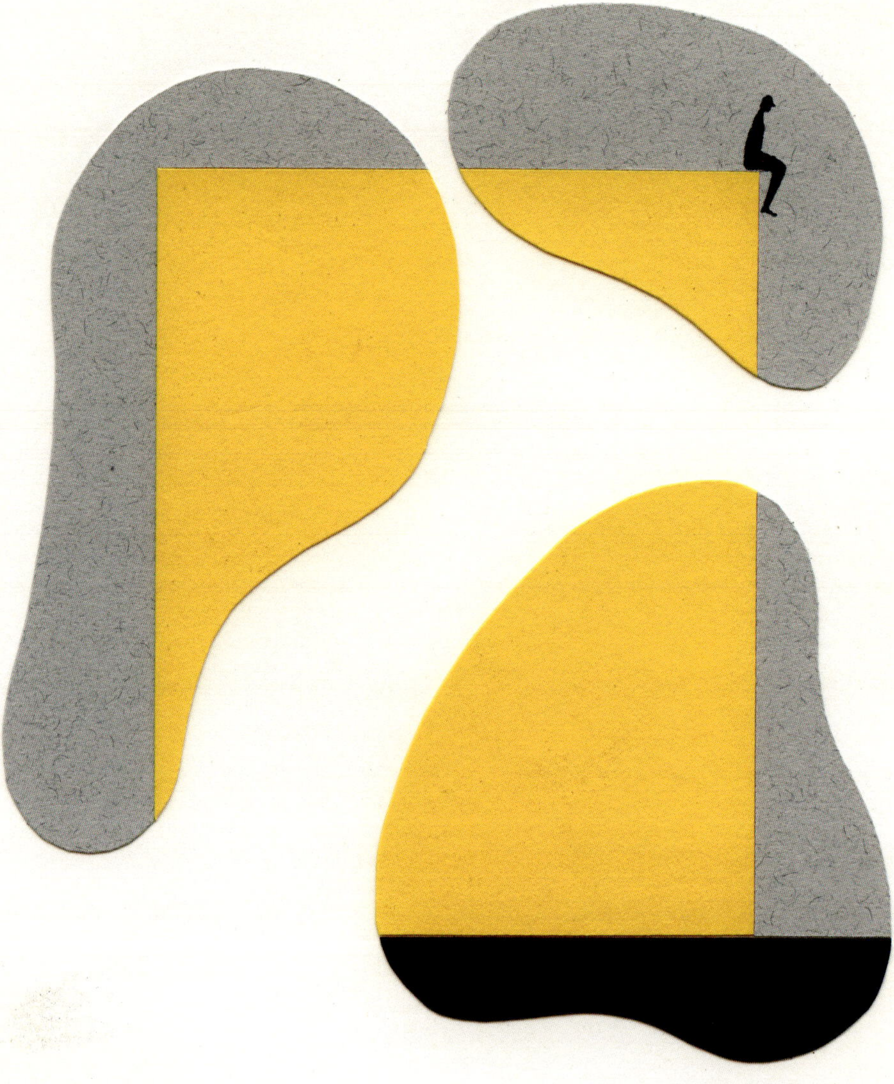

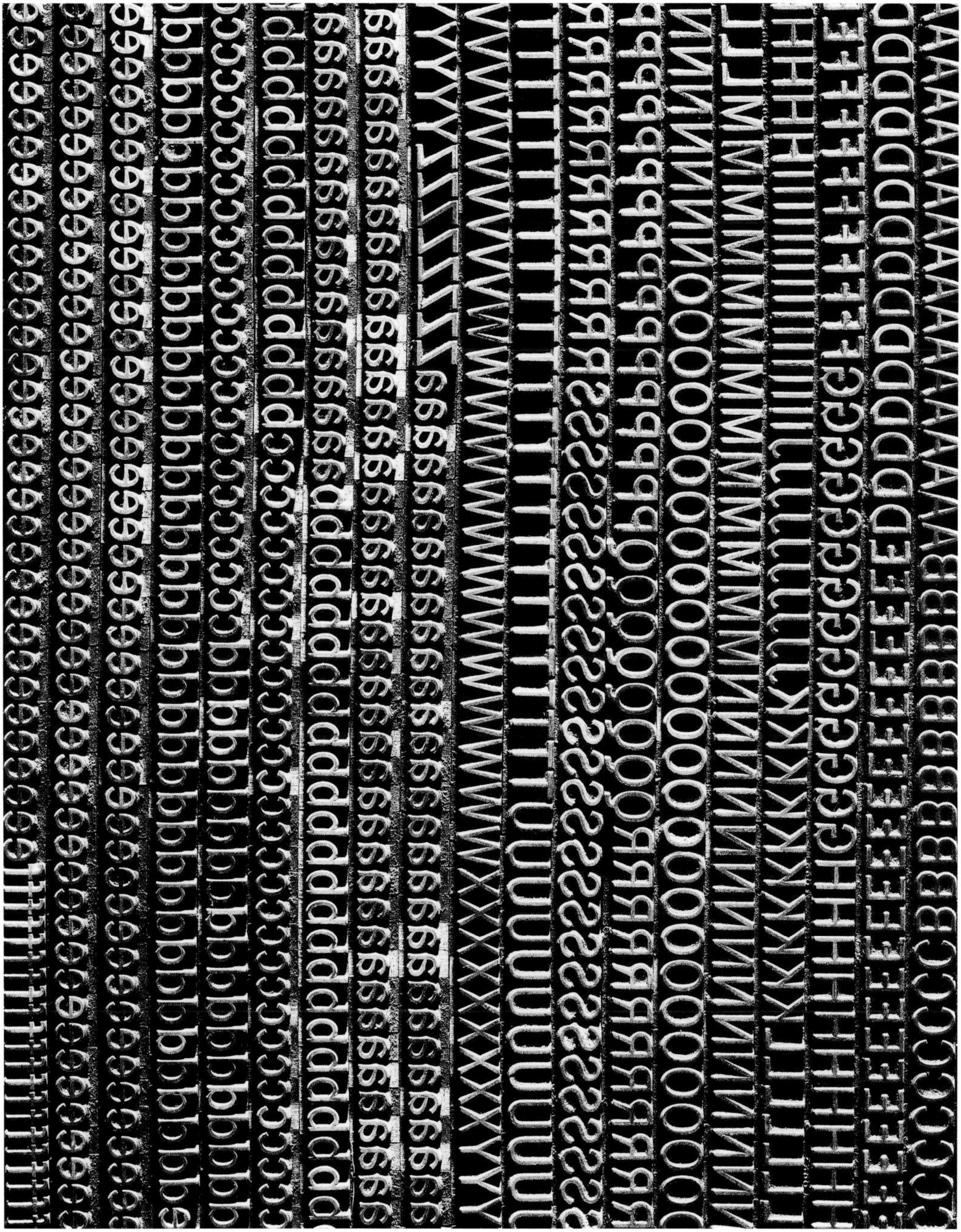

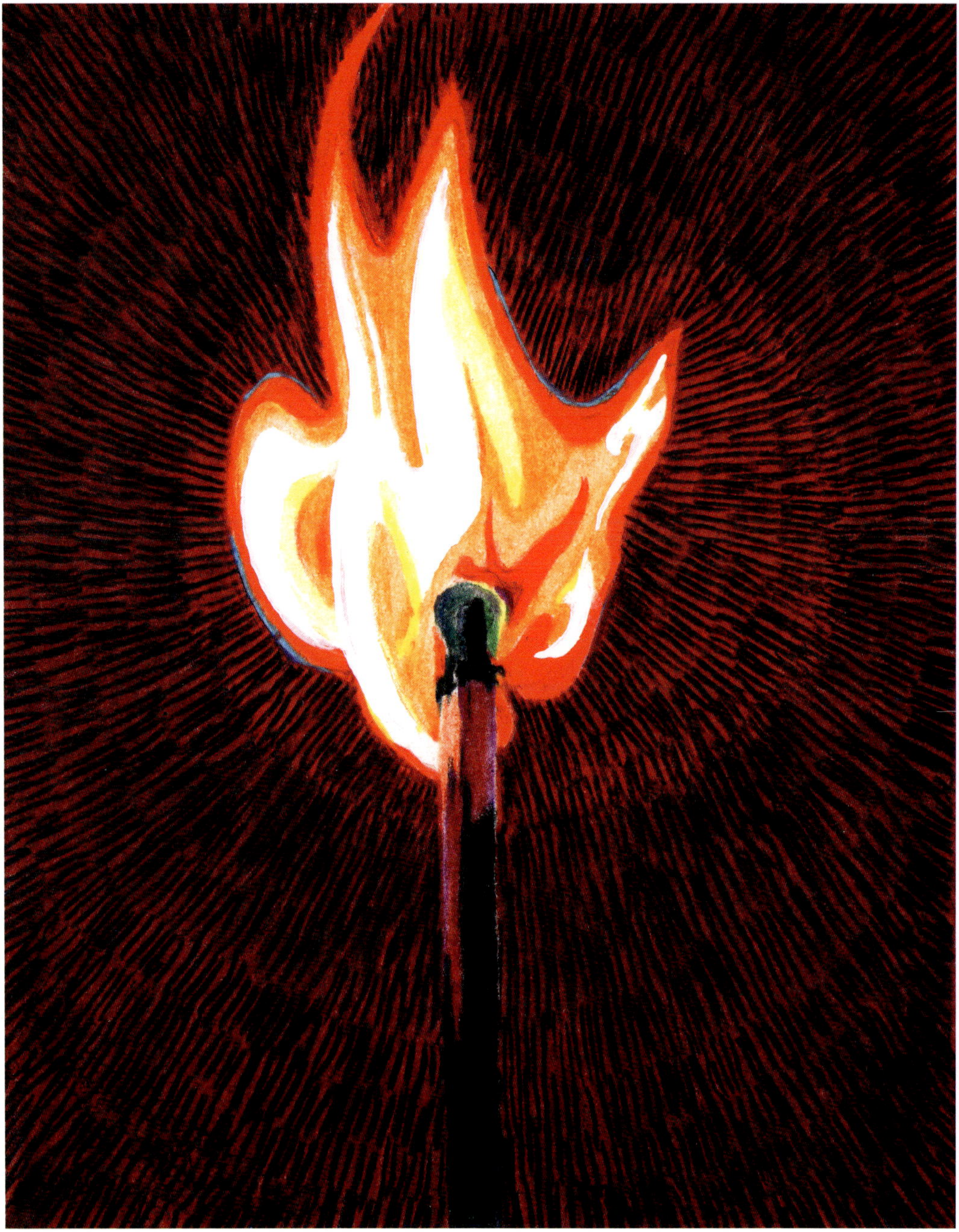

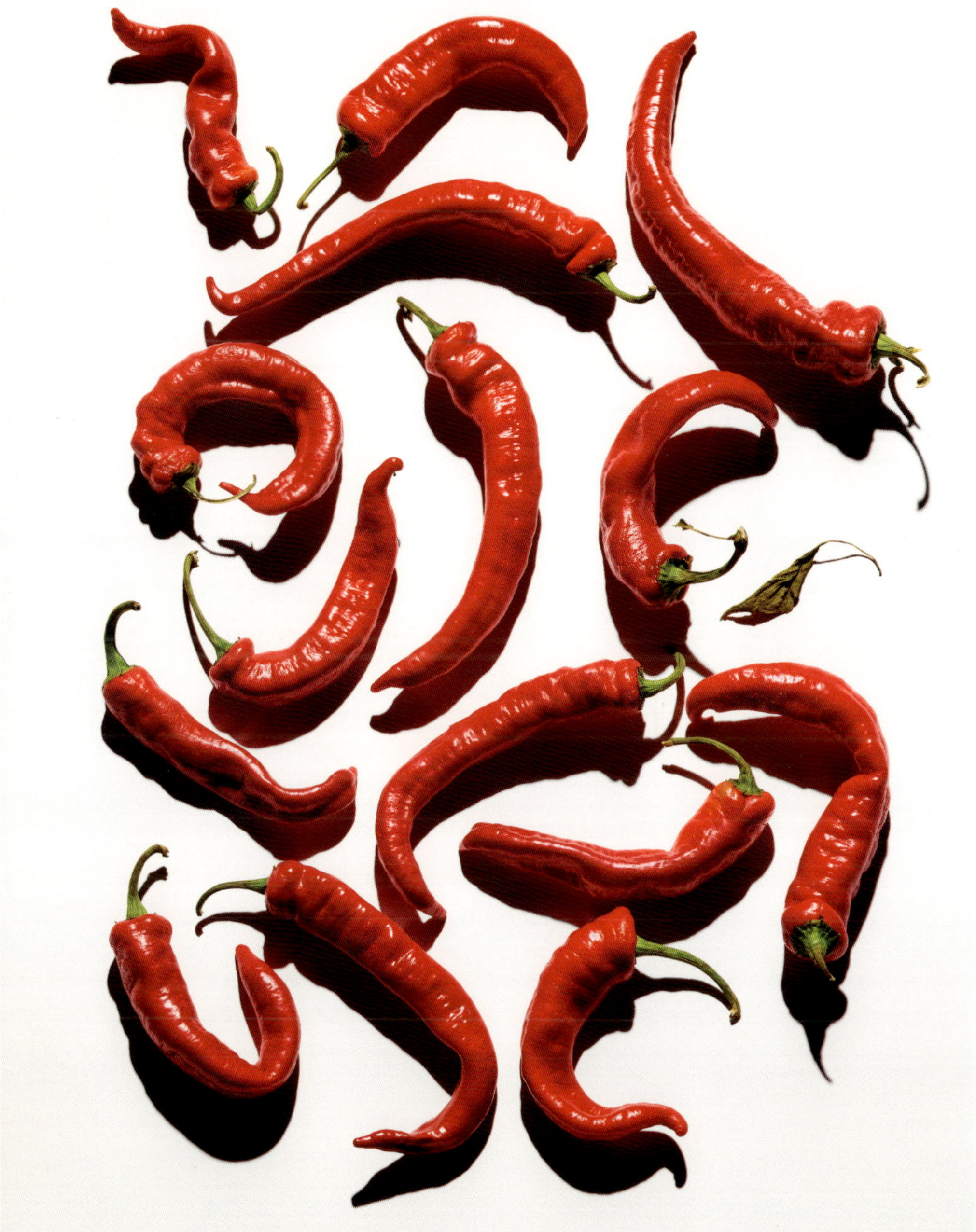

23

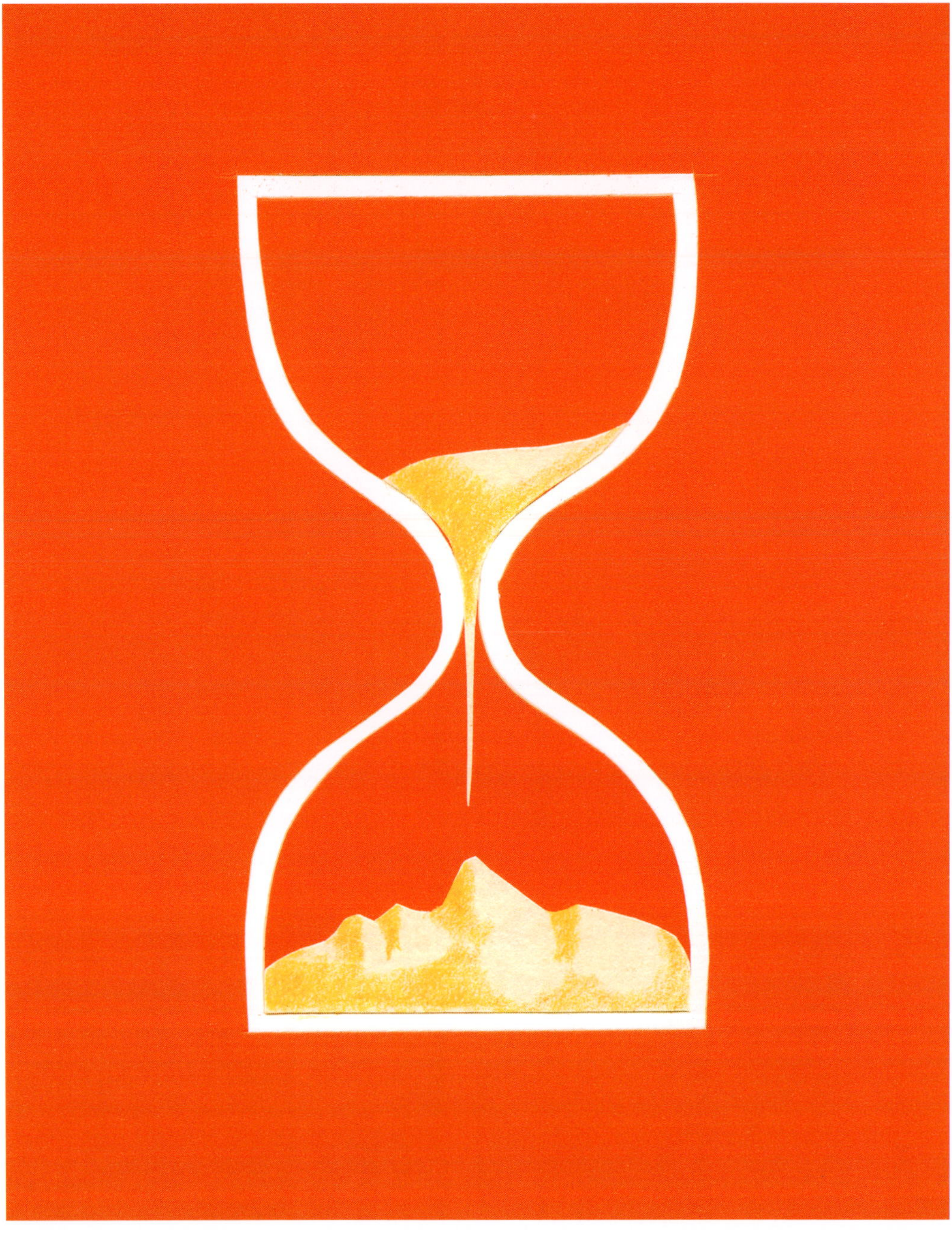

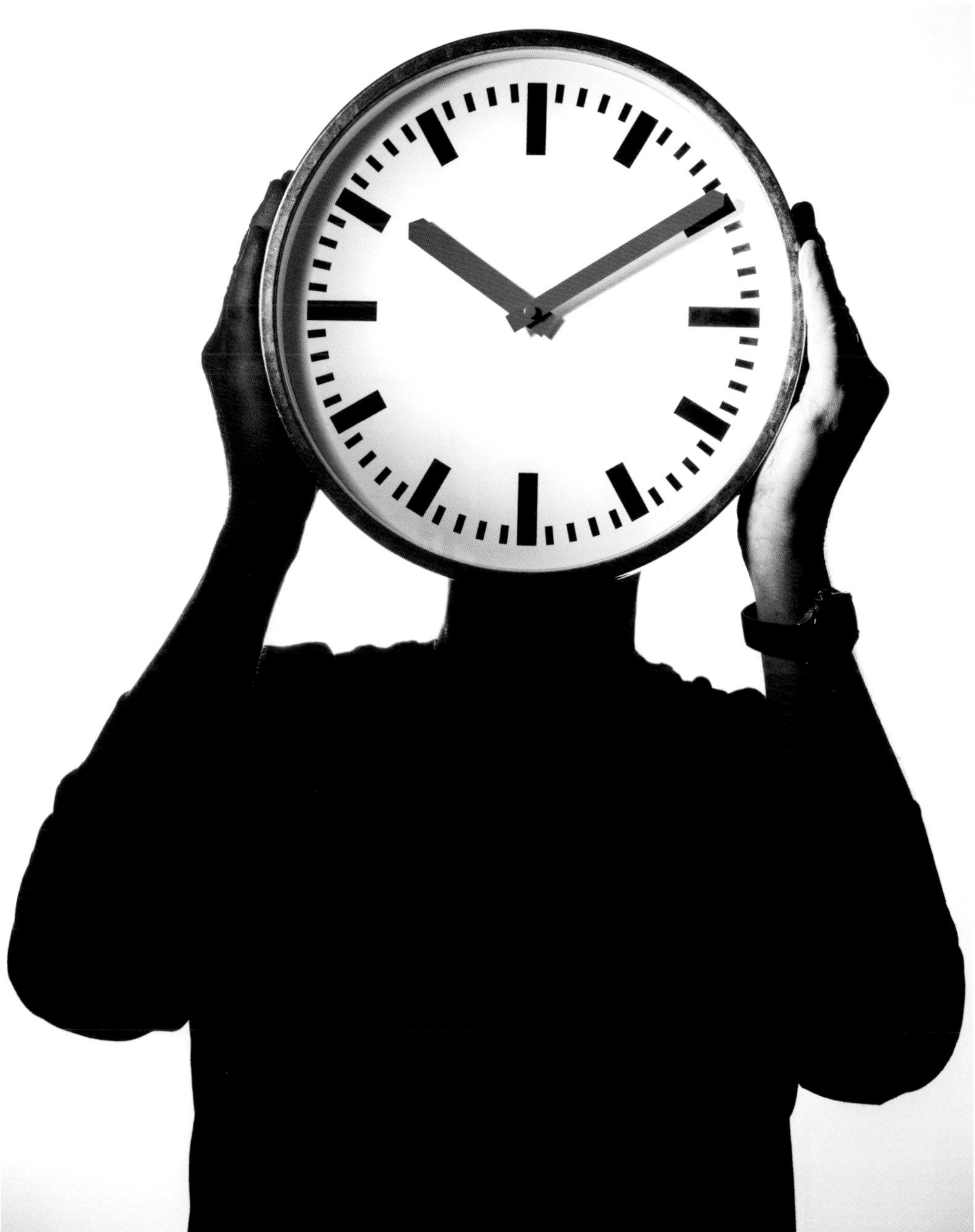

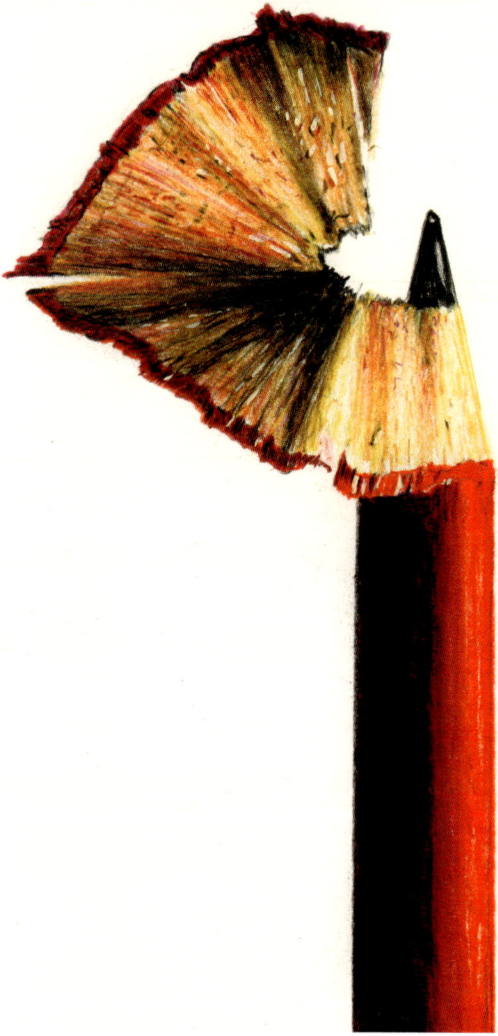

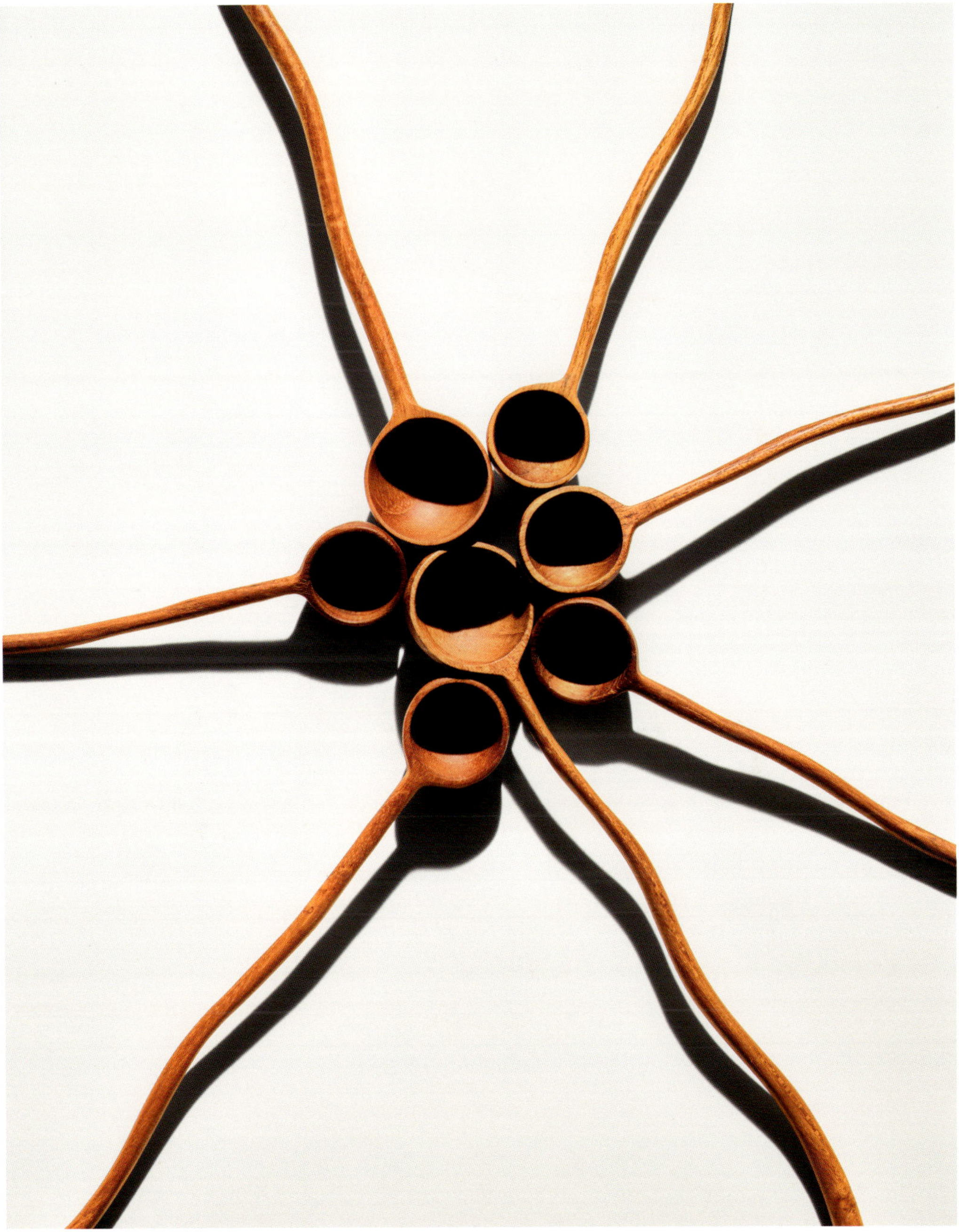

25

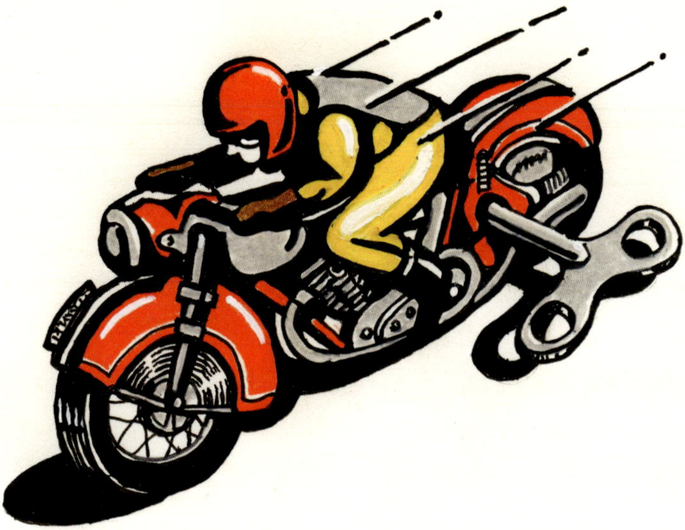

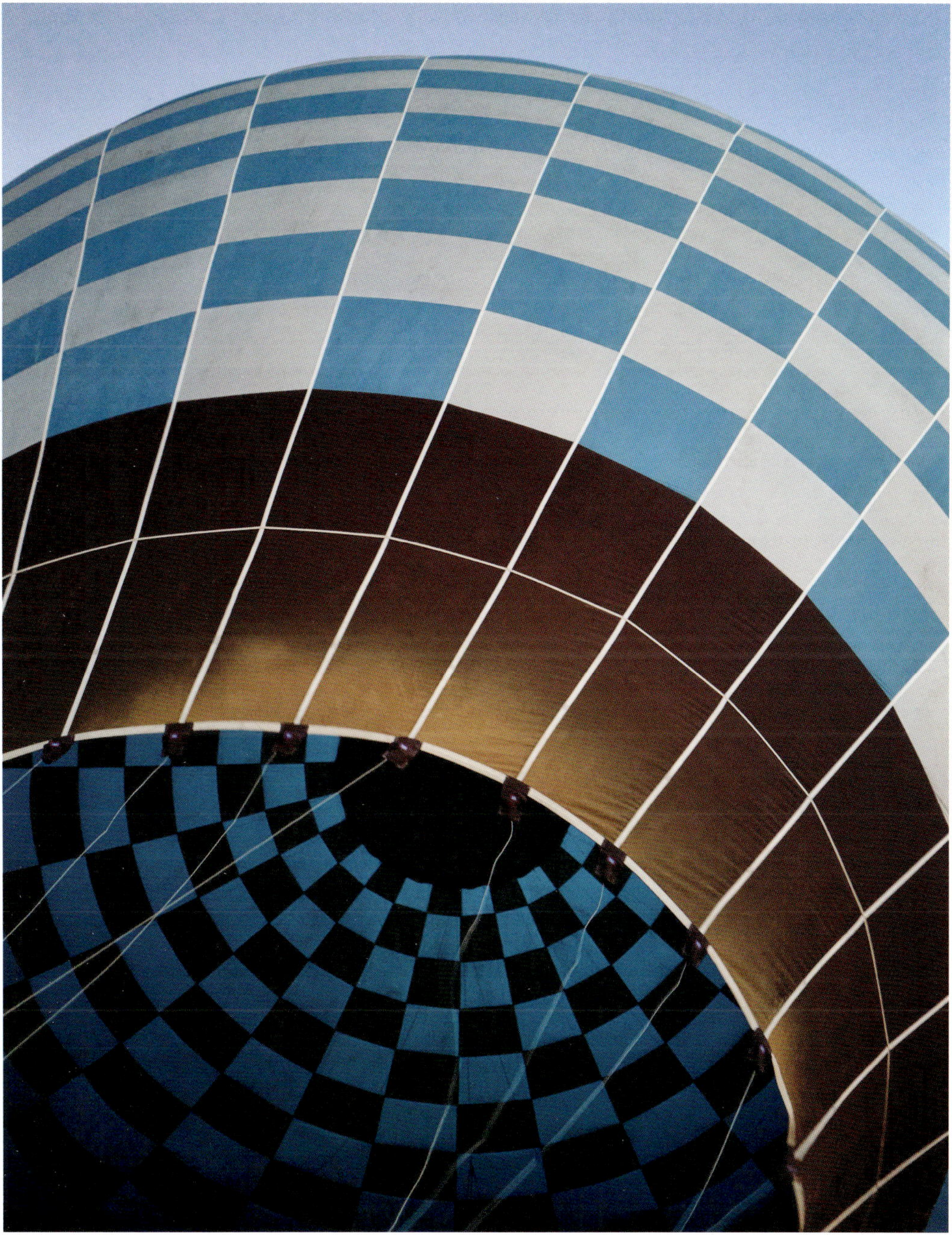

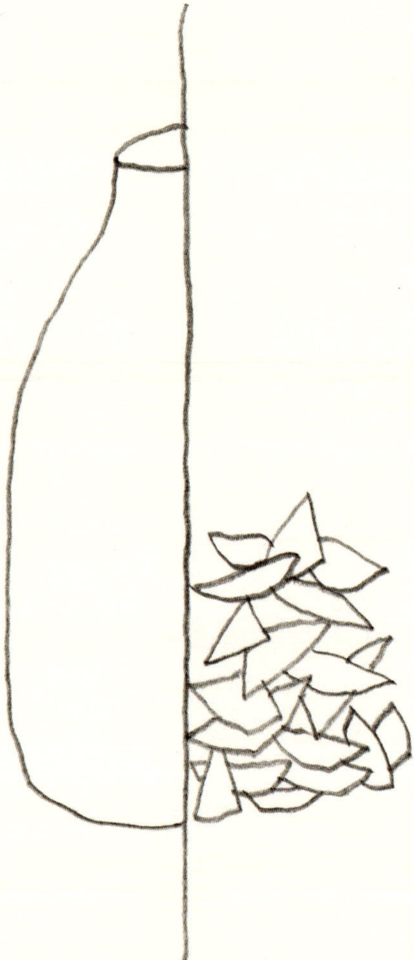

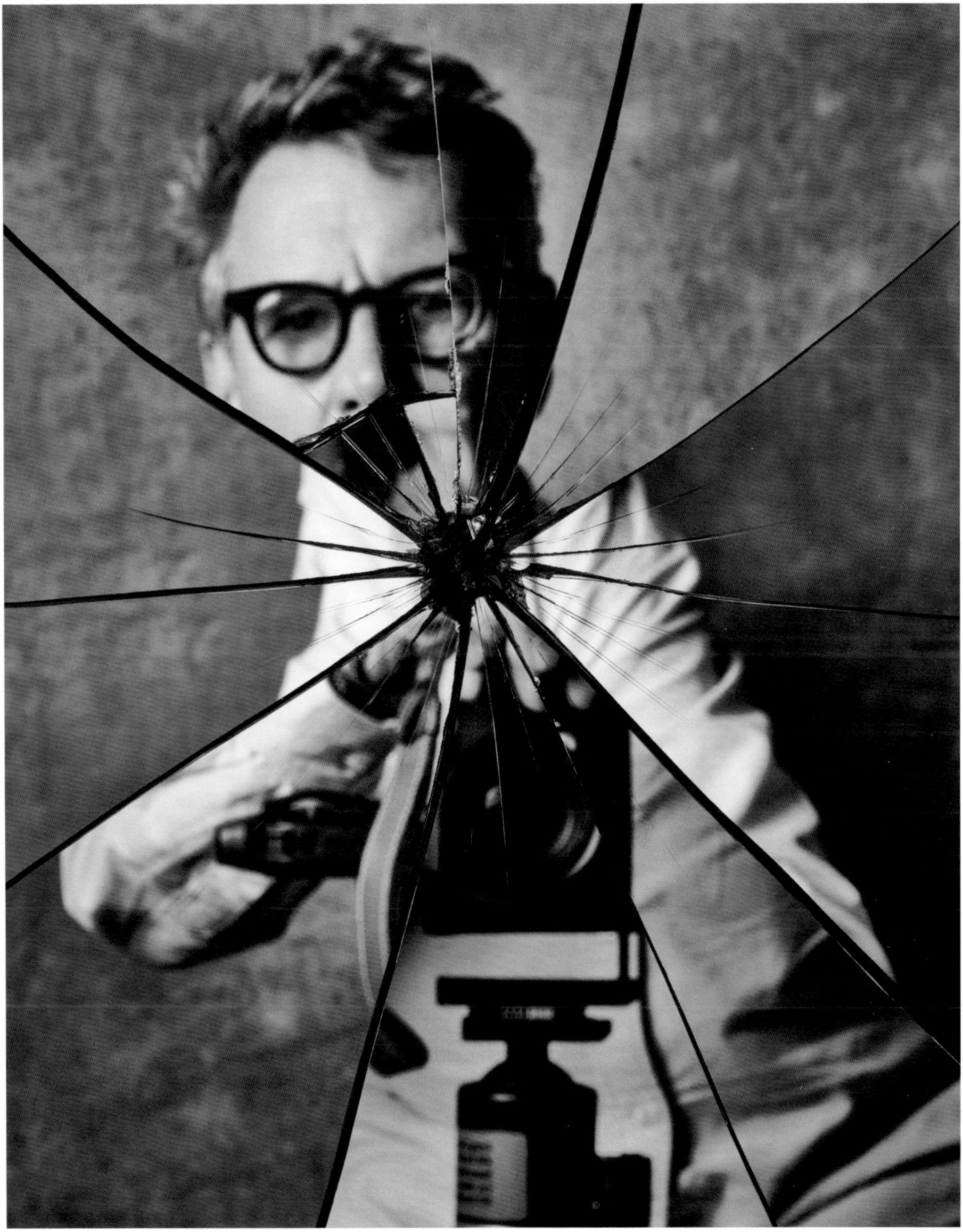

27

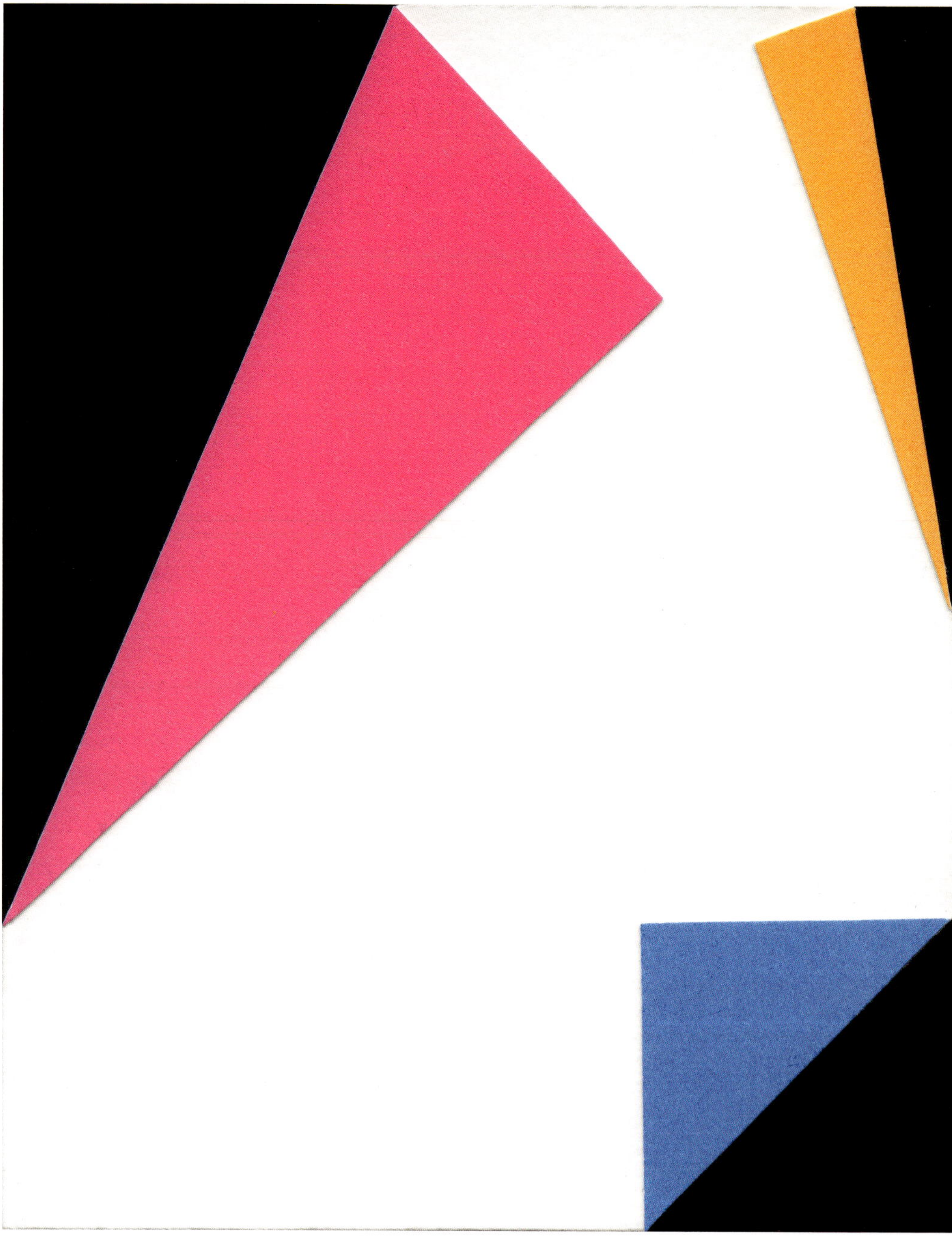

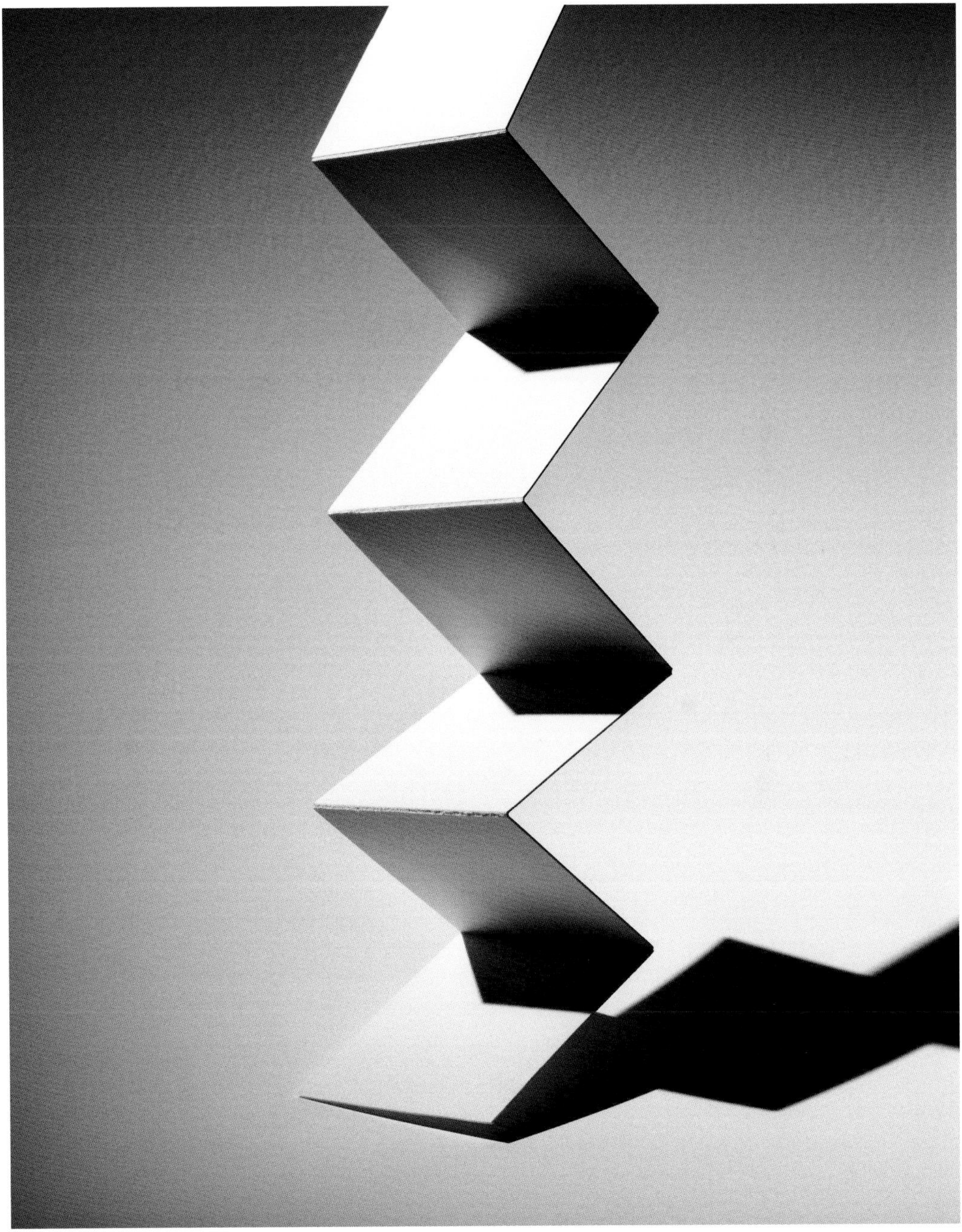

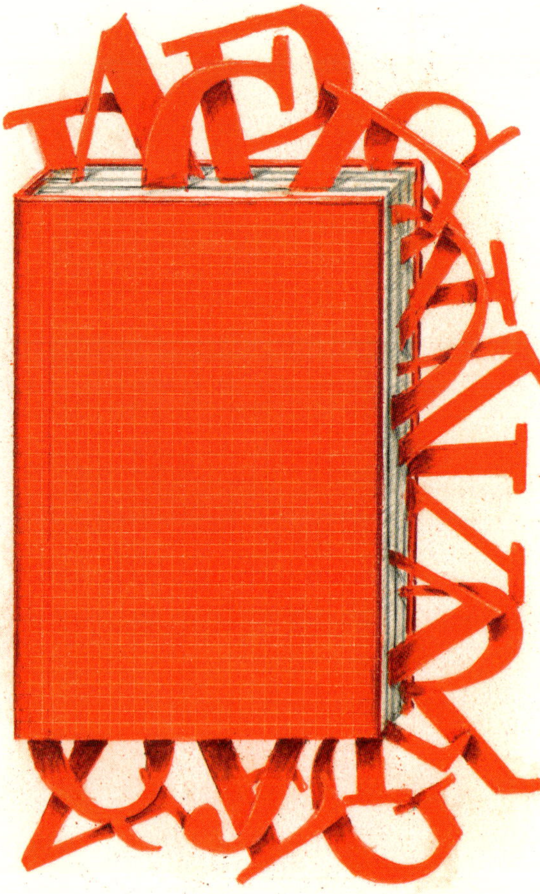

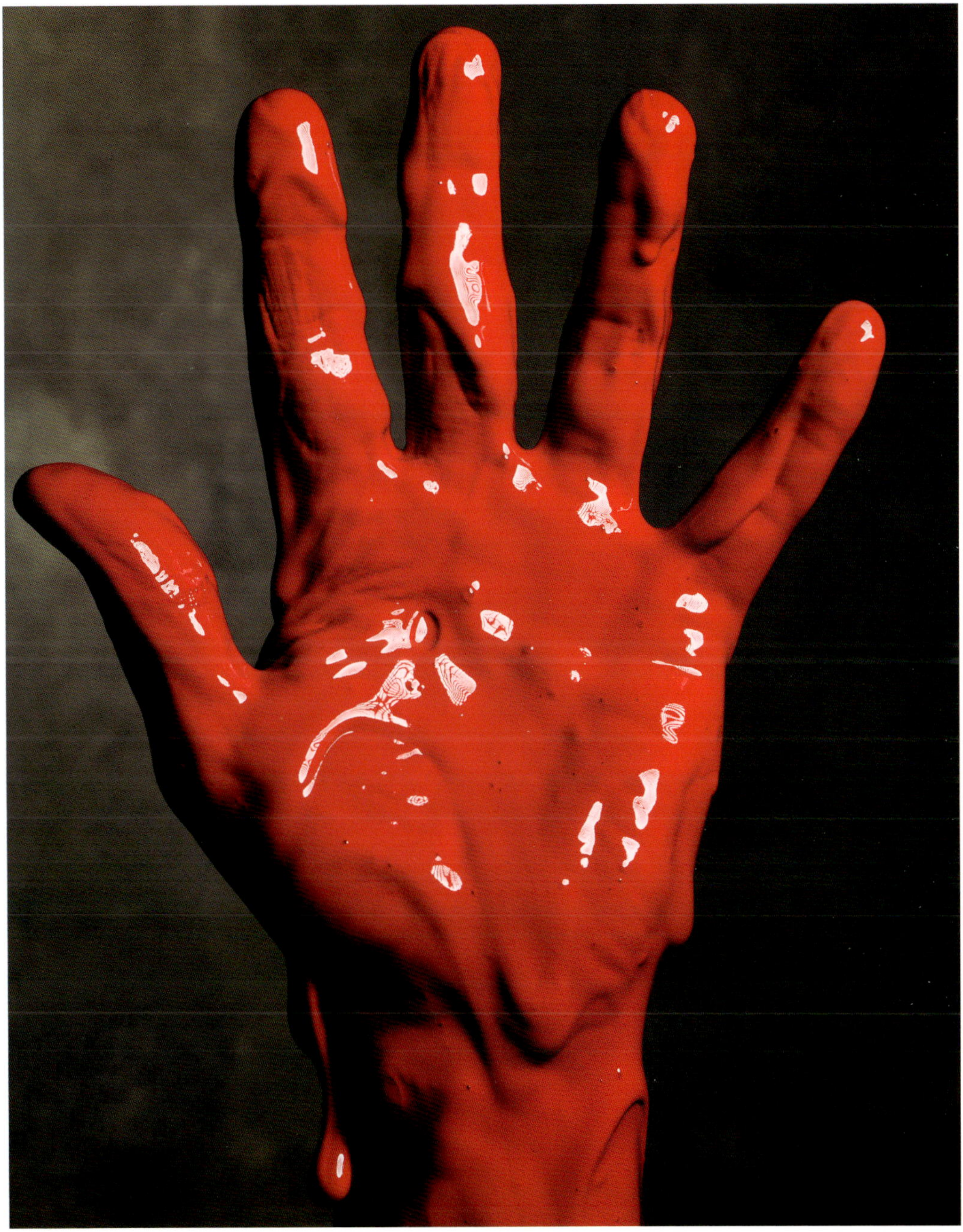

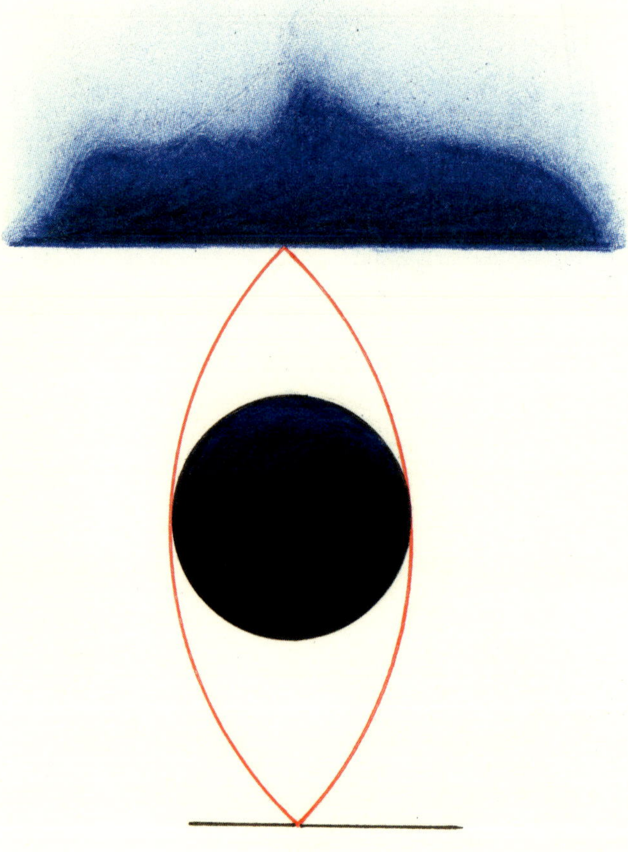

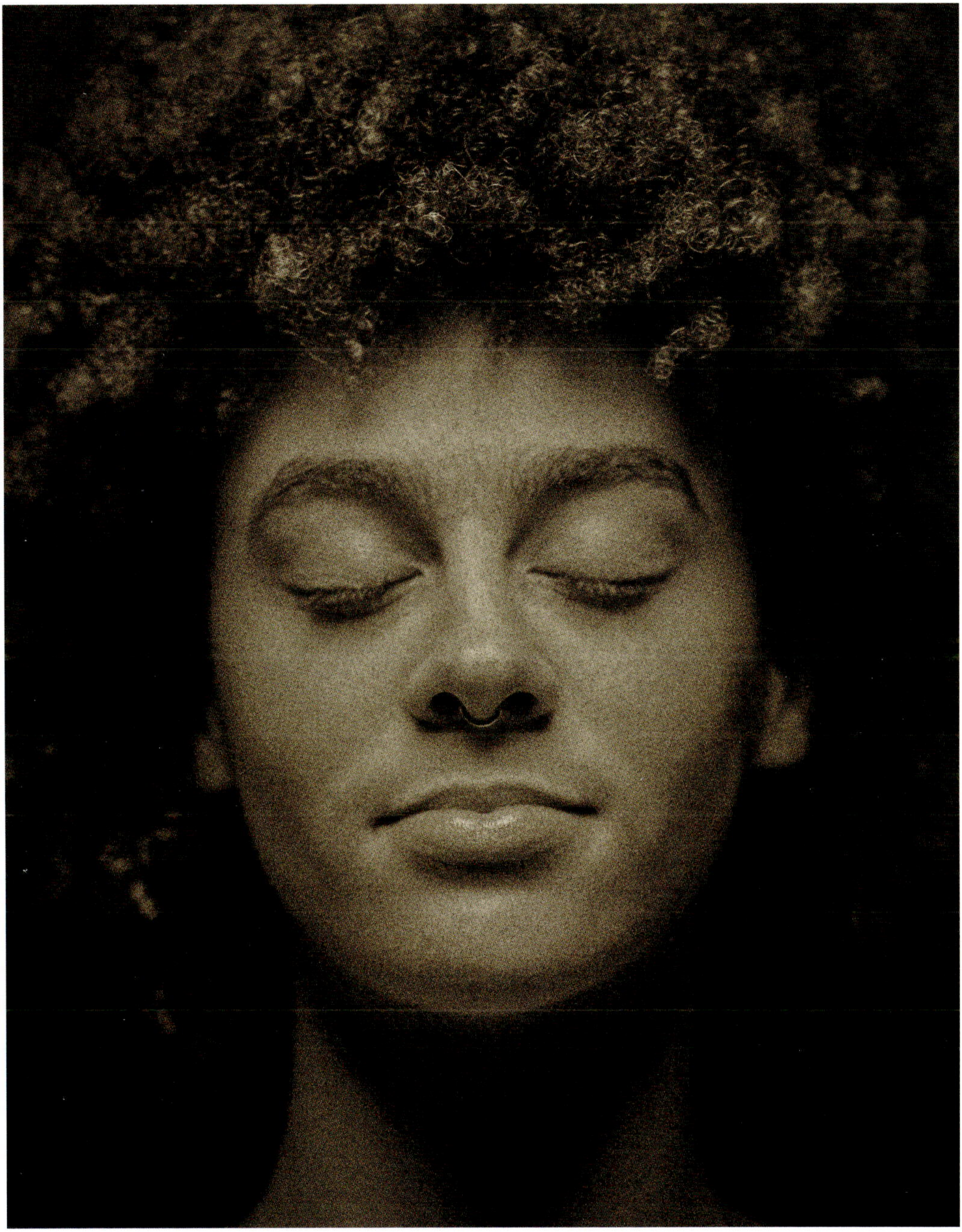

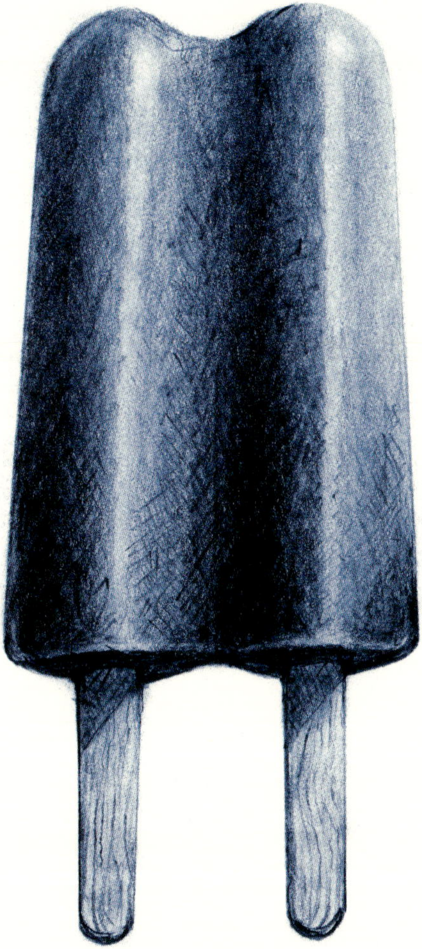

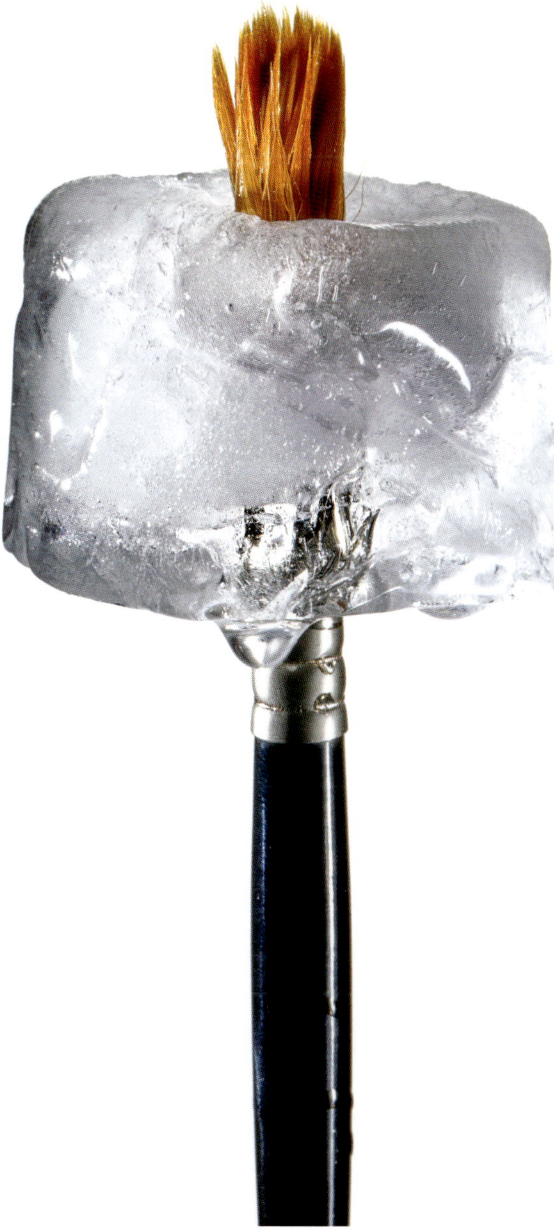

31

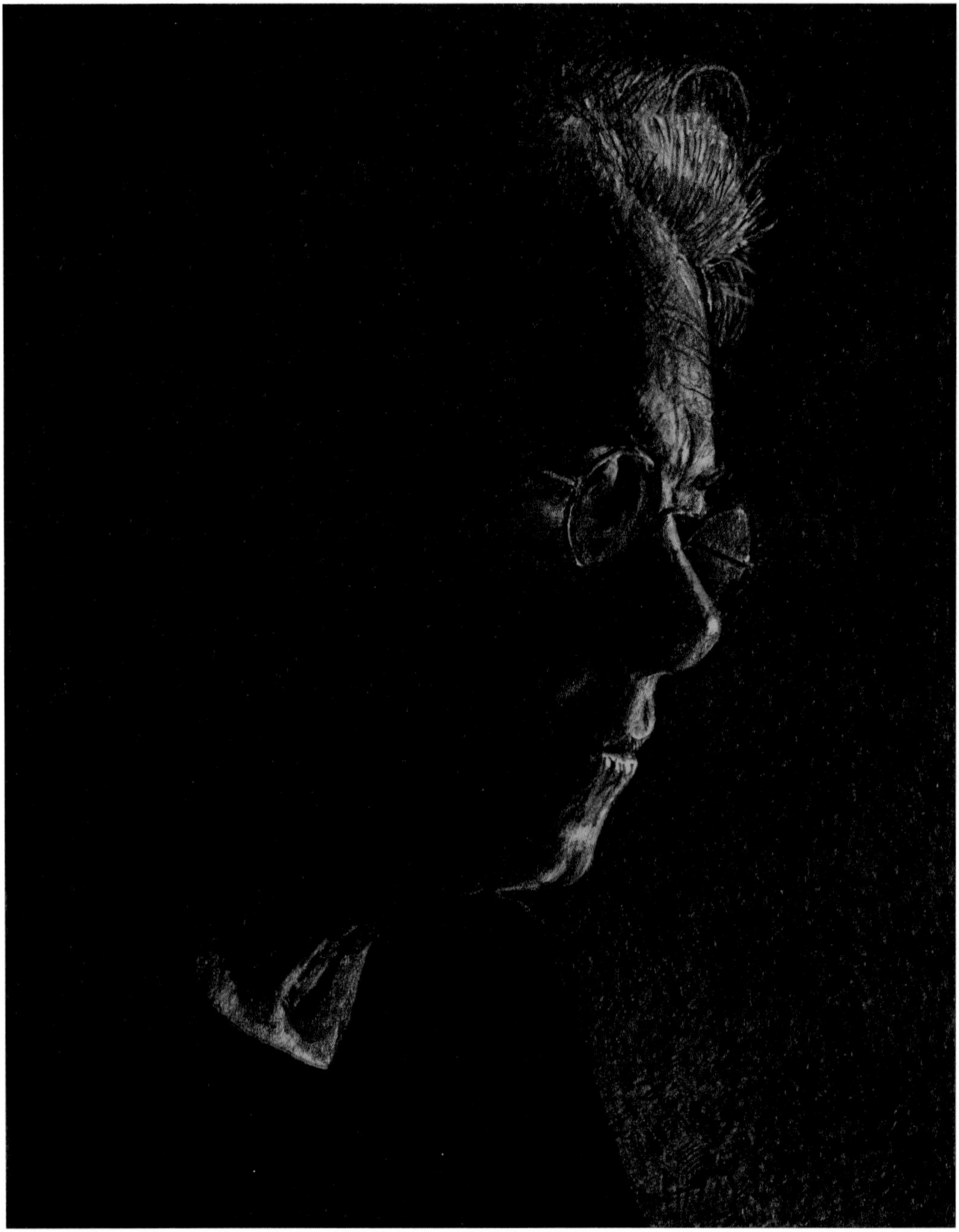

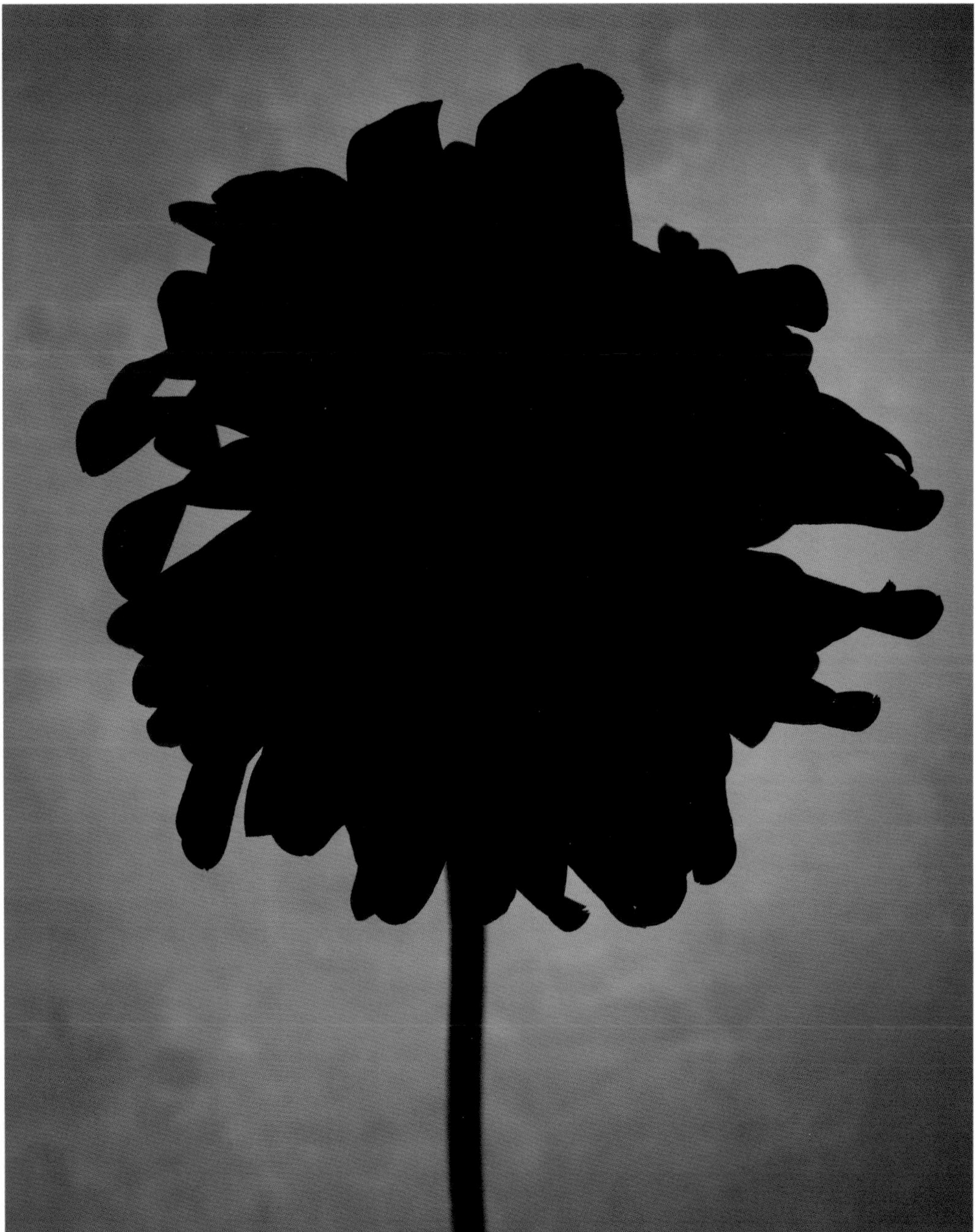

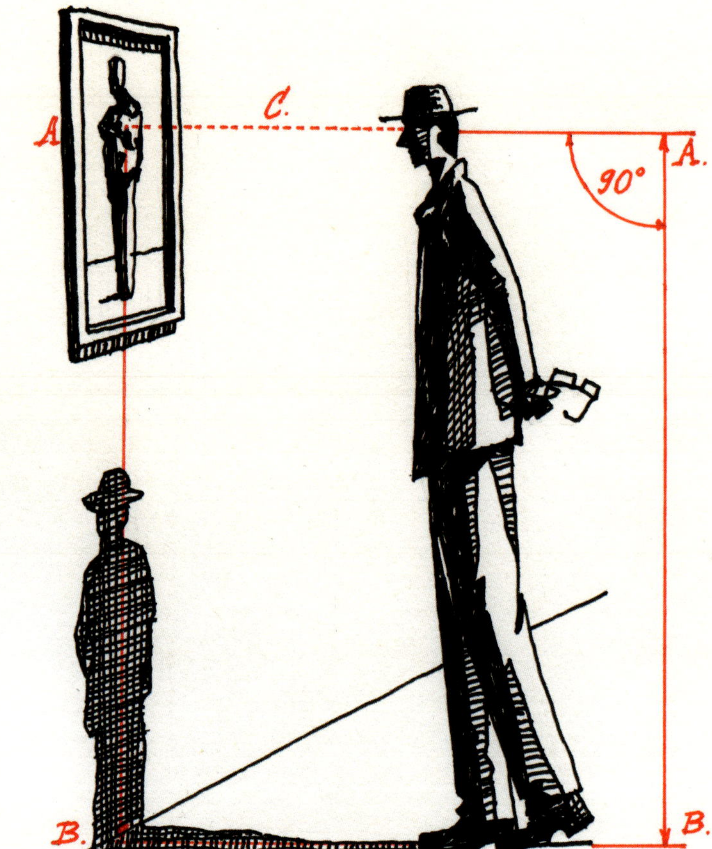

Fig.1

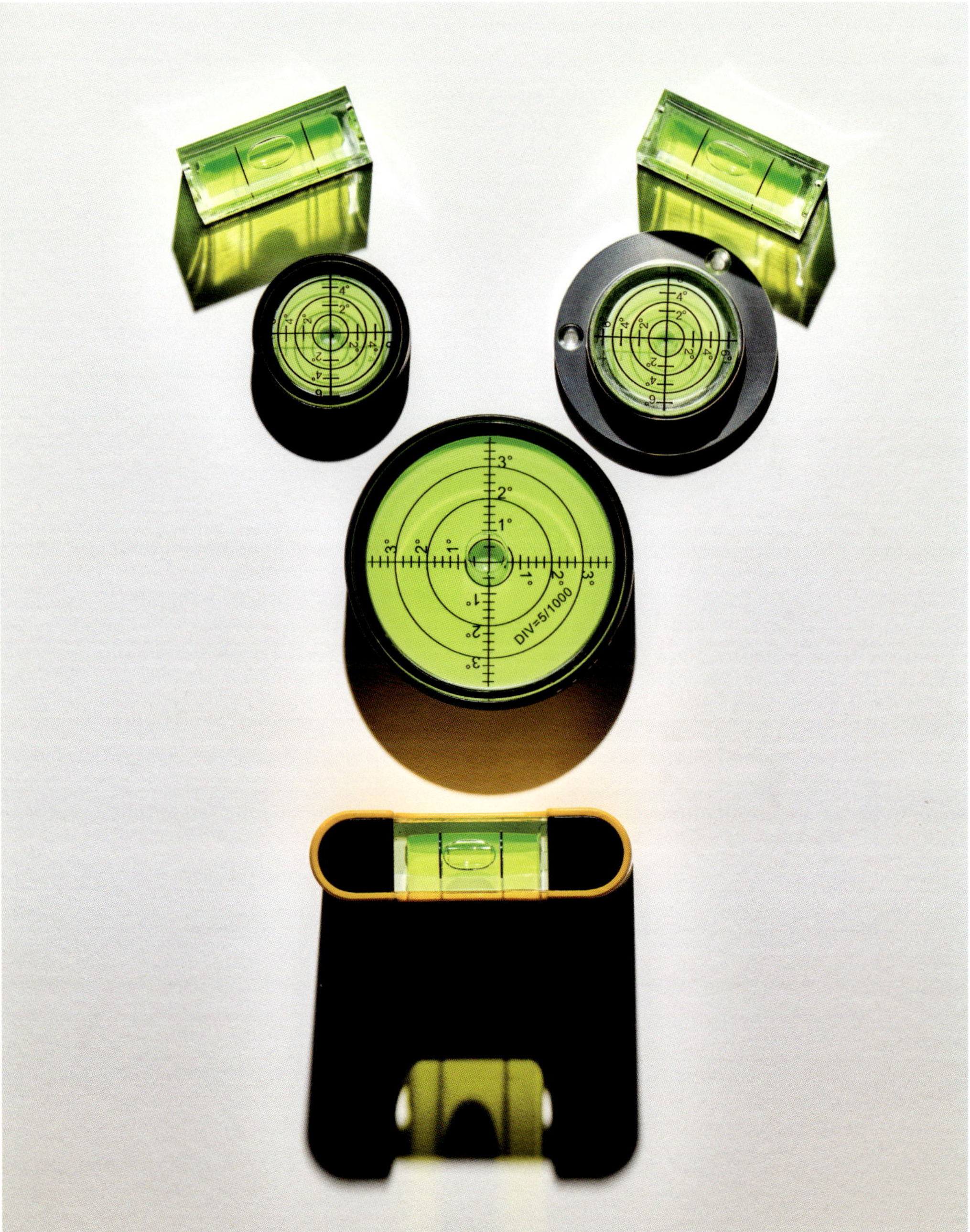
DIV=5/1000

33

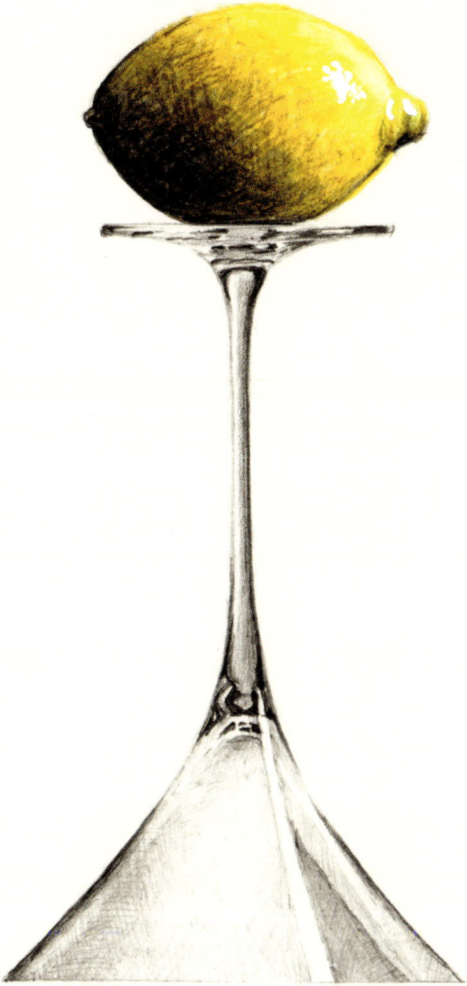

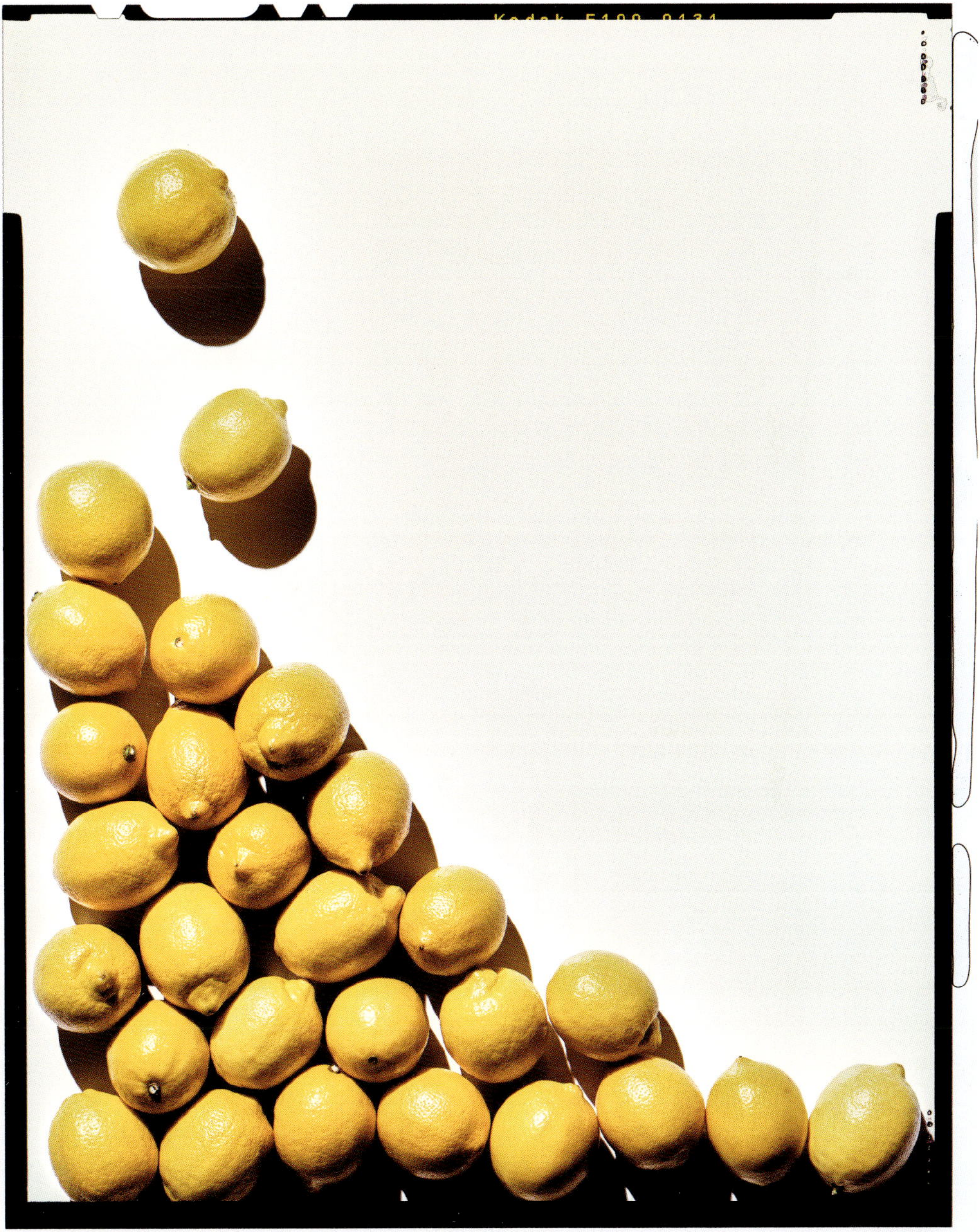
Kodak E100 0131

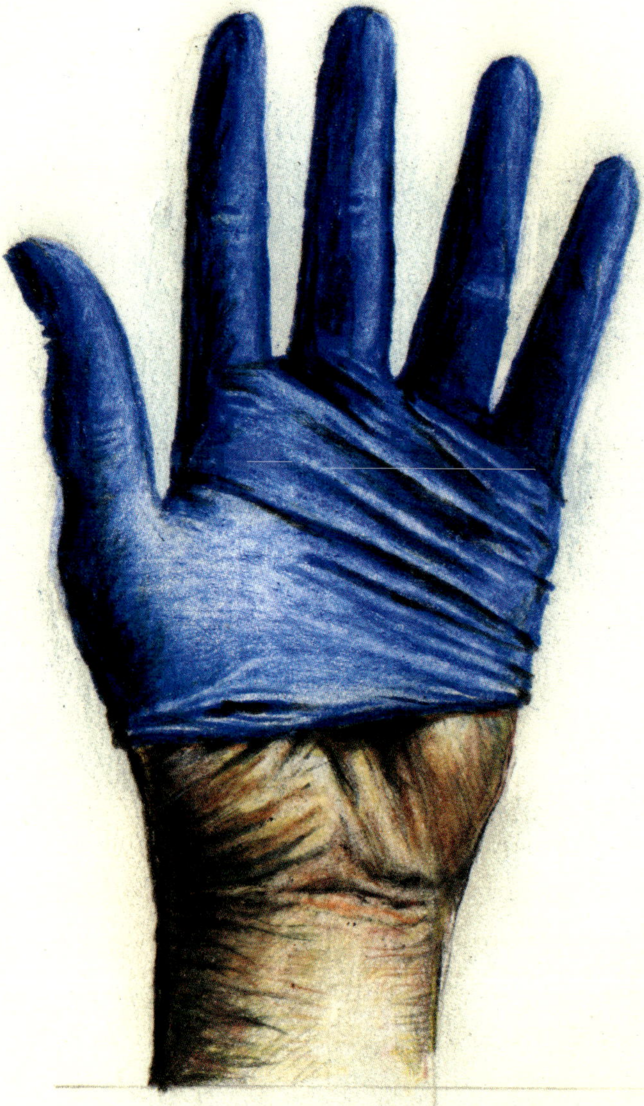

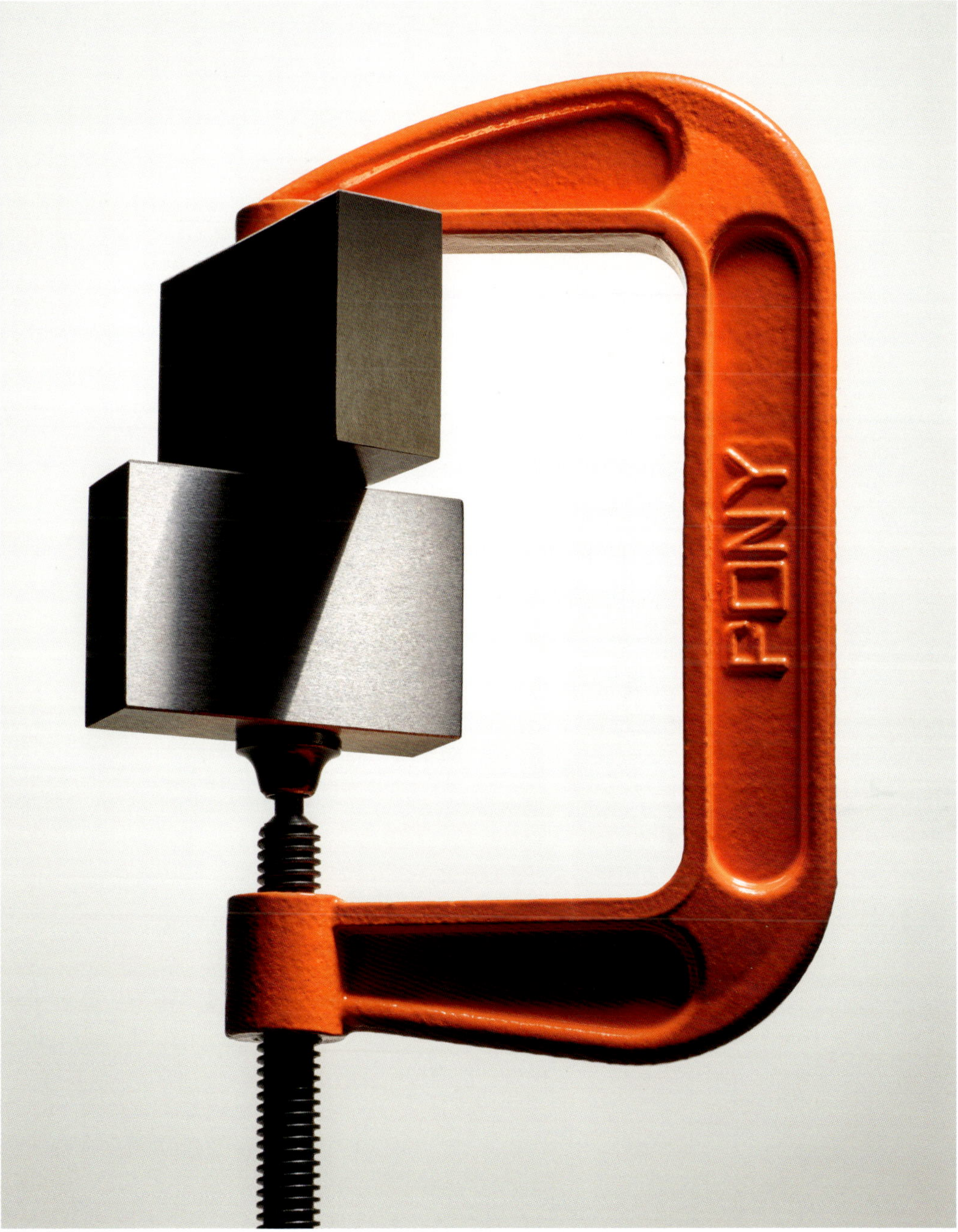
PONY

35

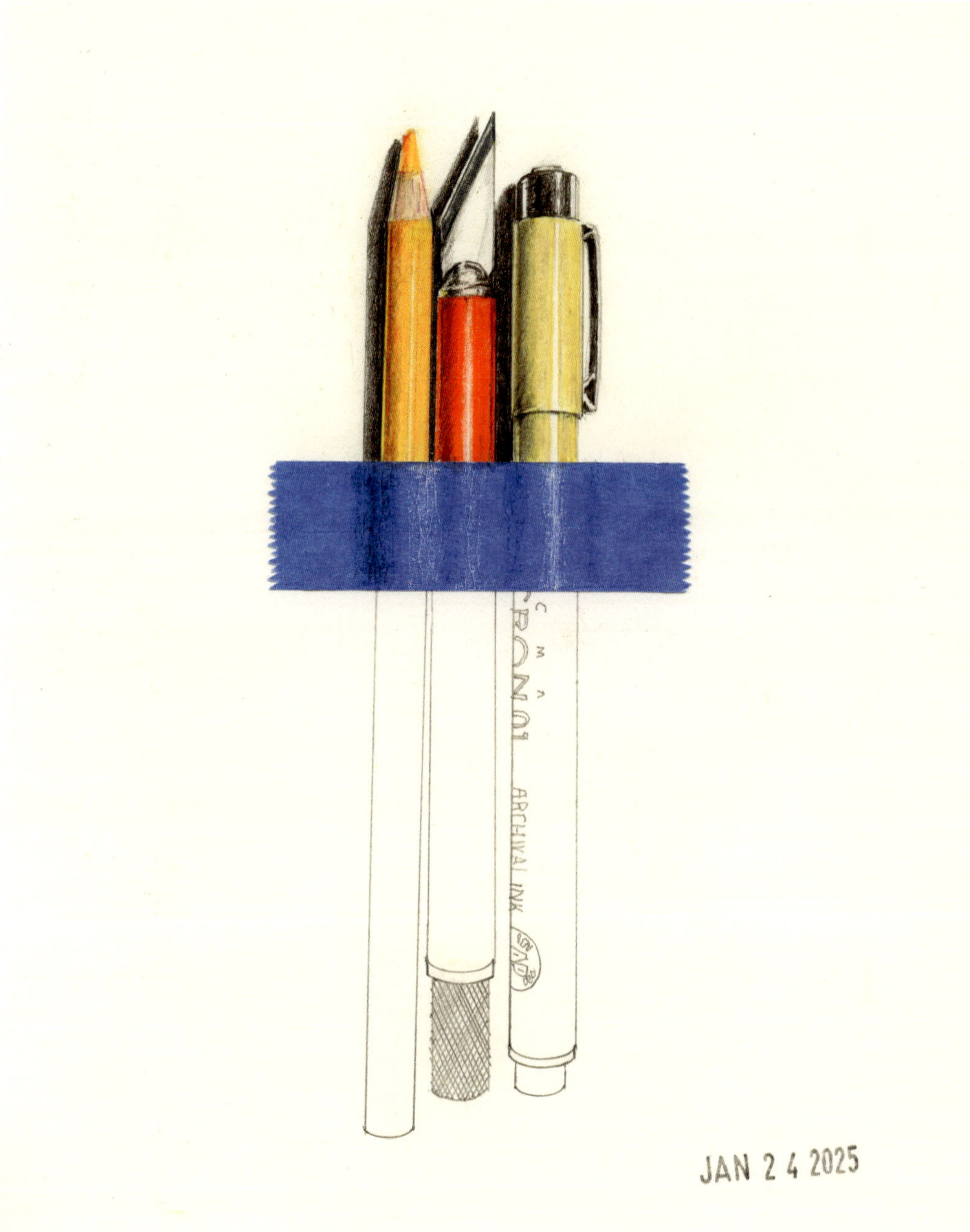

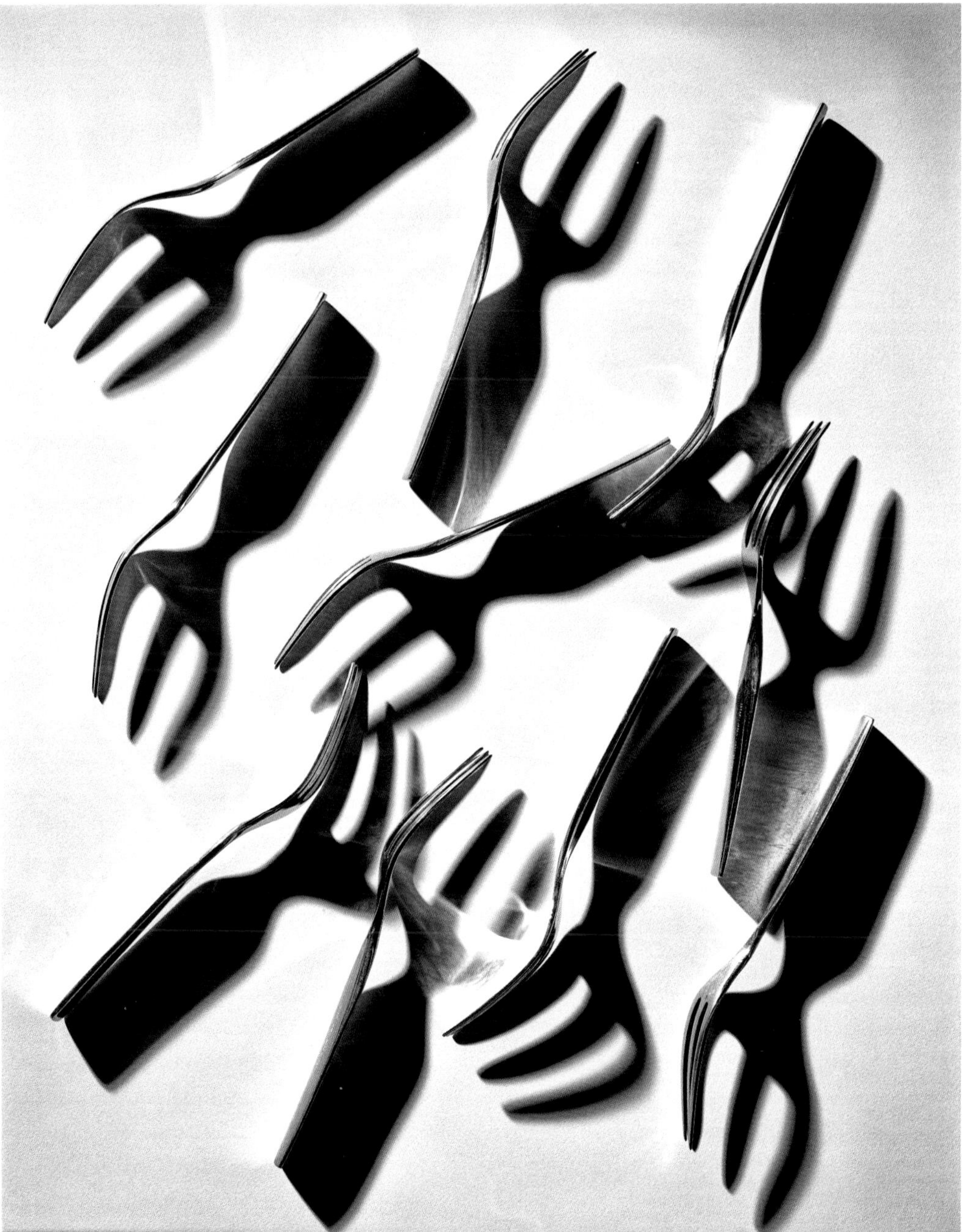

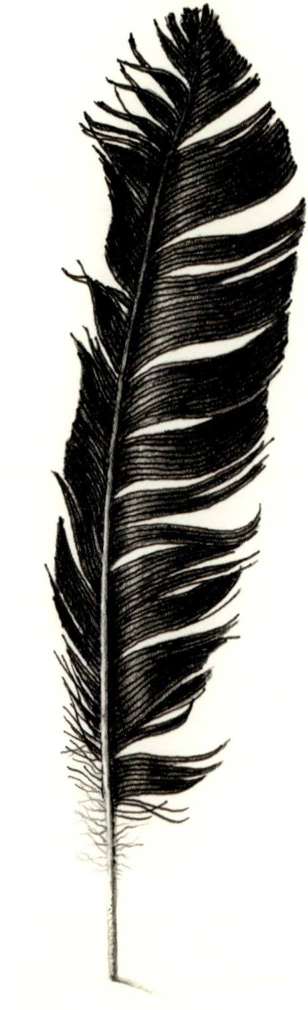

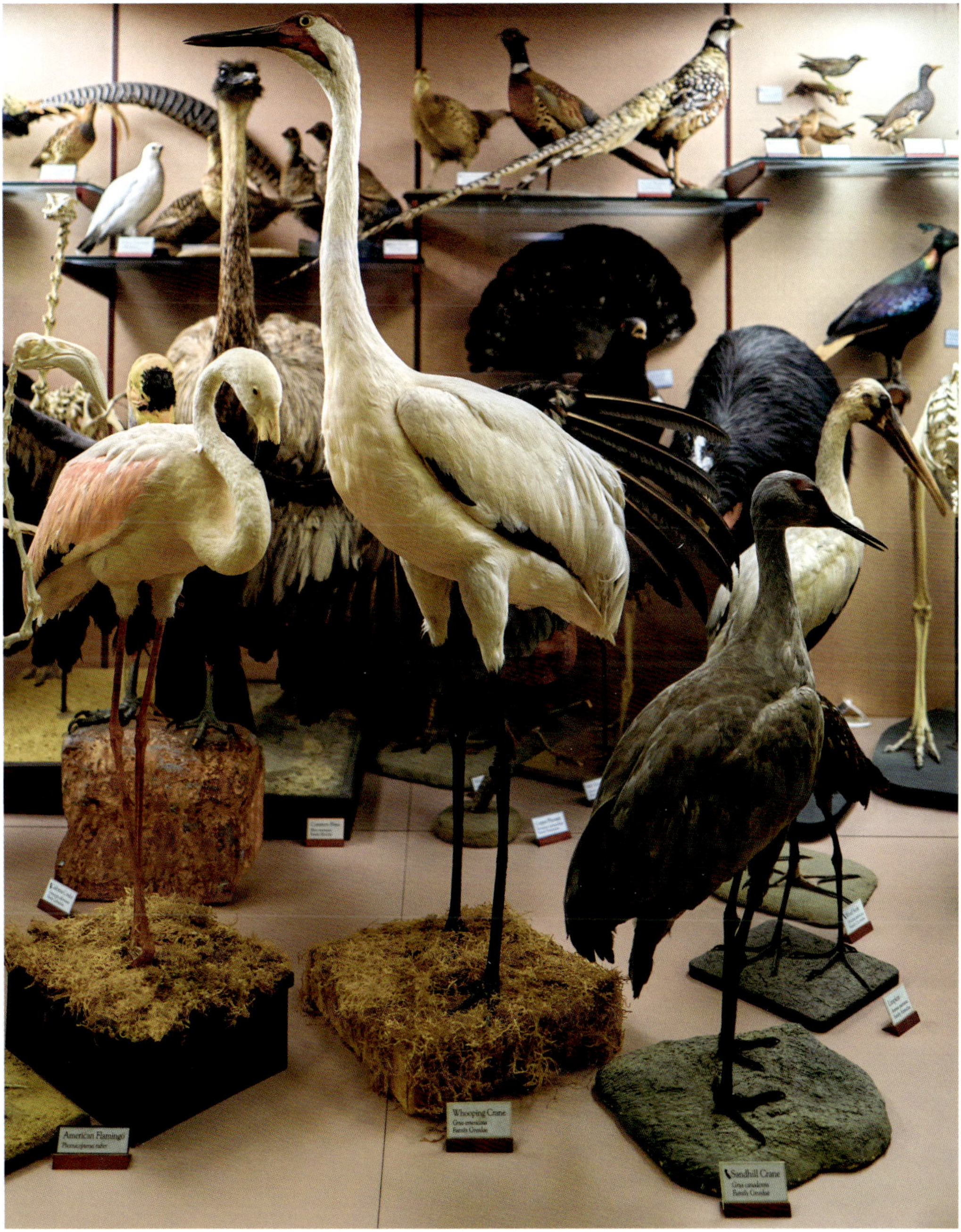

Photograph courtesy of the Natural History Museum of Los Angeles County.

37

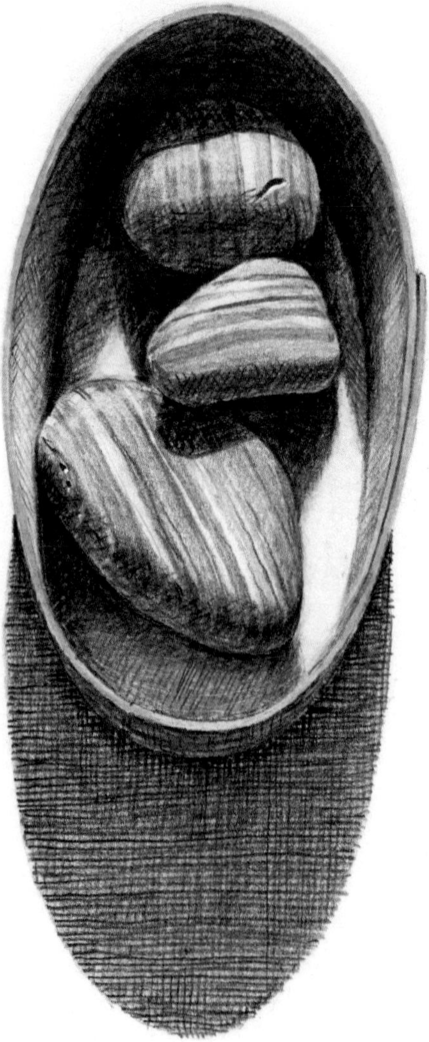

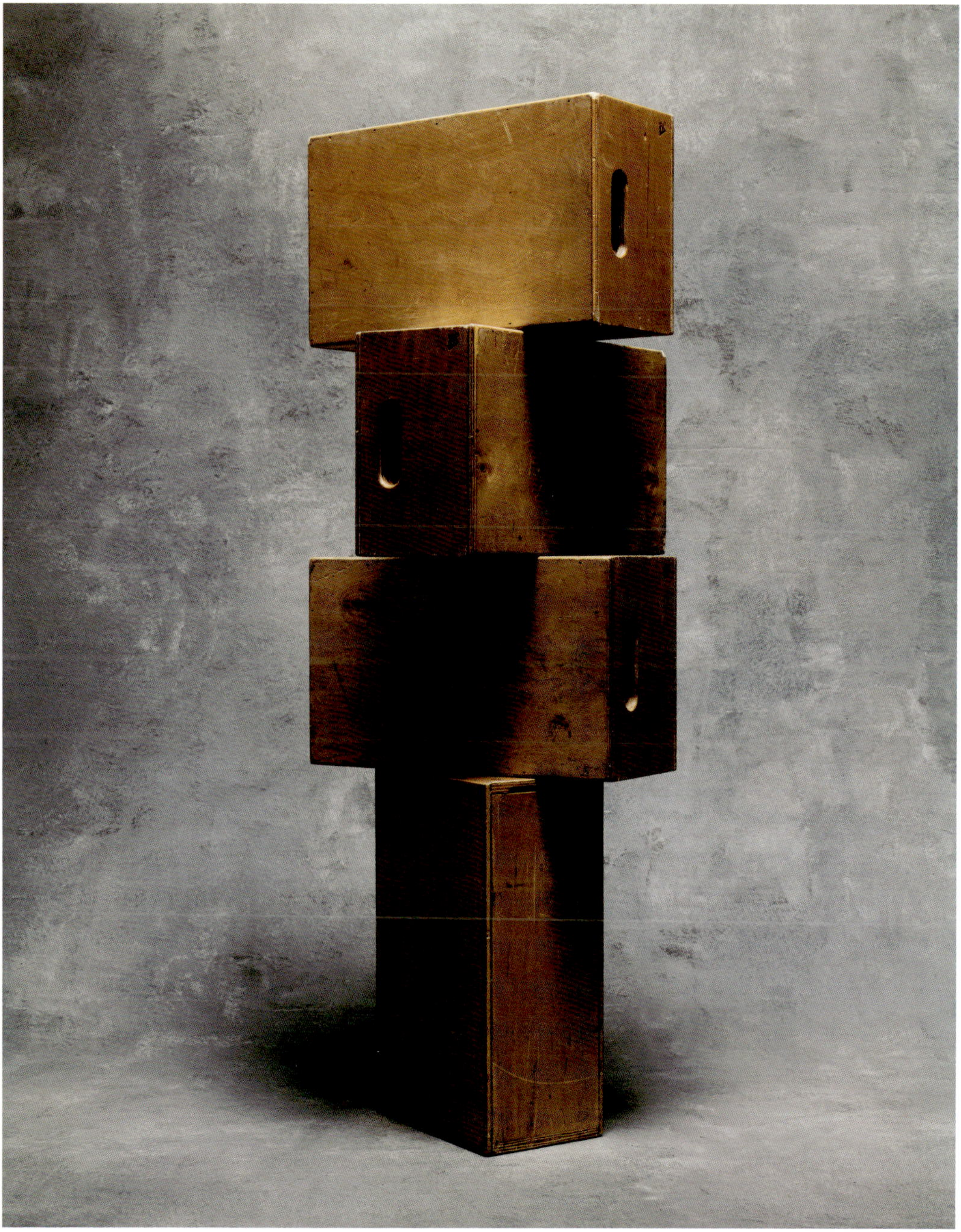

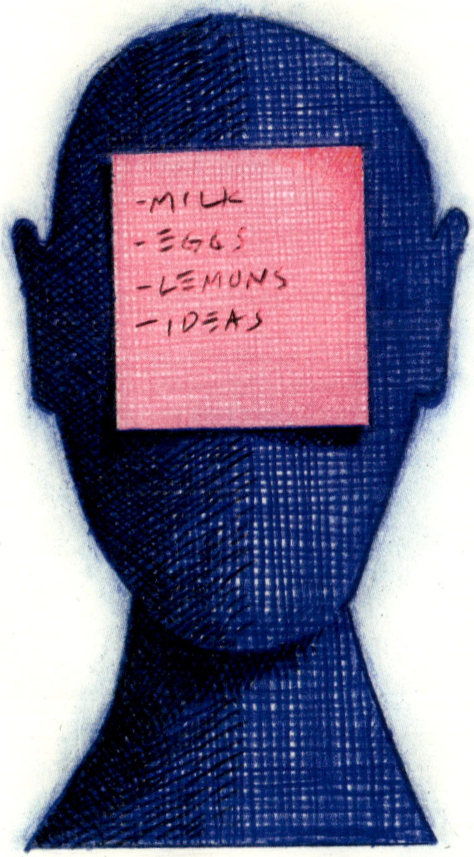
-MILK
-EGGS
-LEMONS
-IDEAS

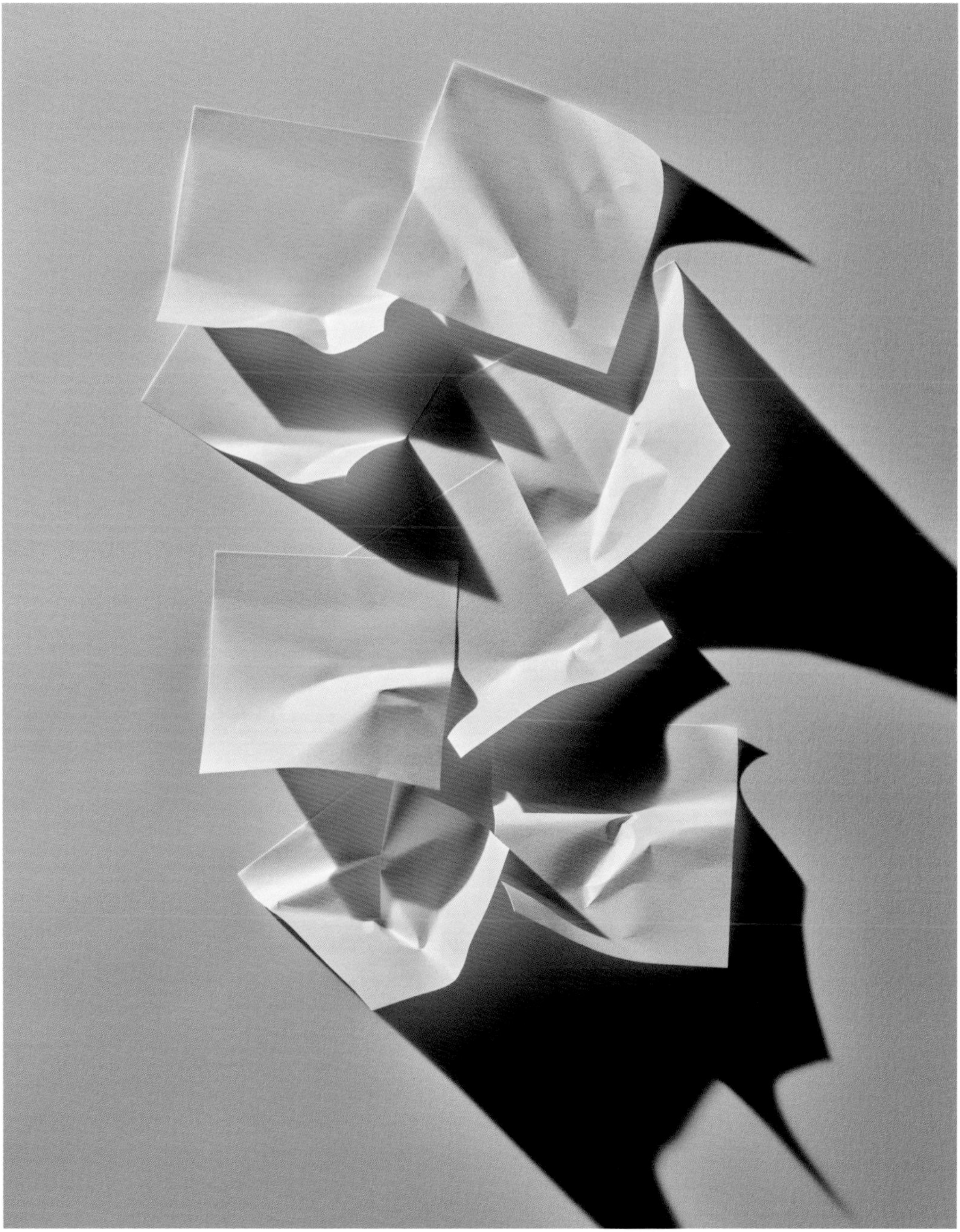

39

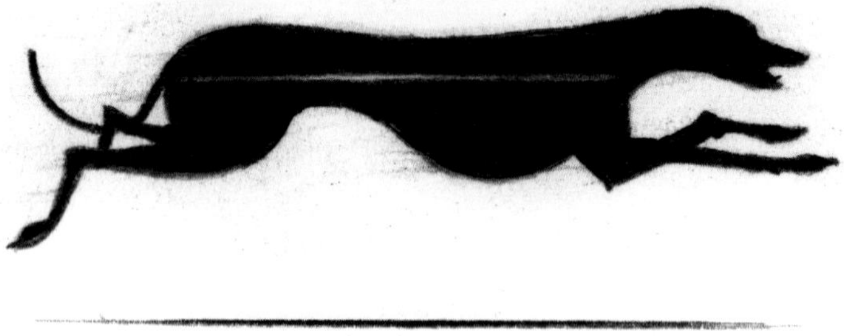

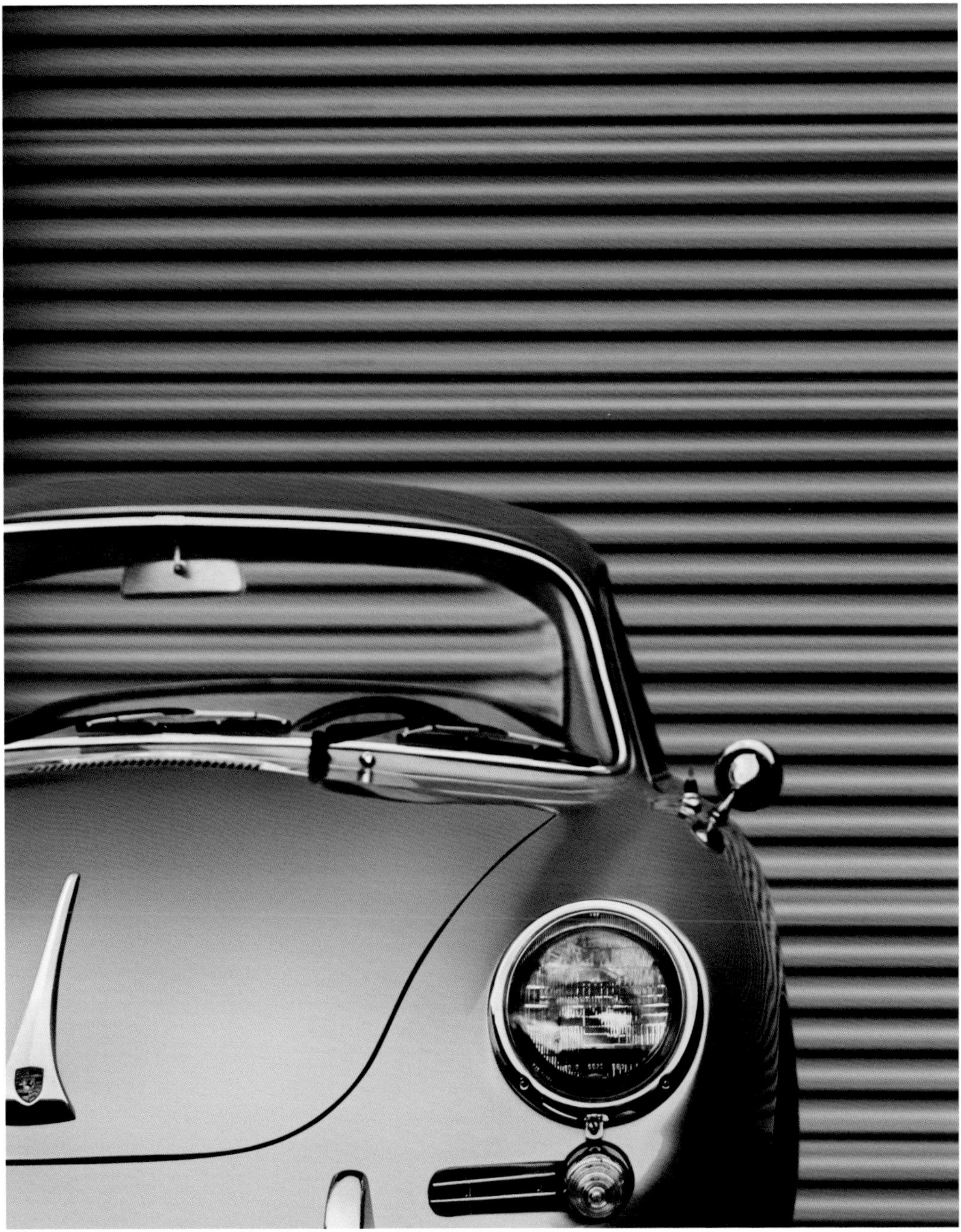

40

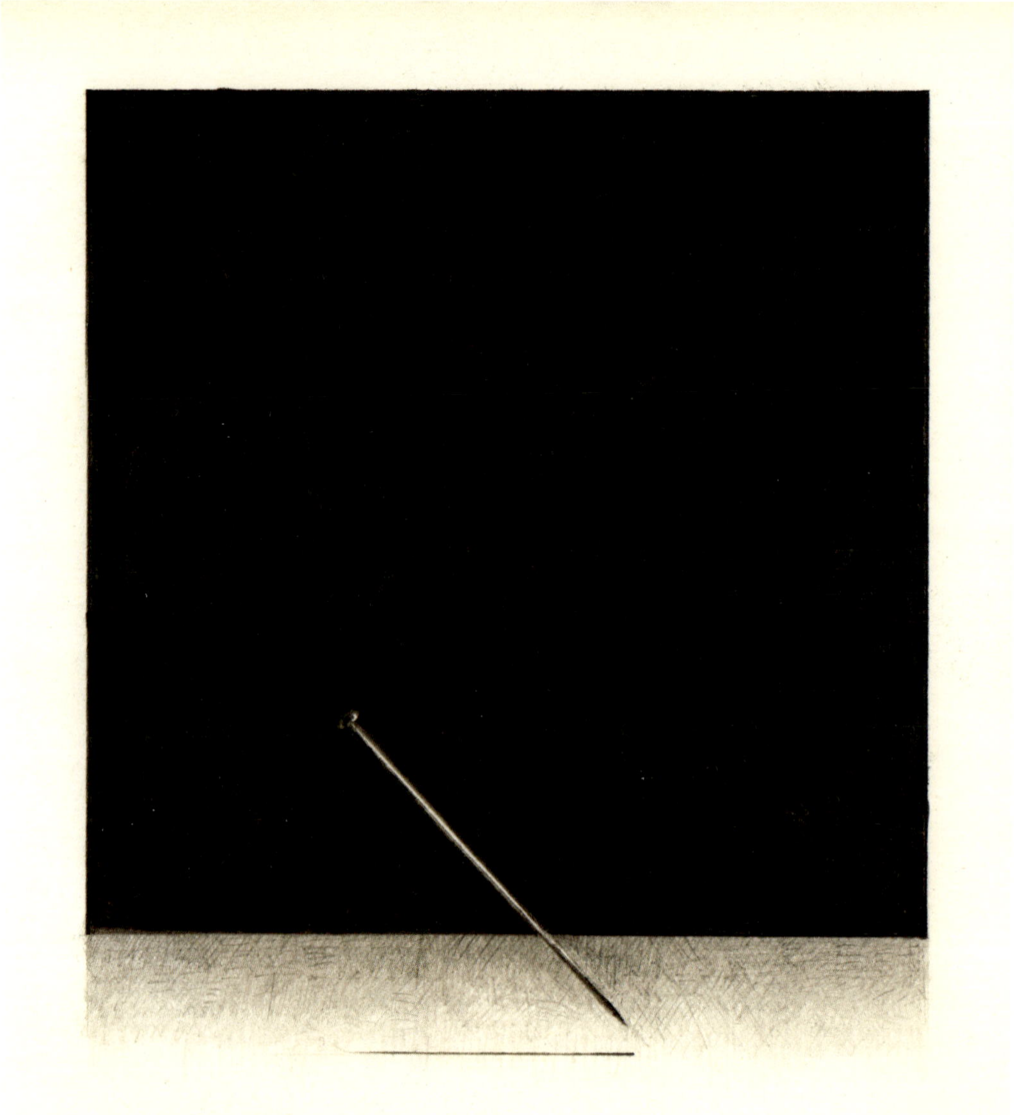

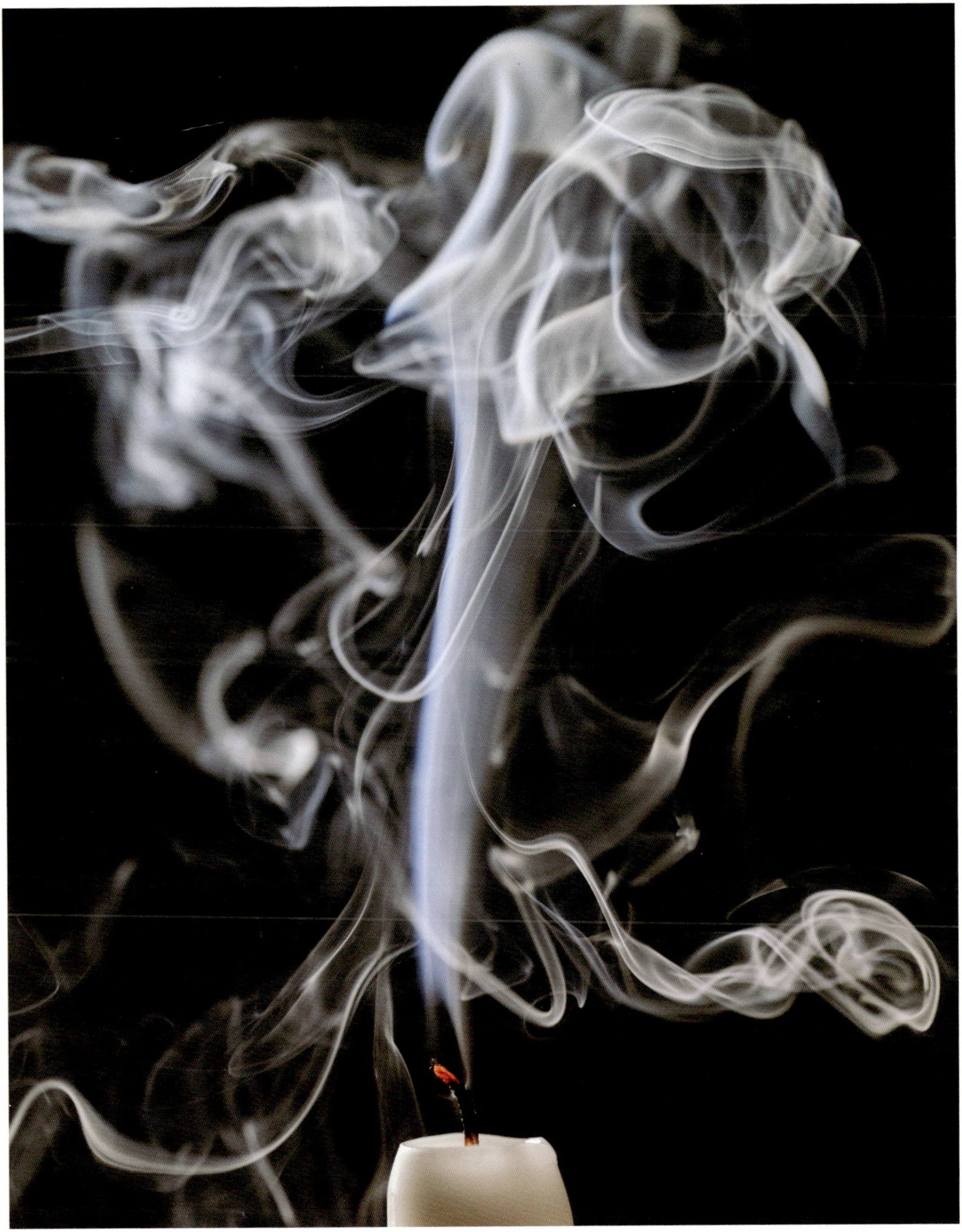

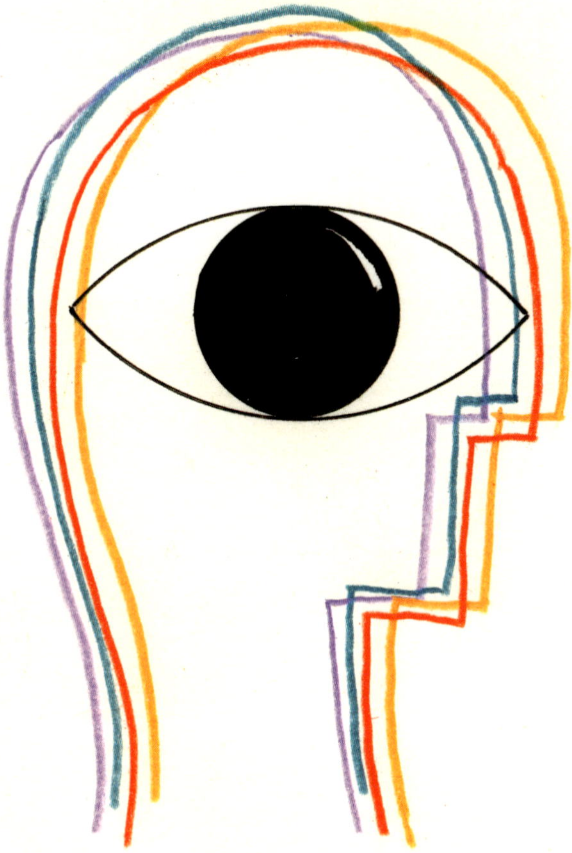

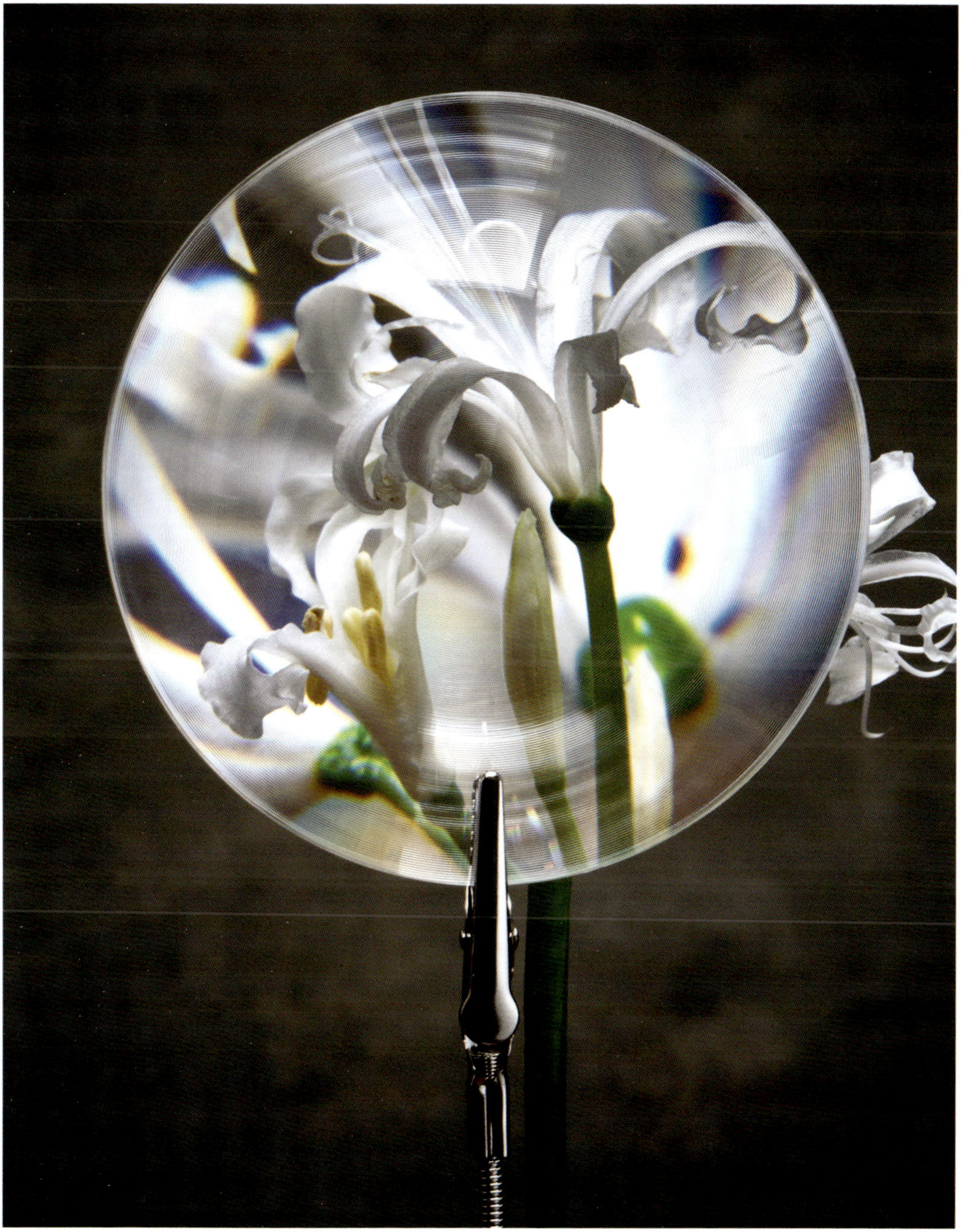

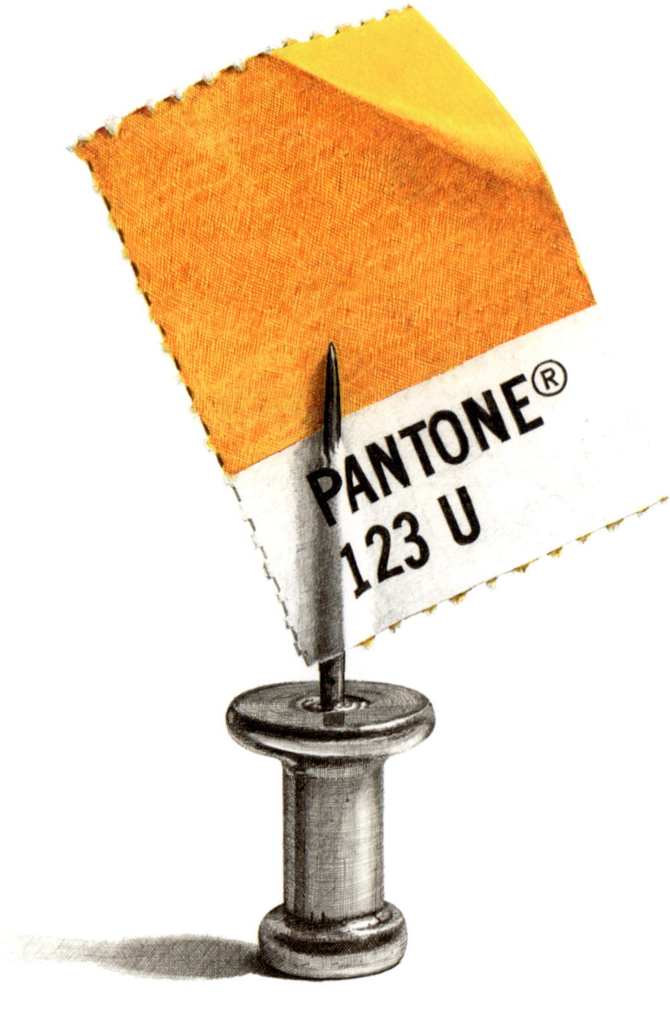
PANTONE®
123 U

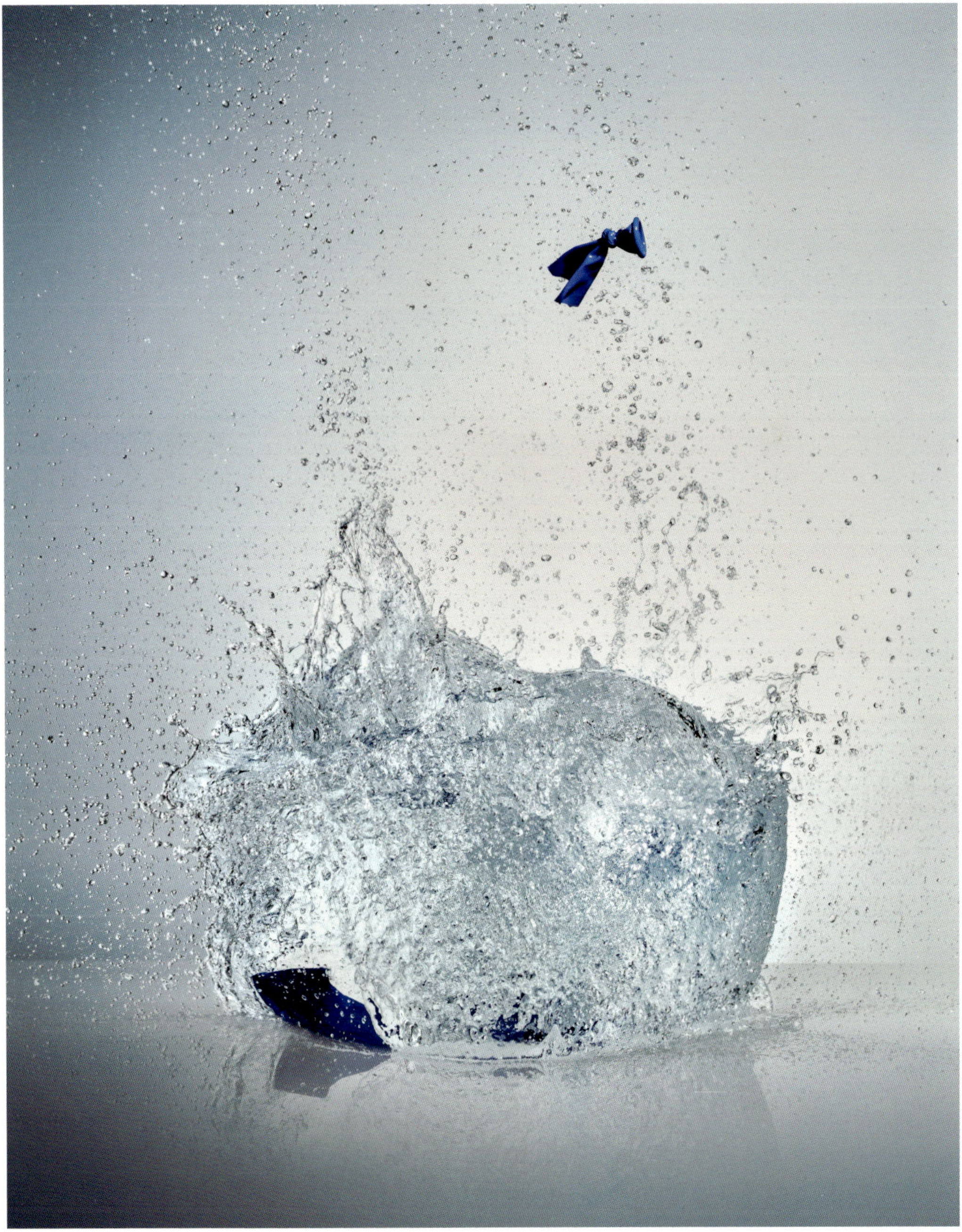

43

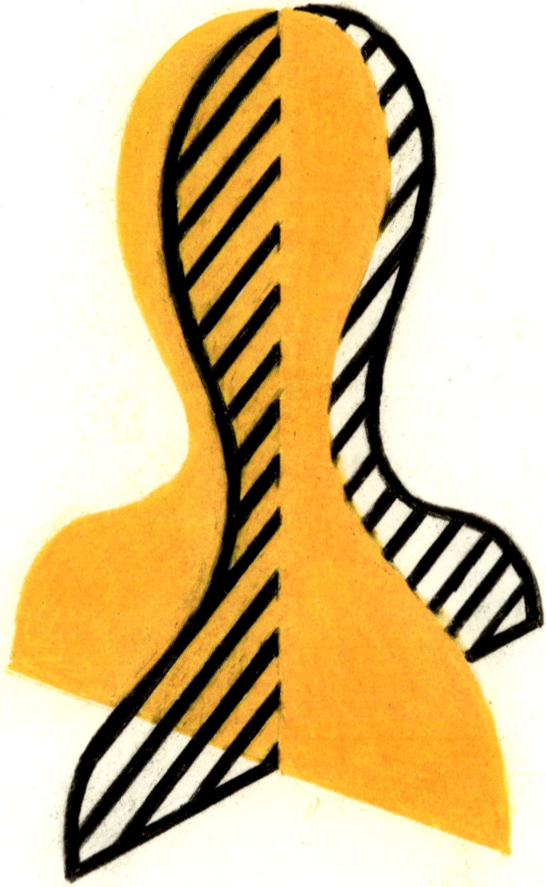

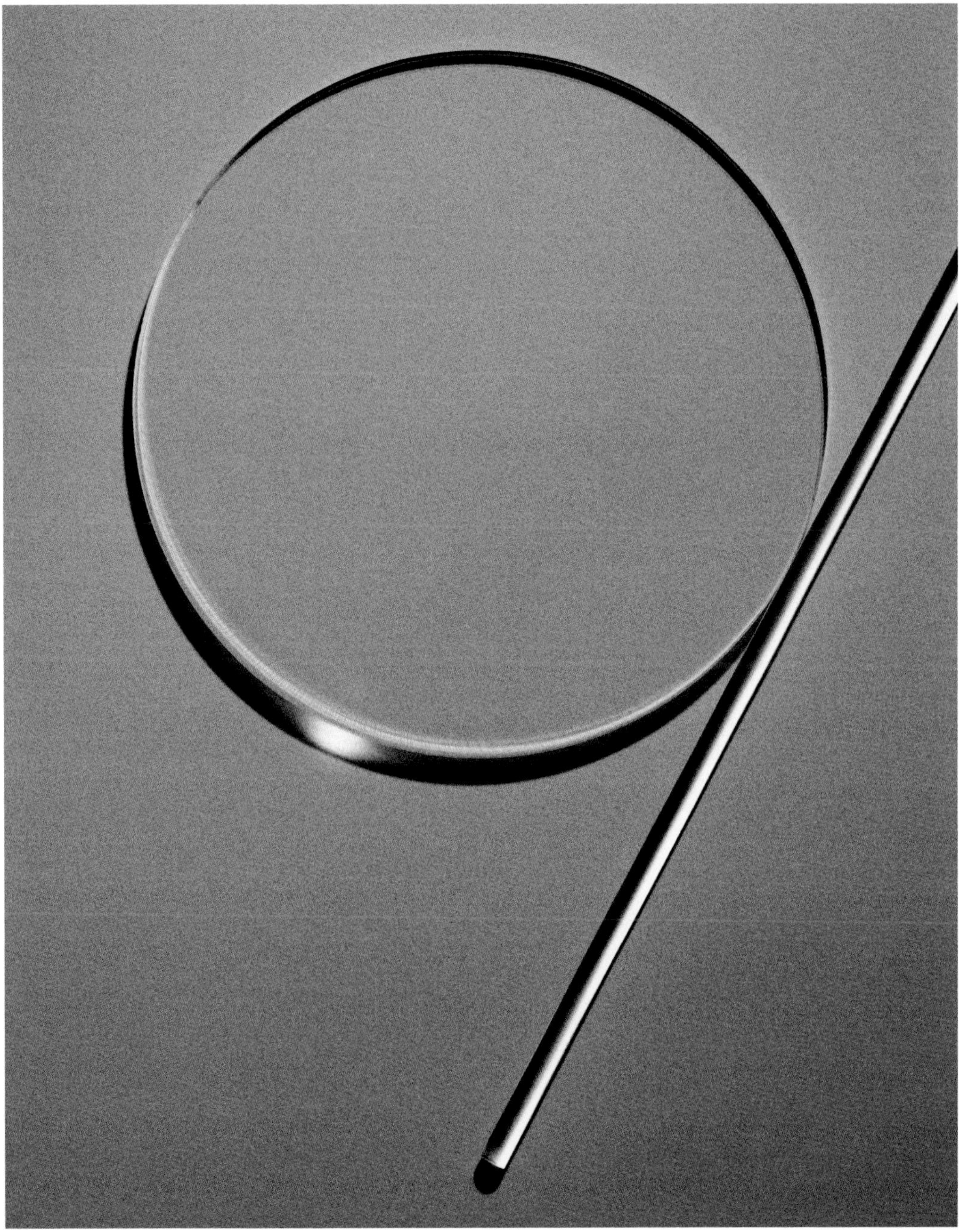

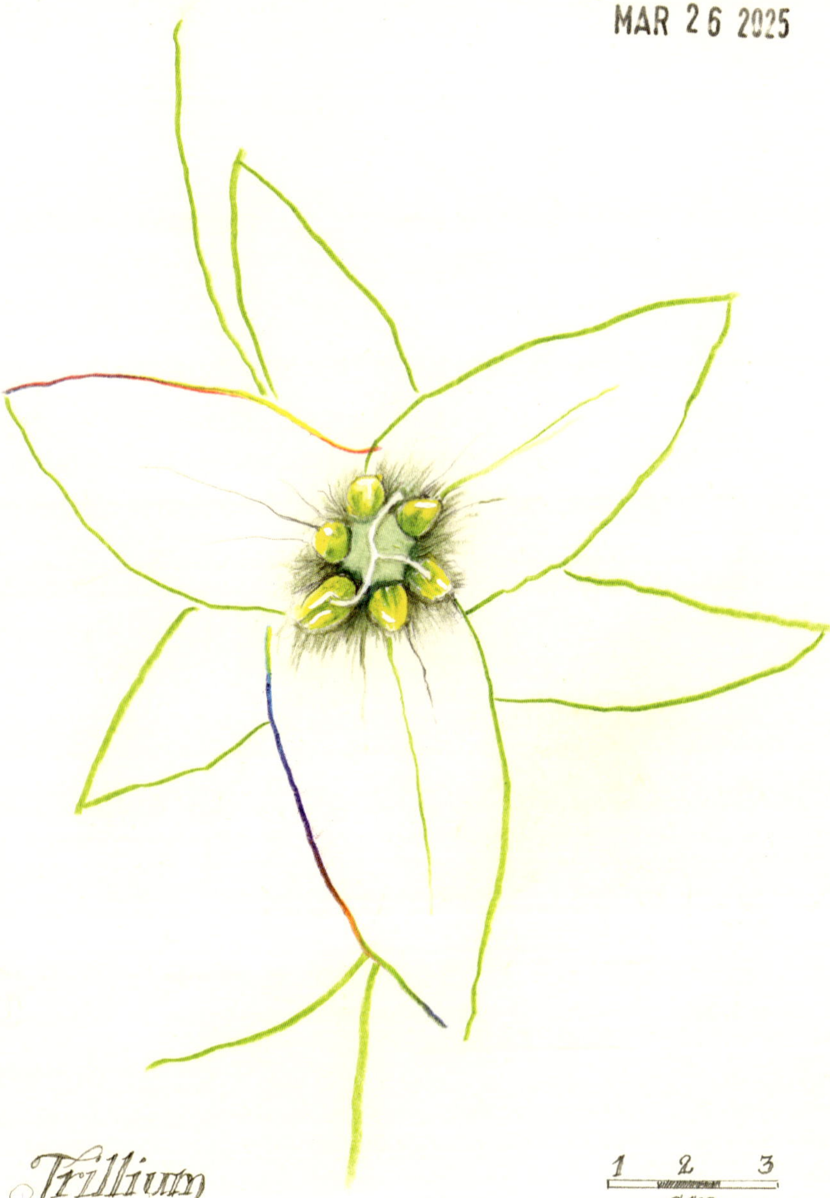
Trillium
1 2 3
cm

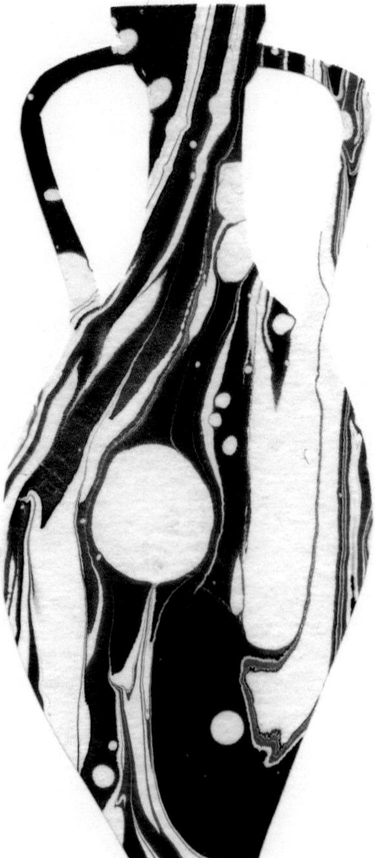

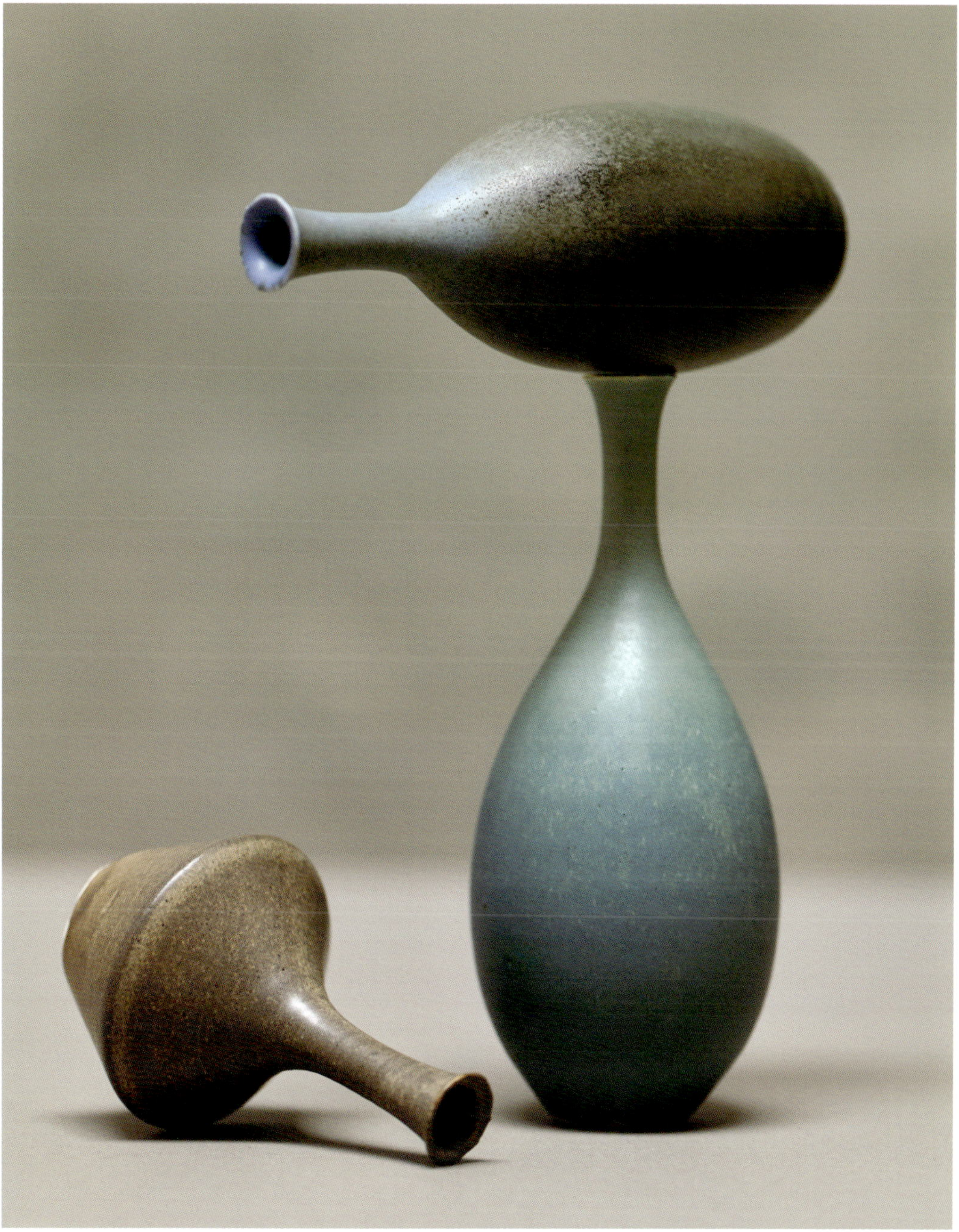

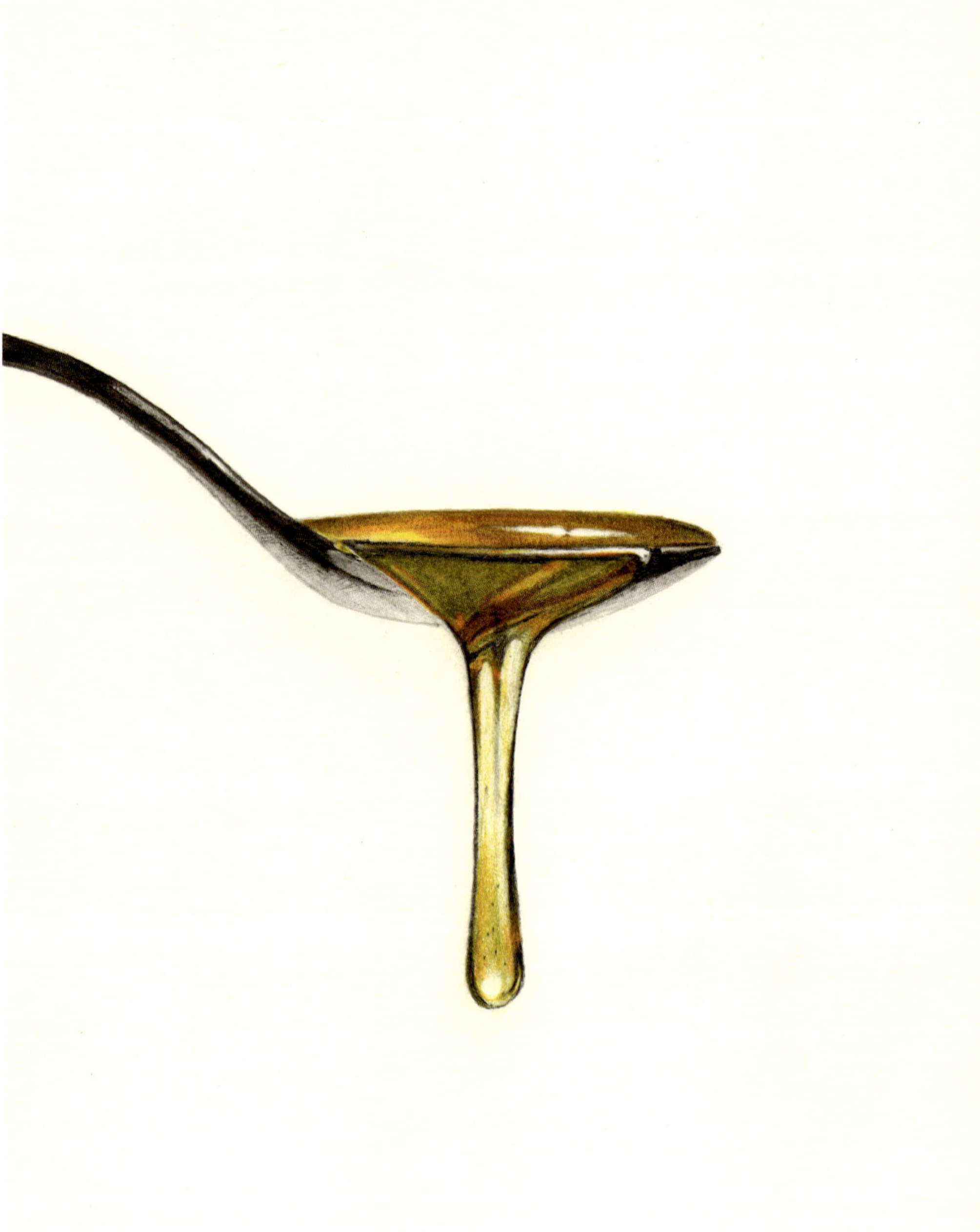

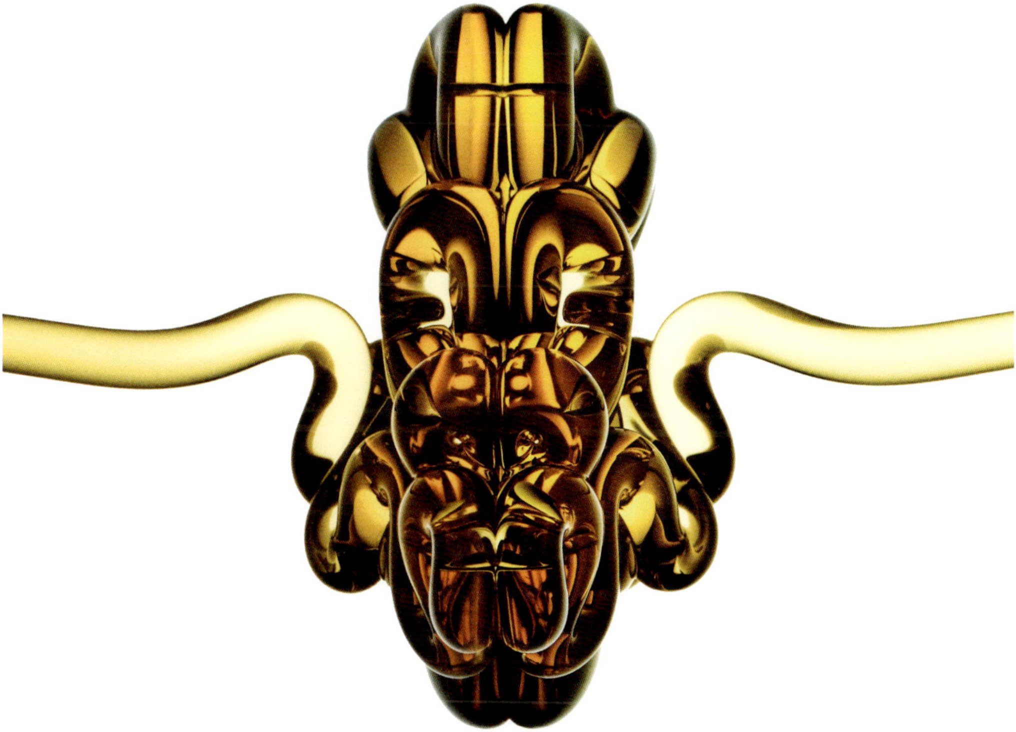

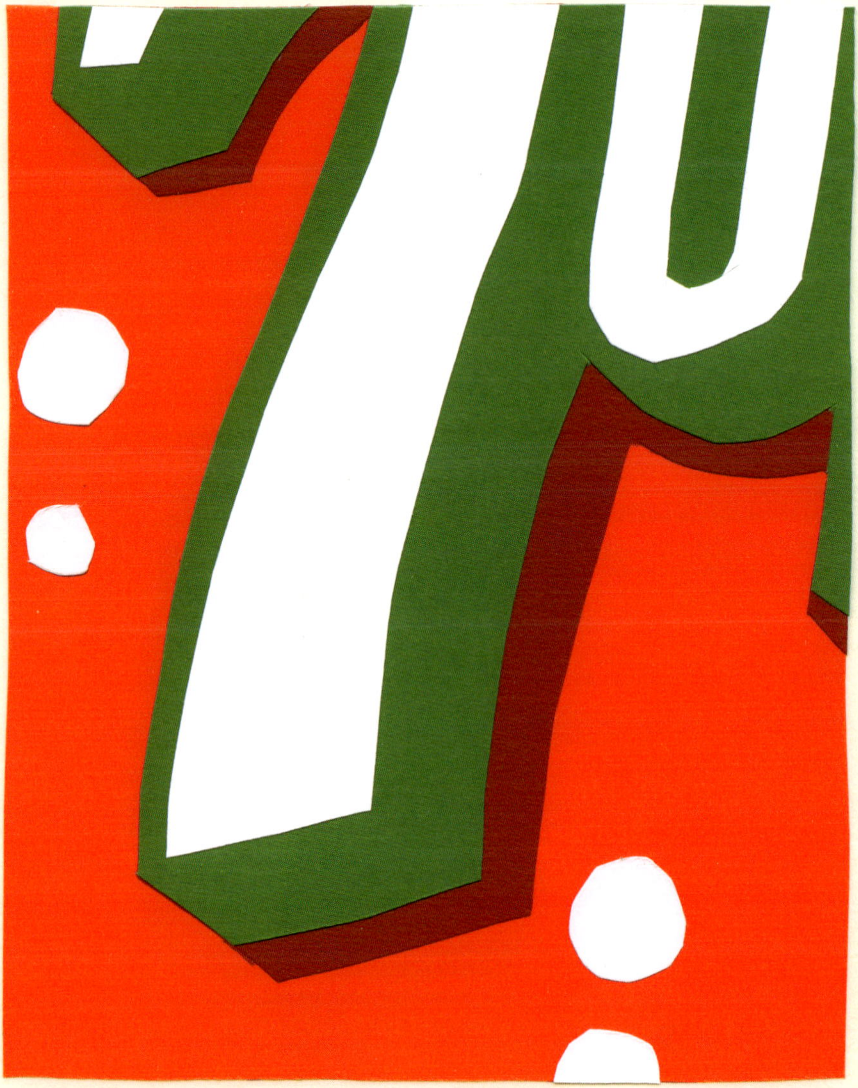

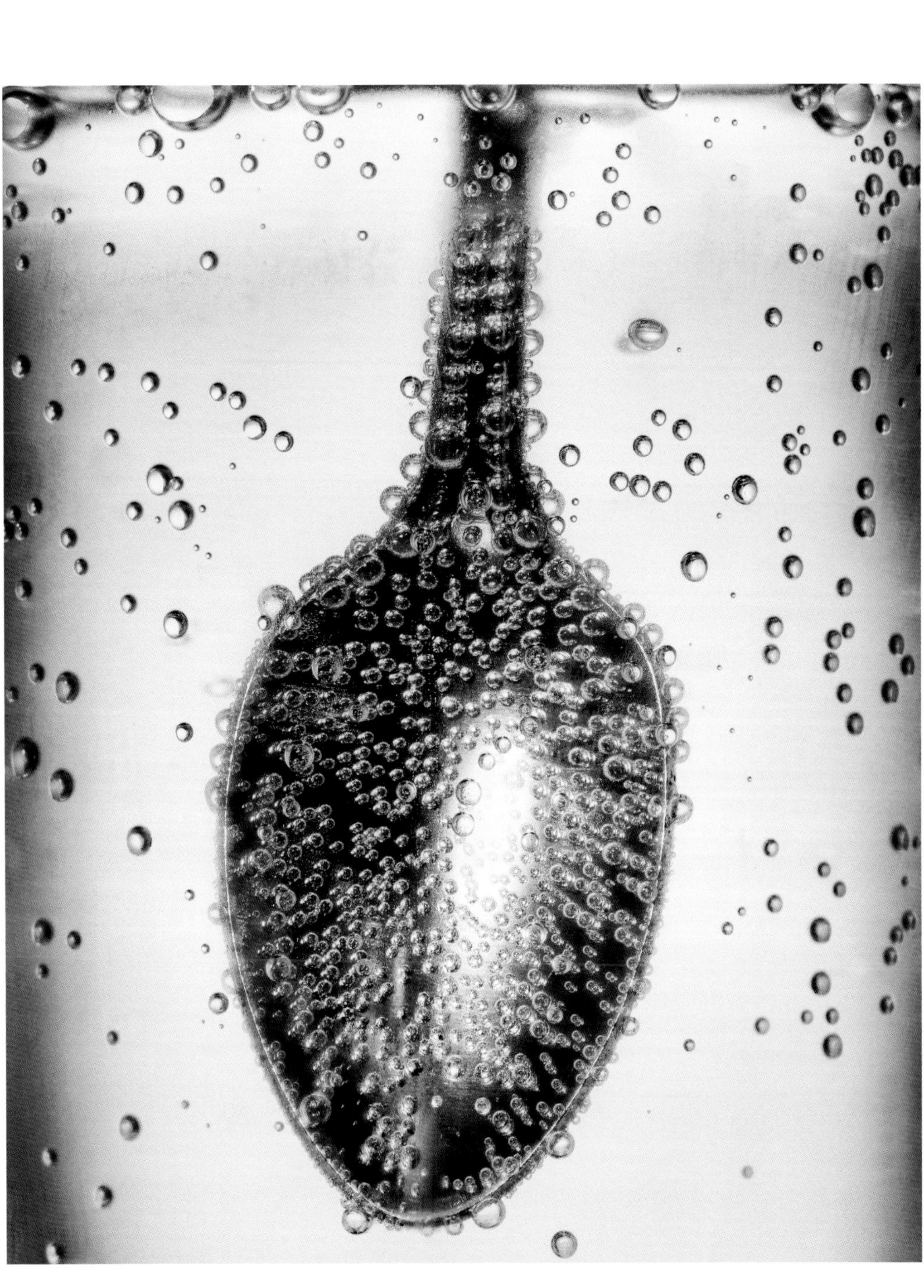

48

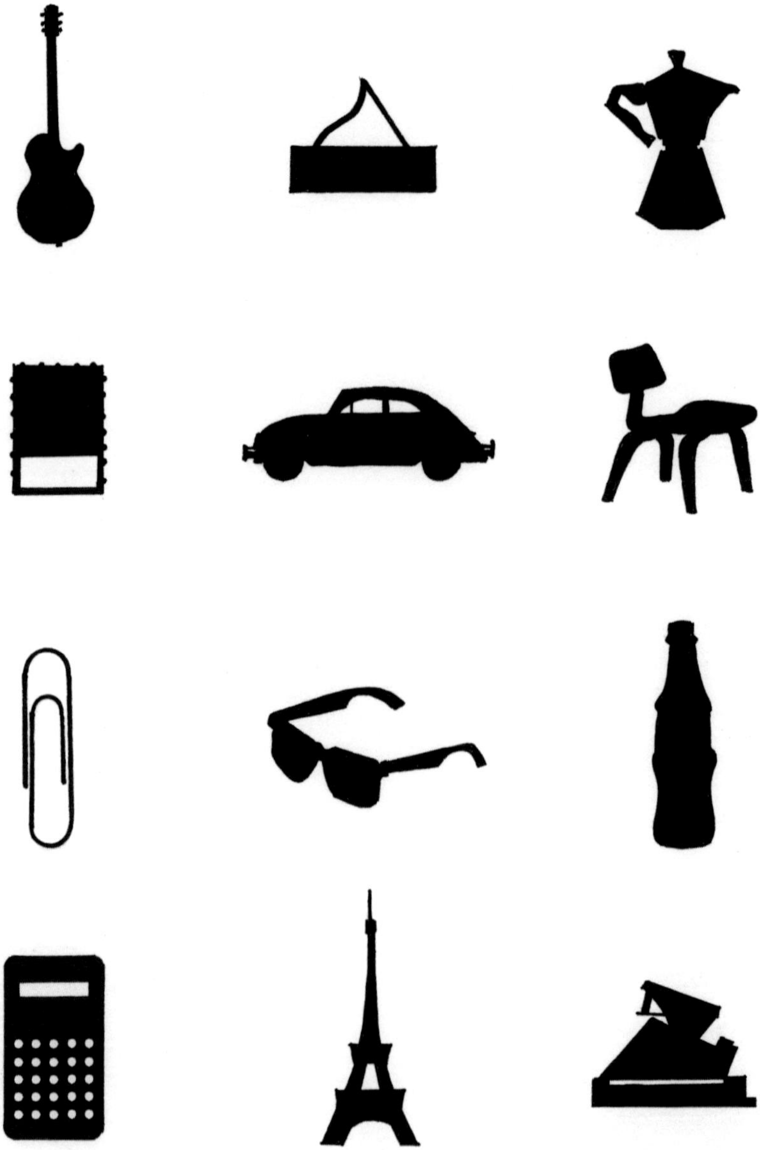

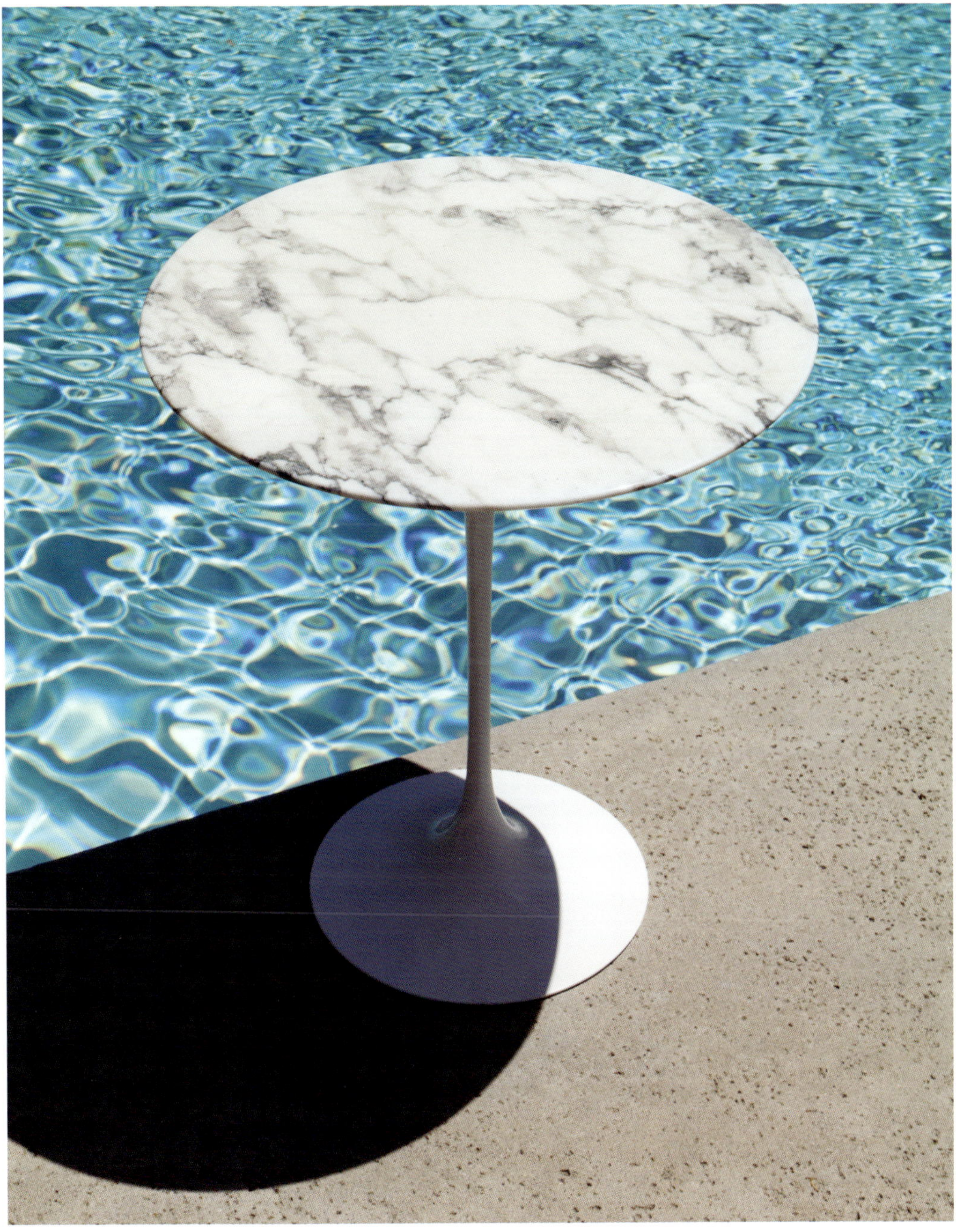

49

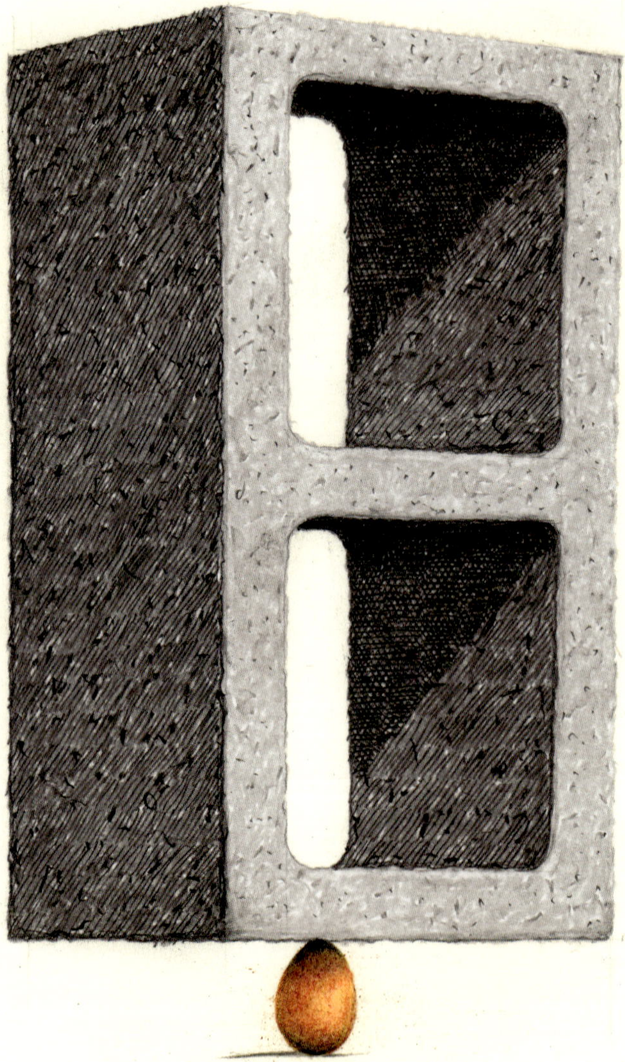

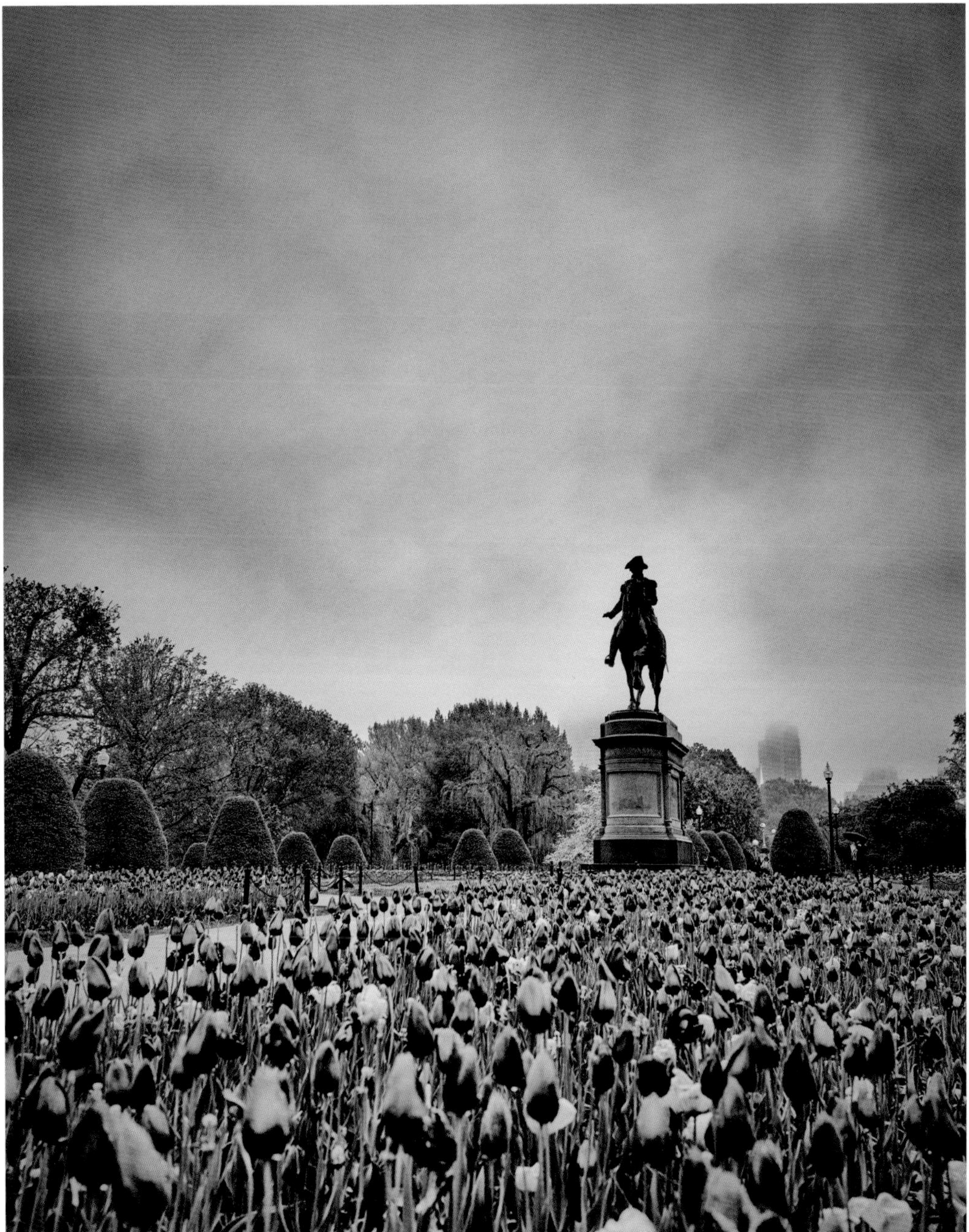

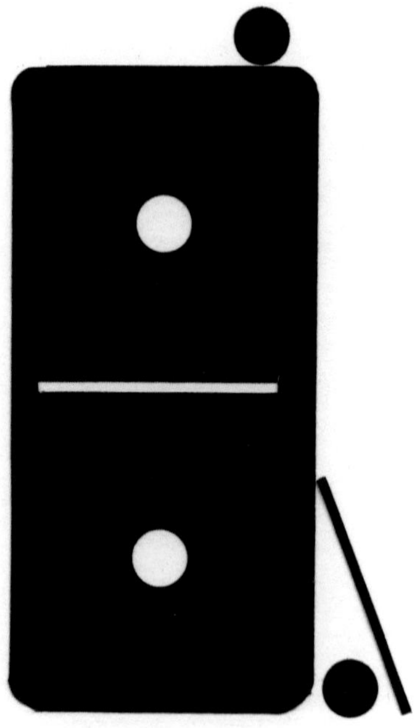

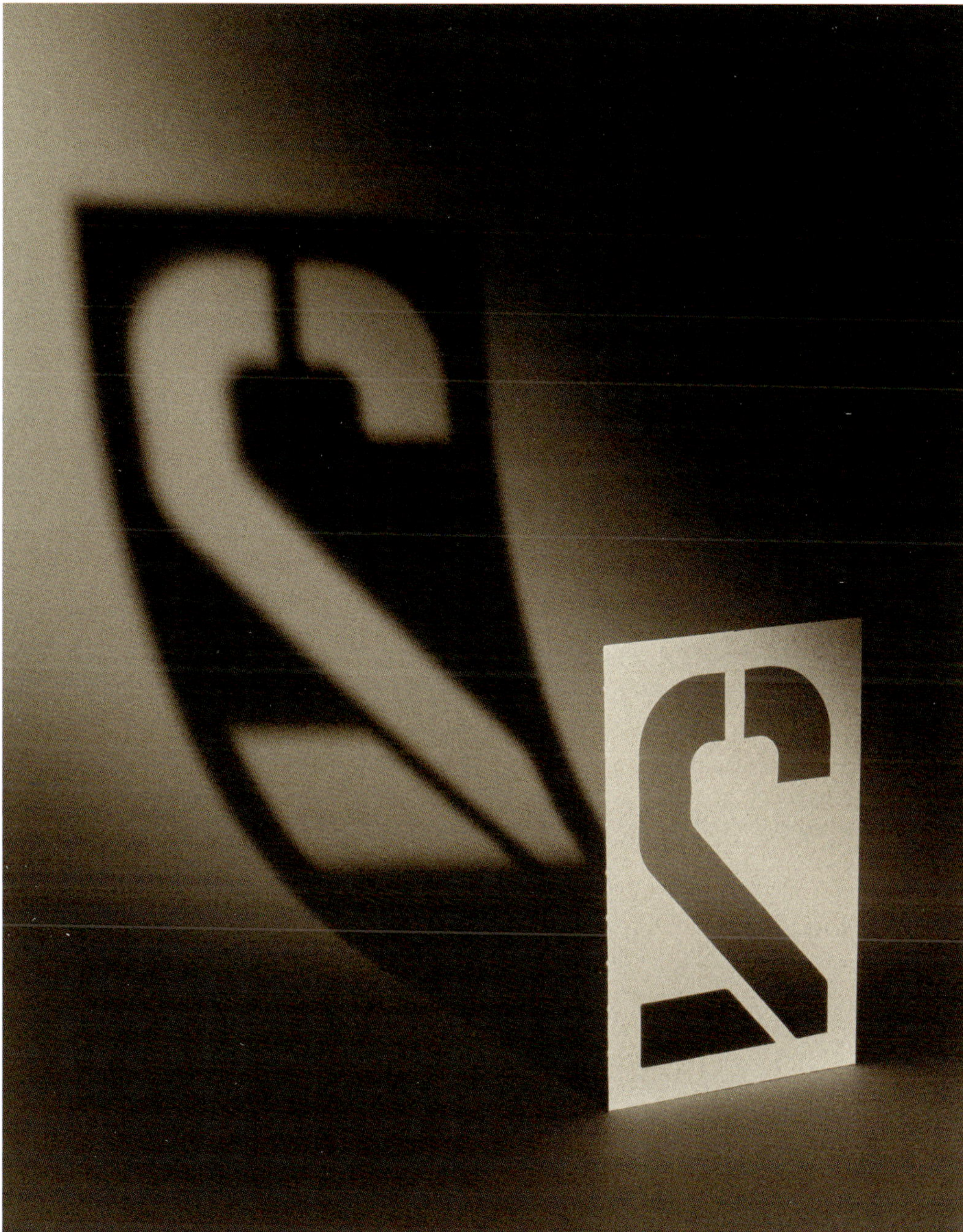

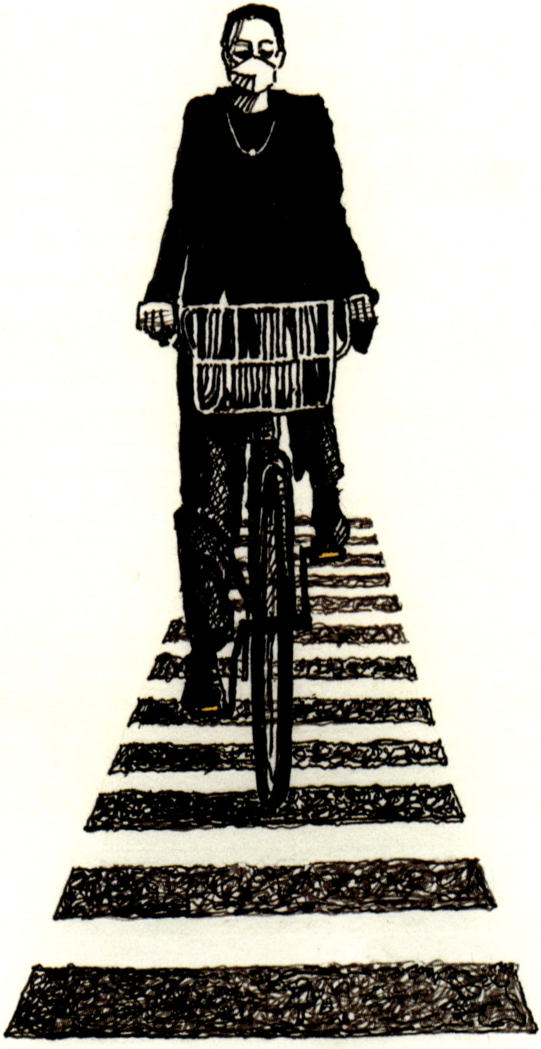

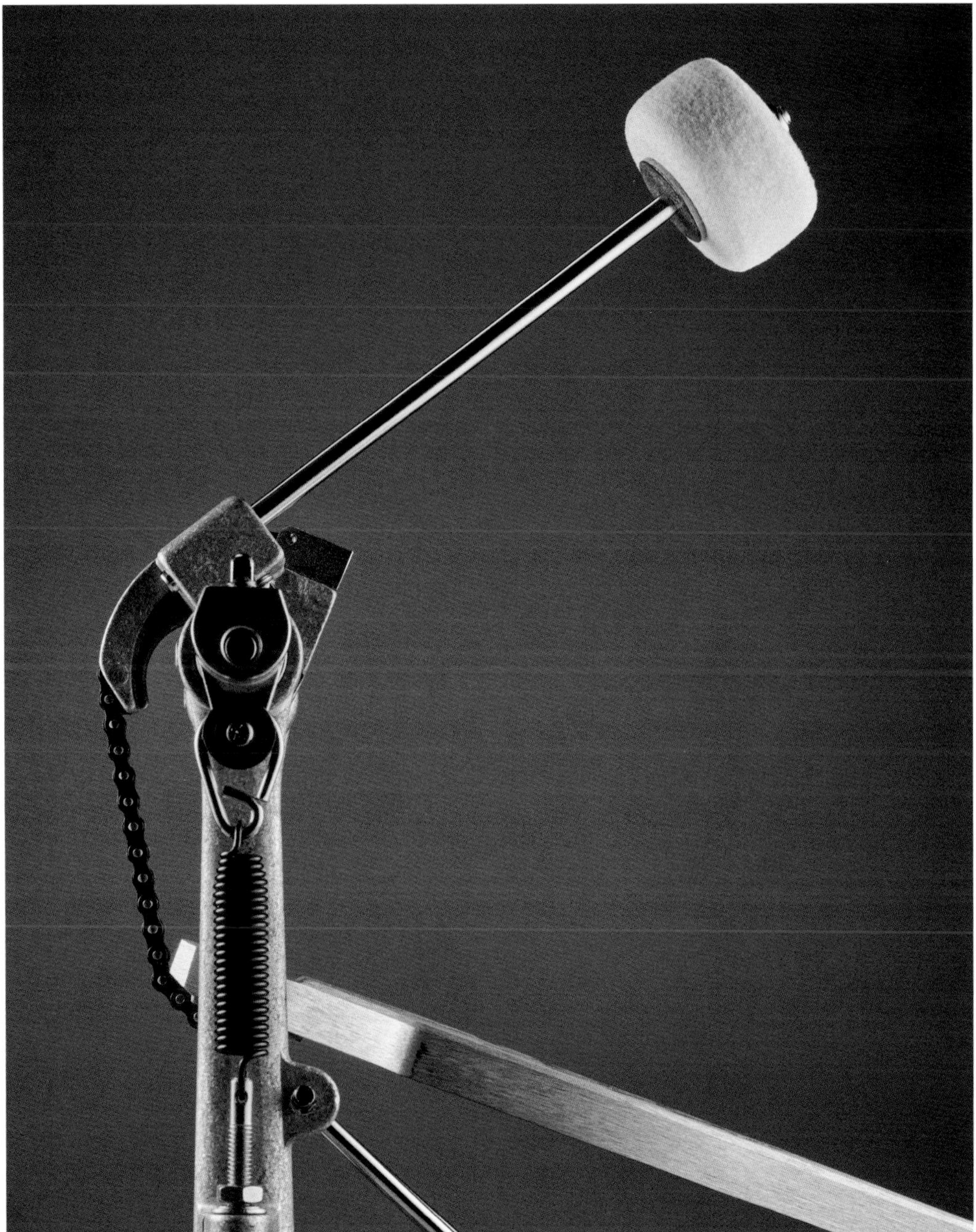

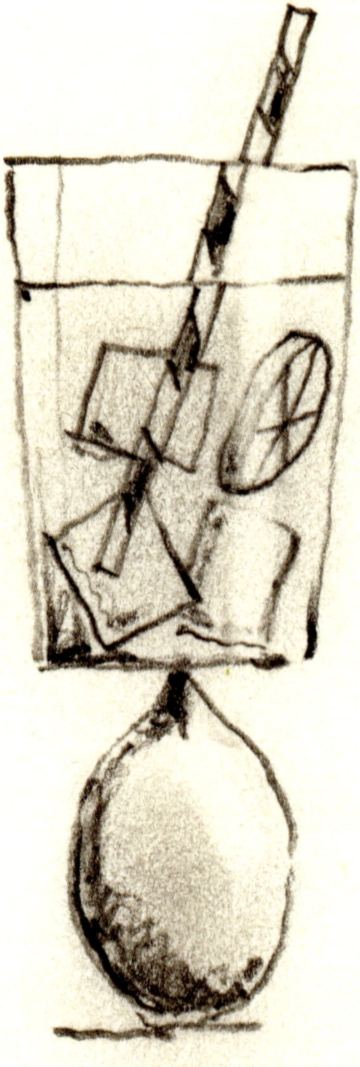

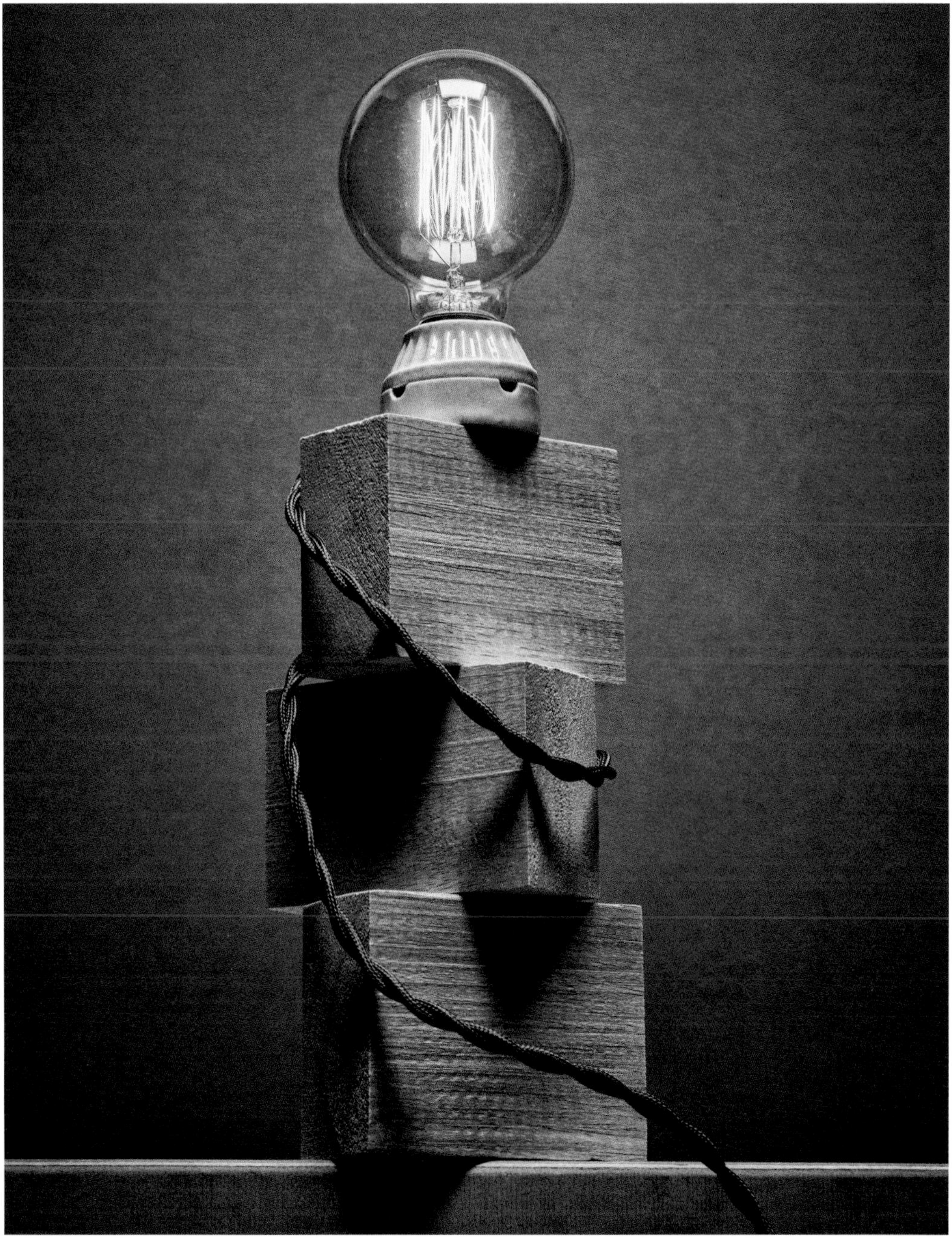

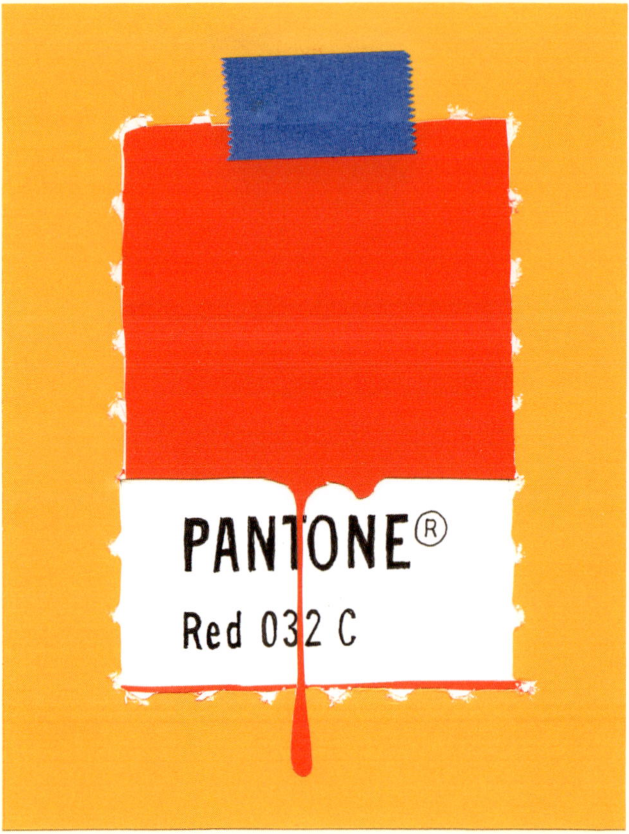
PANTONE®
Red 032 C

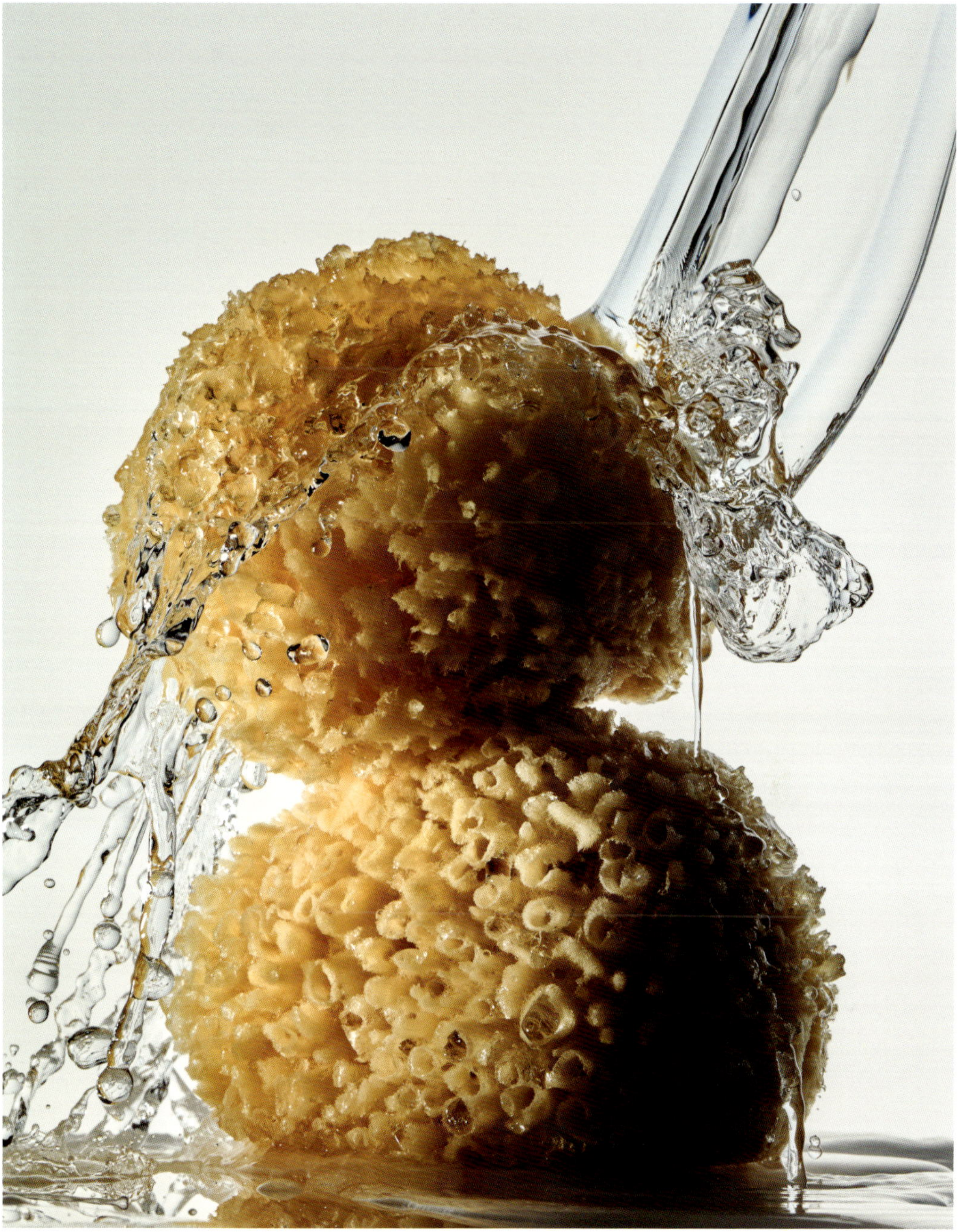

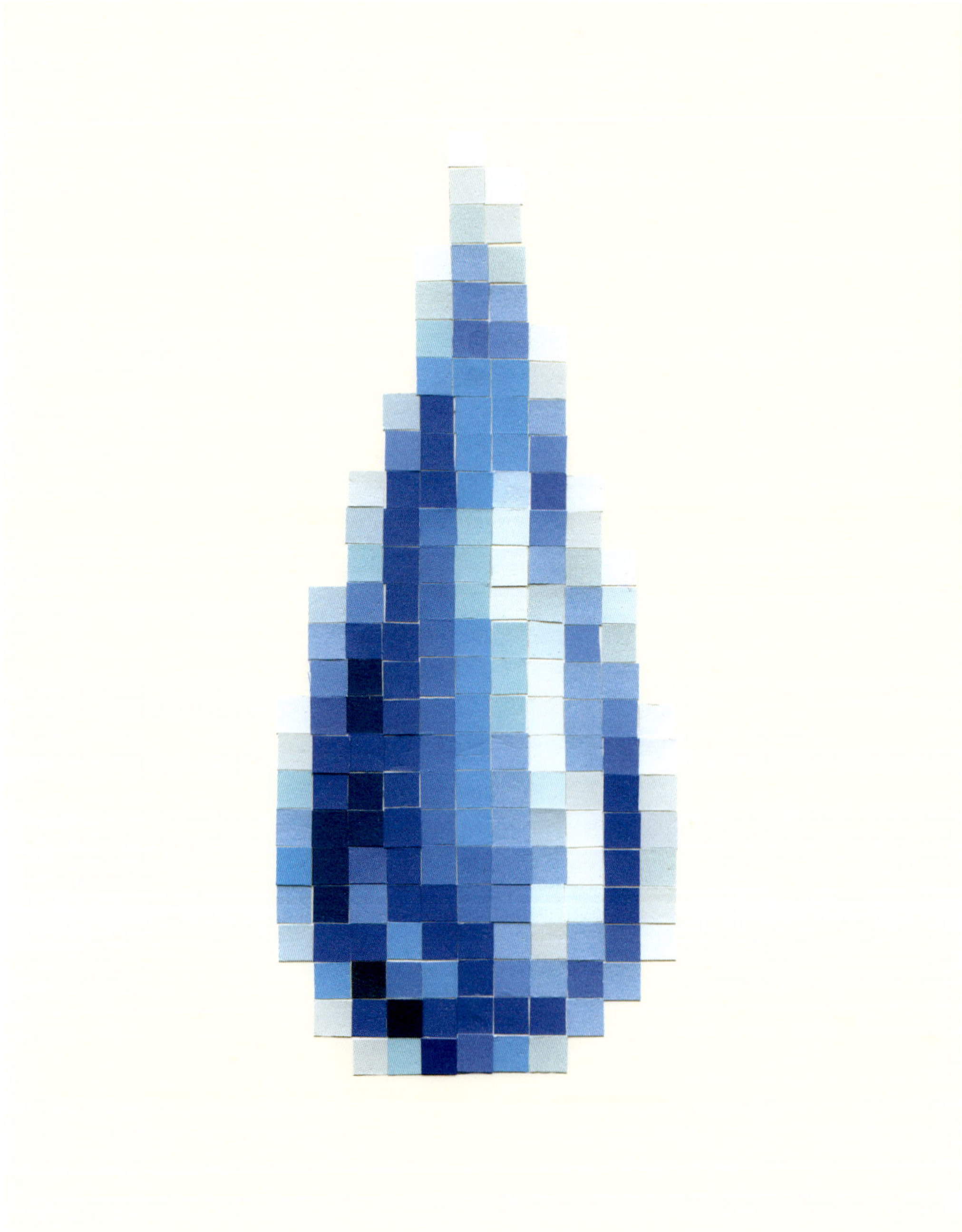

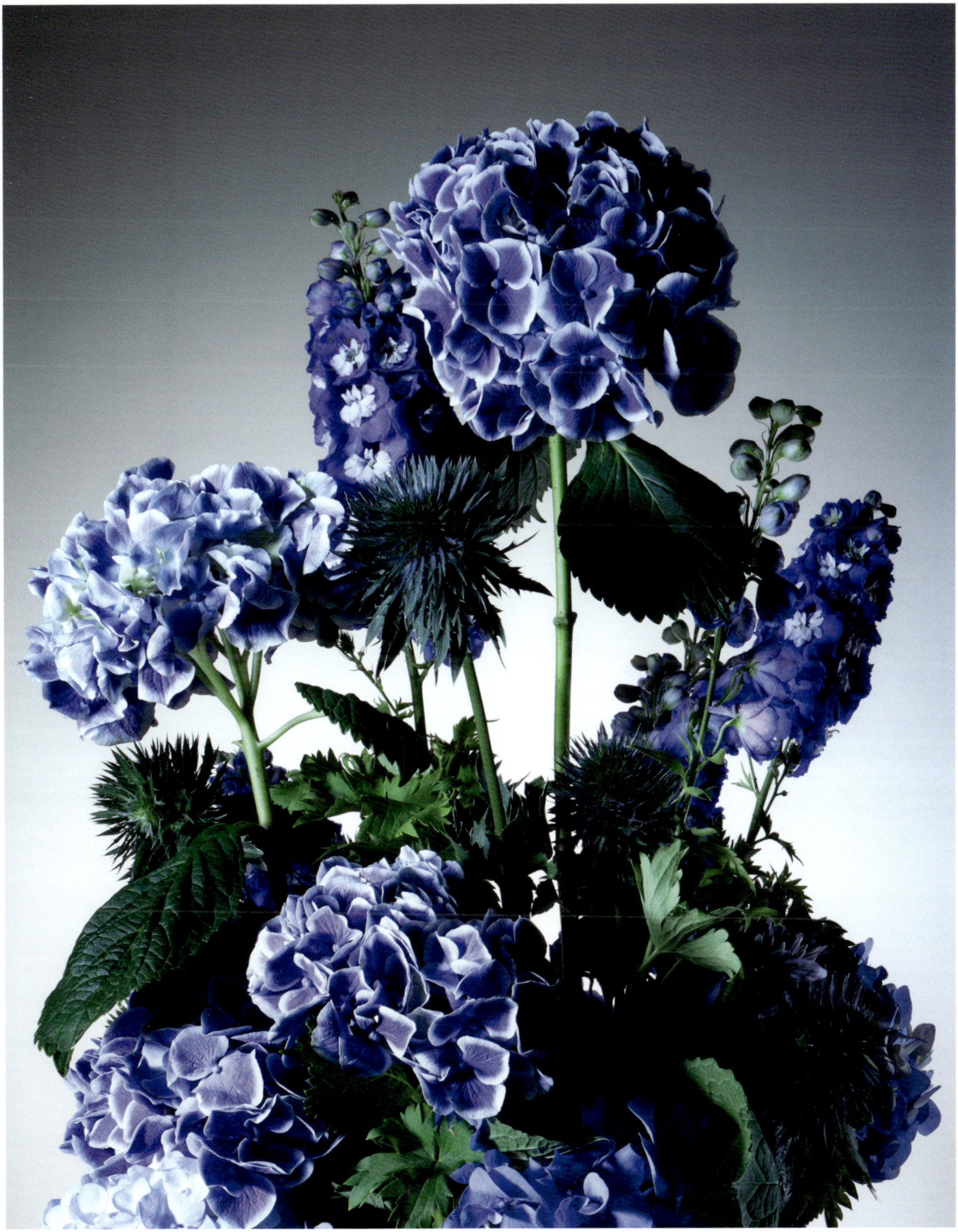

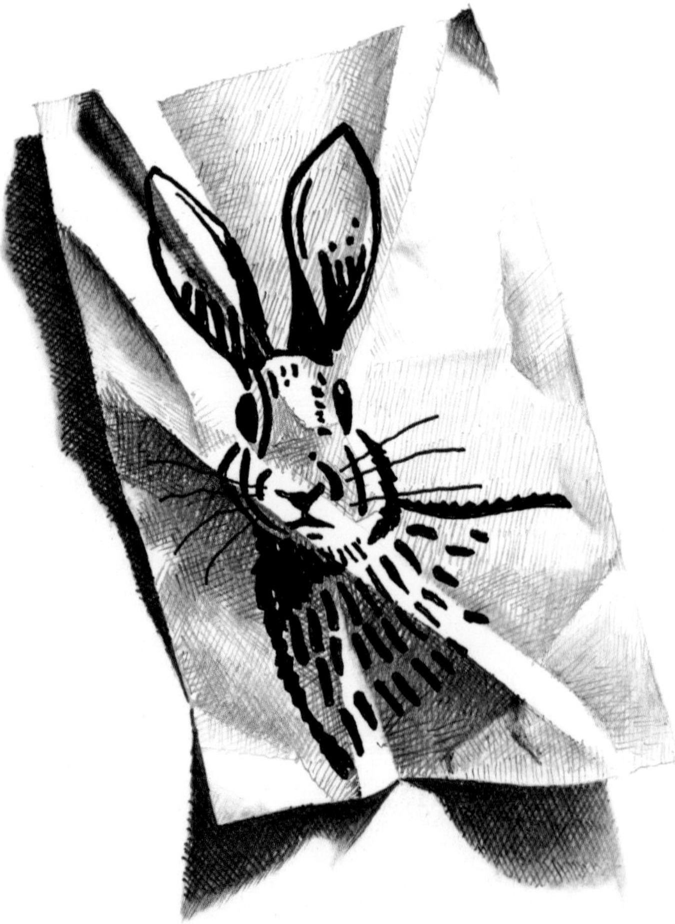

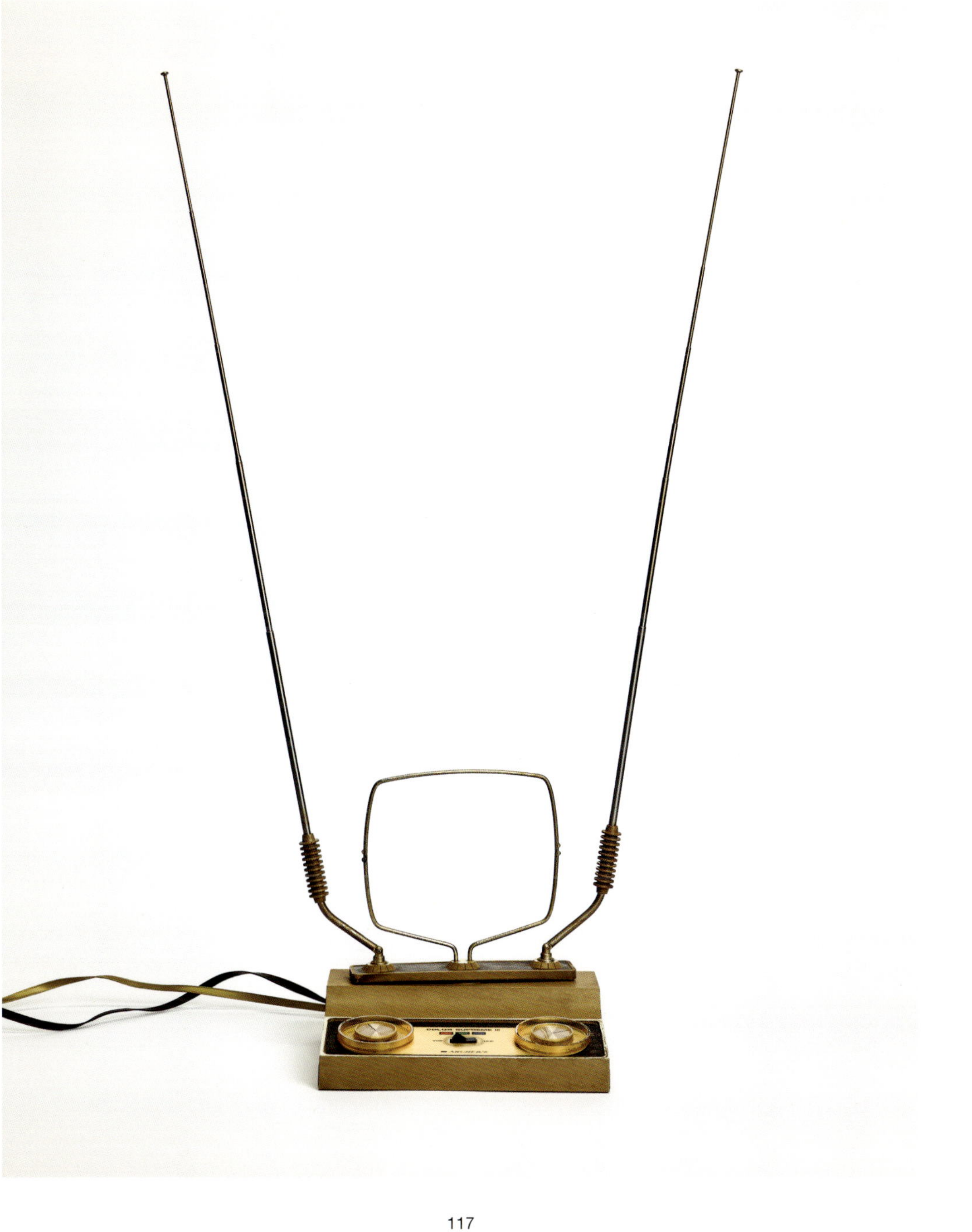

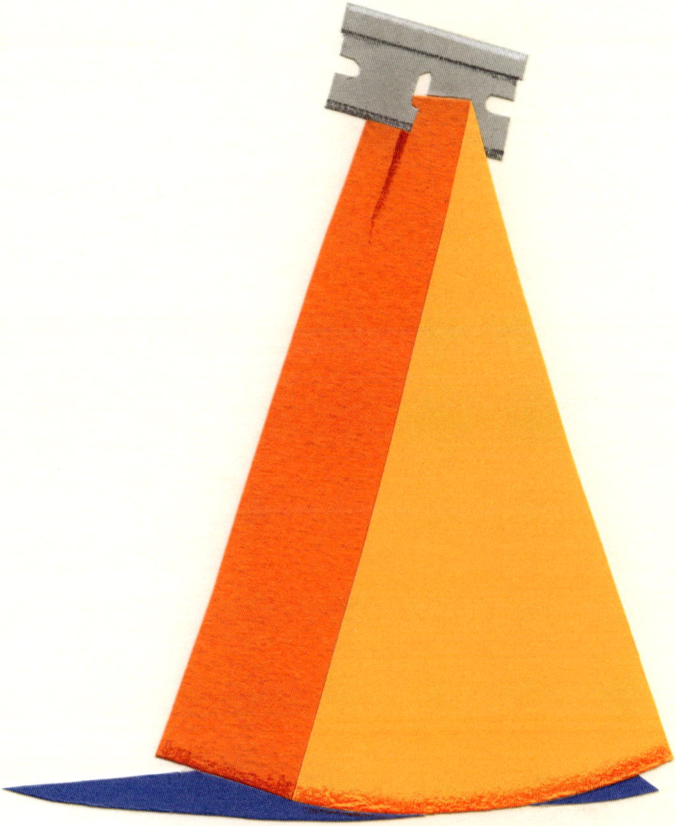

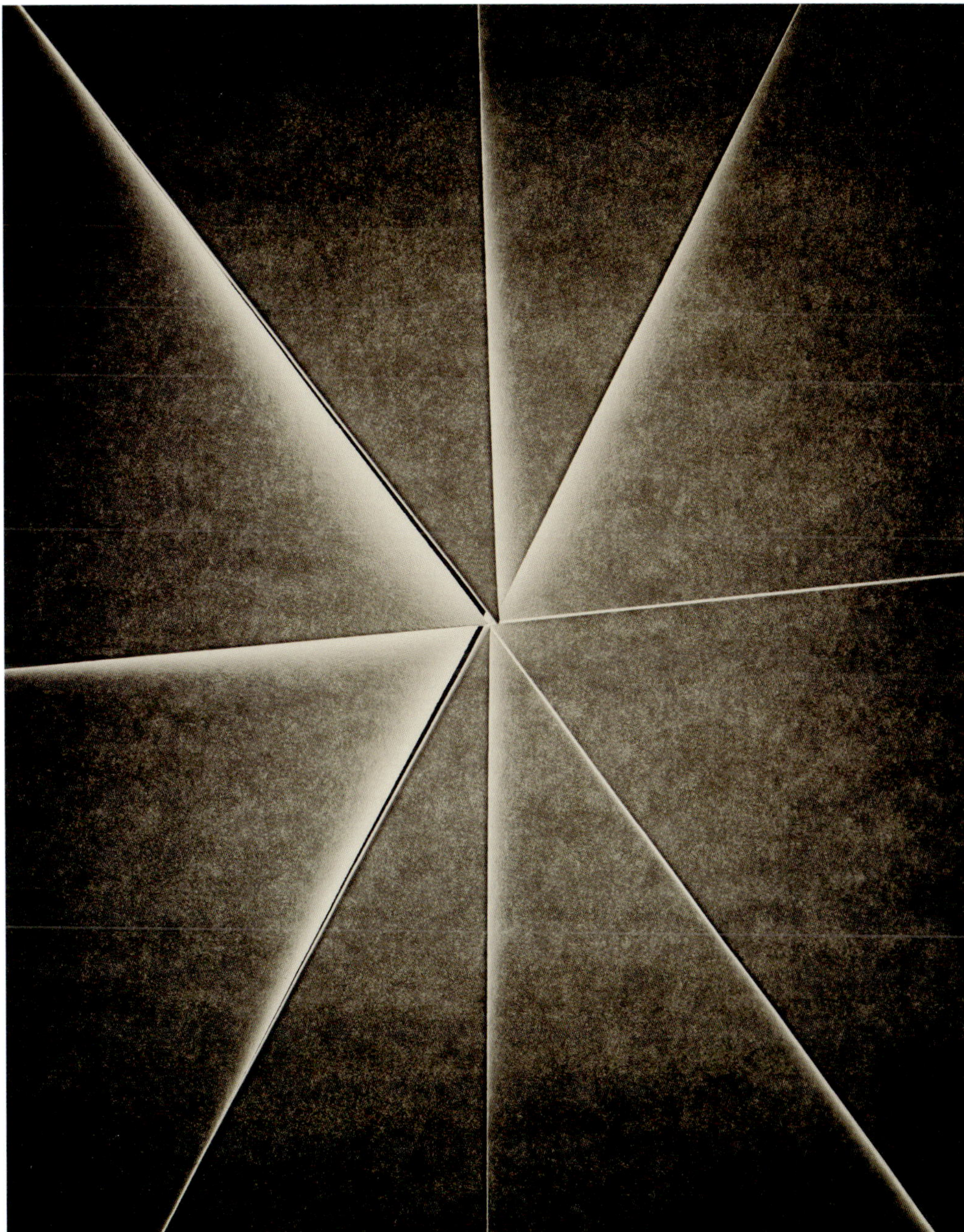

23/2

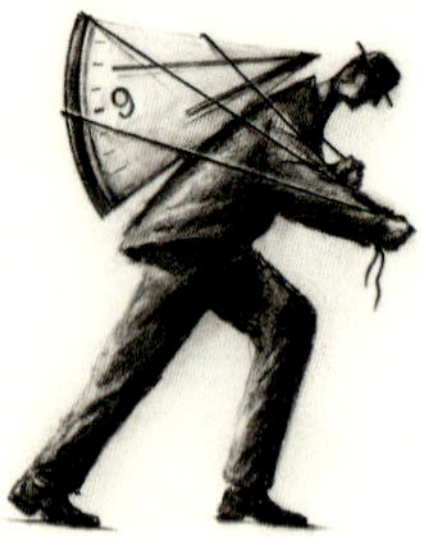

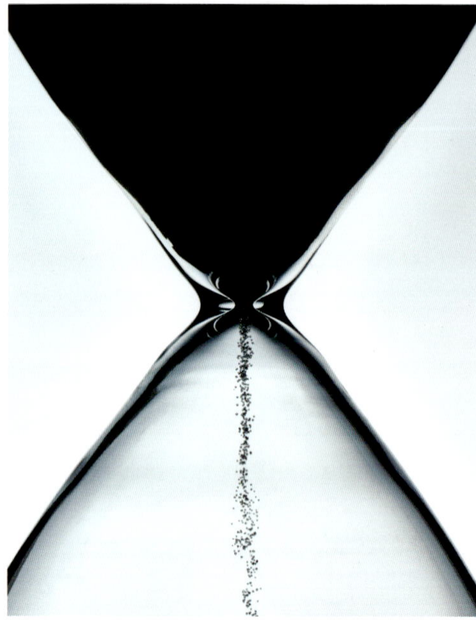

25/2

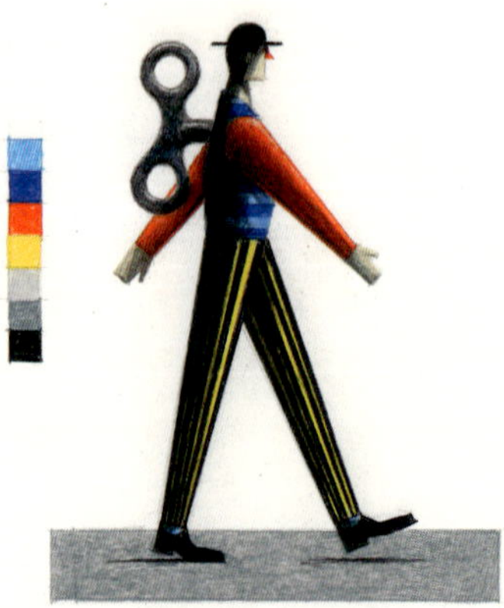

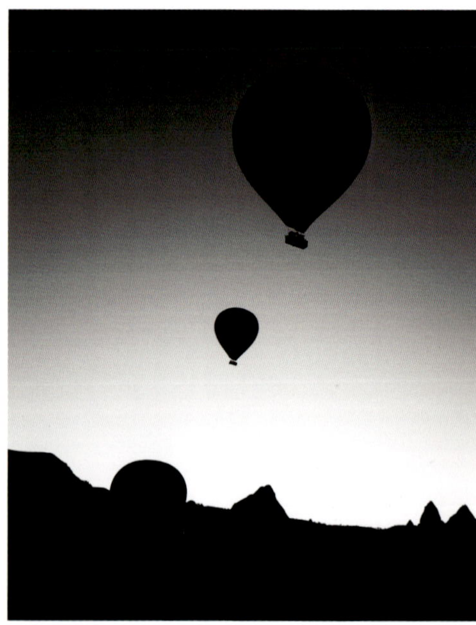

30/2

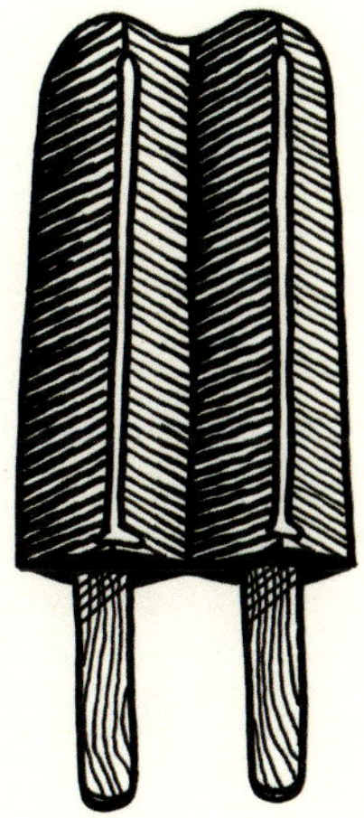

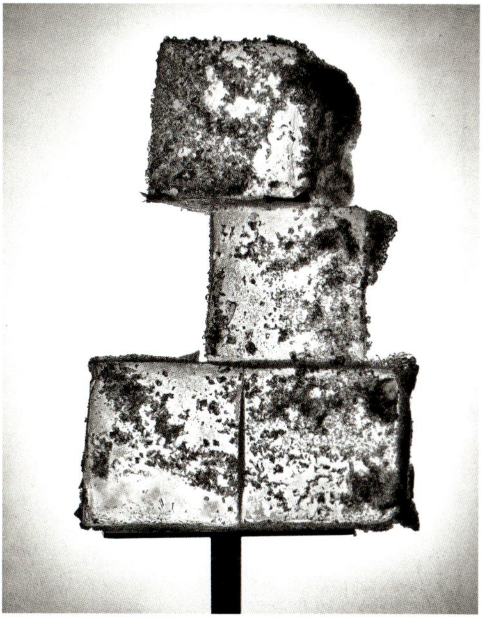

32/2

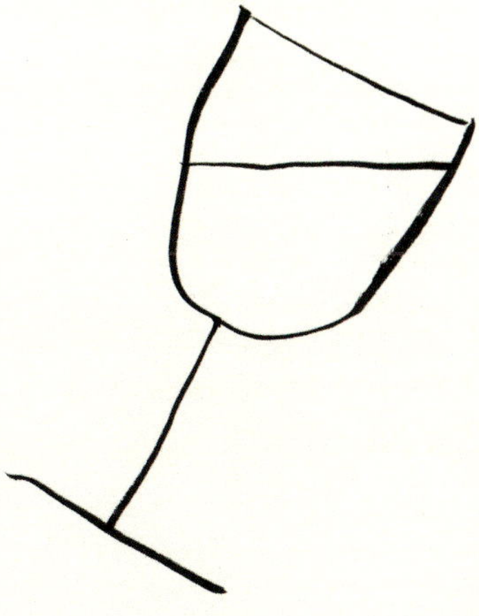

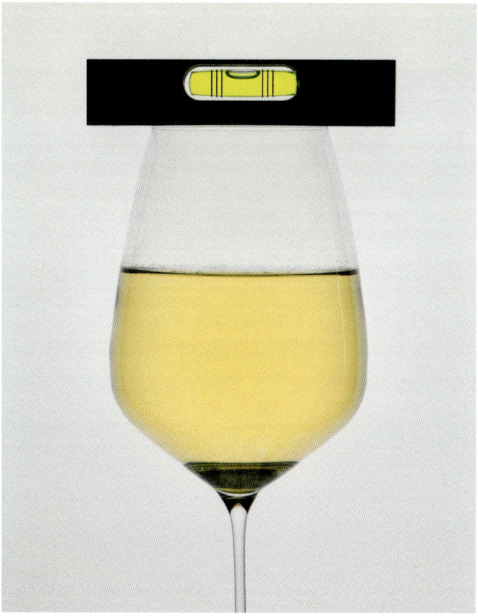

33/2

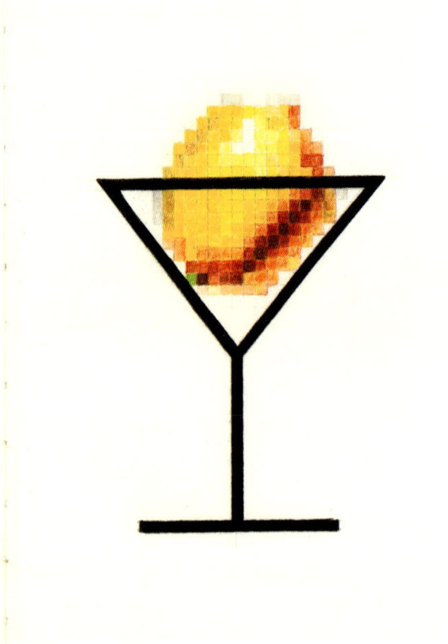

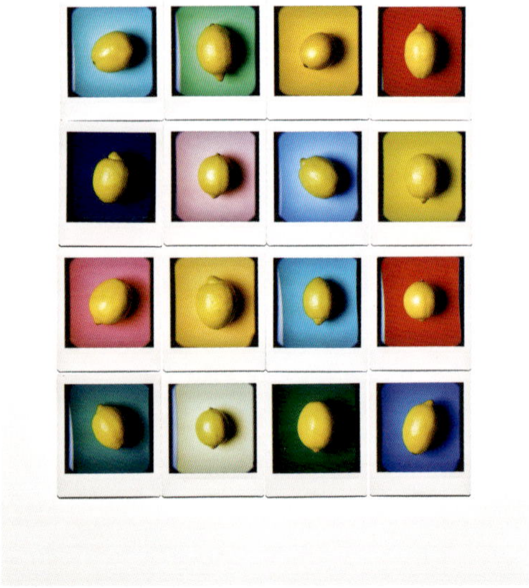

40/2

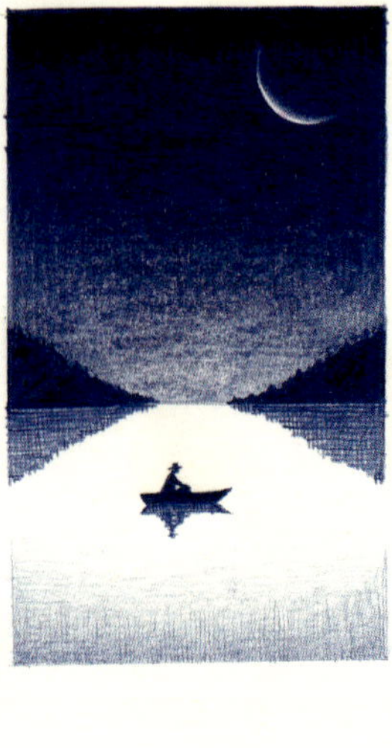

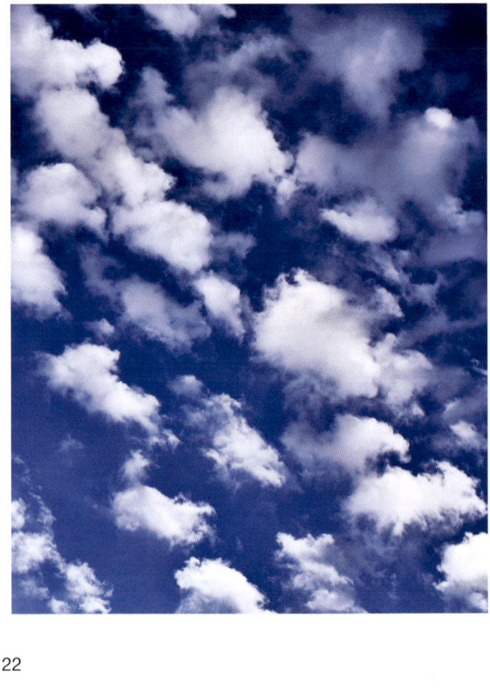

45/2

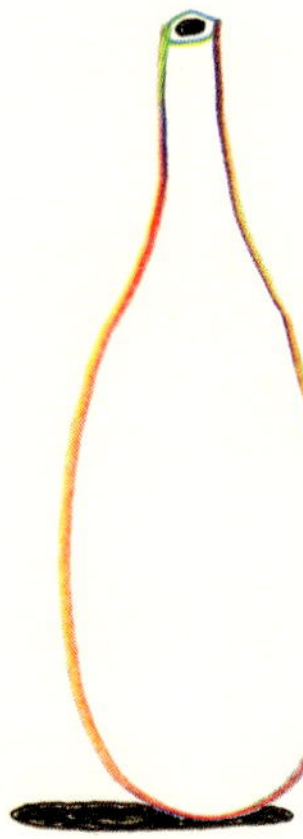

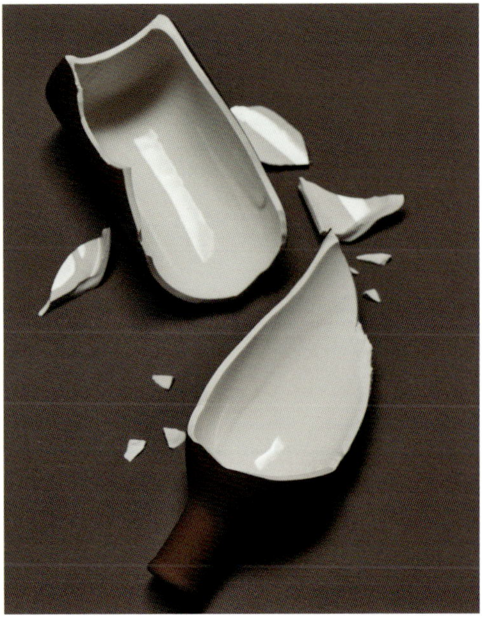

50/2

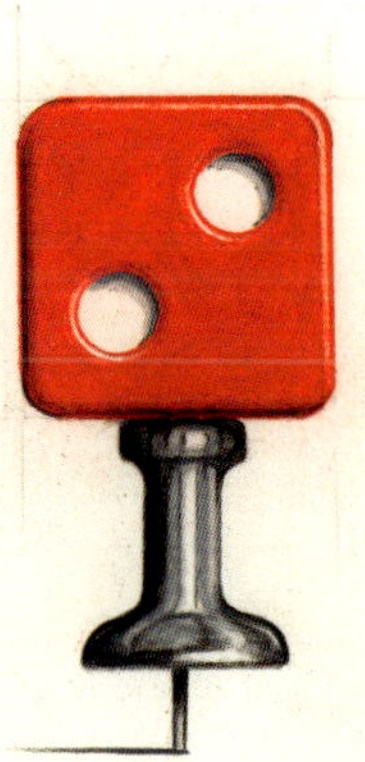

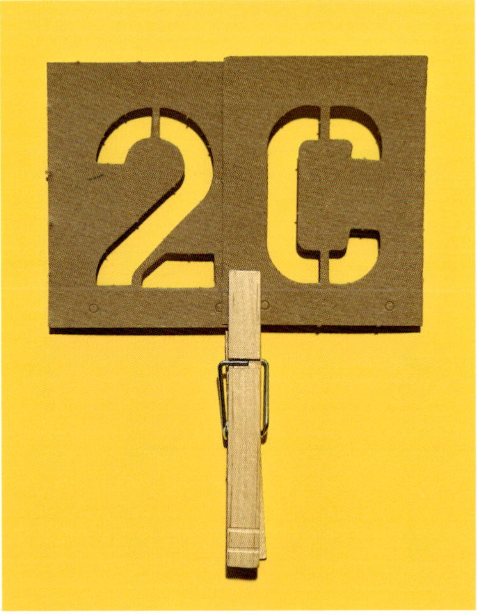

Ideas over execution.
by Craig Cutler

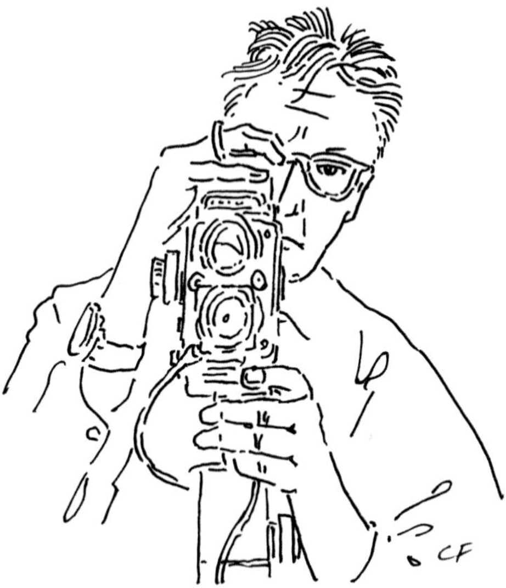

The first time Craig Frazier and I worked on a project together, he couldn't attend the actual photo shoot. He gave me a few guidelines and the freedom to do what I do best. Although I didn't know it at the time, this would become the basis for our year of long-distance collaboration, Project 2 Craigs.

The experiment started on a whim, based on the simple idea of responding to a word prompt in parallel with another creative person, but without knowing what the other was creating. To be honest, I was unsure how far this project would go.

In the beginning, we both came up with interesting ideas to solve the words, and I felt confident with the results. This is what we are good at. However, three weeks into the project, I began to view the scope differently. I tried to anticipate what the other Craig was thinking and come up with something that would surprise me and get better once placed alongside his solution. Some of the words were easier to photograph, and some were more suited for an illustrator. The challenge intensified as each week passed. Our anticipation for the weekly reveal was amplified by the fact that Craig and I have never met.

For me, this project was about exploring concepts and nurturing ideas, rather than creating the perfect photograph. A mediocre photograph with a concept will be remembered long after a beautiful photograph that has none. I've always been more excited about coming up with ideas and sketches, and felt that the execution of the idea was more of a formality. I typically spend a few days playing in my sketchbook before shooting anything.

The beauty of this project was that once you put it out there, it was done, and it was time to move on to the next word. It was a creatively liberating process—to have the freedom to make decisions and pursue a direction without any external constraints. None of the images had to be adjusted to appeal to a panel of tastemakers, so I jumped in any direction I felt the impulse to explore. I was not trying to create a photograph that would please everyone.

One thing I appreciated about this project was that after receiving our word, we had exactly one week to submit our image. There is nothing worse than having too much time to overthink, over-manipulate, and over-produce. Everything had to be created from elements that were inexpensive to produce. I felt like I was back in school.

Halfway through the project, it became a mind game—denying my first ideas, trying to outwit my creative partner, whom I knew was in full swing. The further in we went, the more intense it became and the more fun we had. The weekly word became an obsession. Everything I saw, every place I went, had that week's word floating above my head. Good ideas can come from anywhere.

It is important to note that the images Craig illustrated or I photographed were only half of the story. It wasn't until the two images were placed alongside each other that the expression reached its full potential. The best part about this project was the weekly reveal, when I saw for the first time how Craig was thinking—sometimes we took a similar arc, and other times completely divergent. My favorite words were the ones that drove us to two different places, as we tried to outmaneuver each other with a less-than-obvious solution.

Looking back on this experiment, I realized it was a wake-up call for creativity, particularly in the age of AI. It reminded me that learning (and relearning) to use and trust your mind's eye is an essential creative practice. Coming up with ideas has always been the fun part for me. Conceptualizing within this mystery tandem with another artist definitely changed how I thought and allowed me to move in directions I could have never imagined. Project 2 Craigs proved to me the value of the spark within us.

Signs, not destinations.

by Craig Frazier

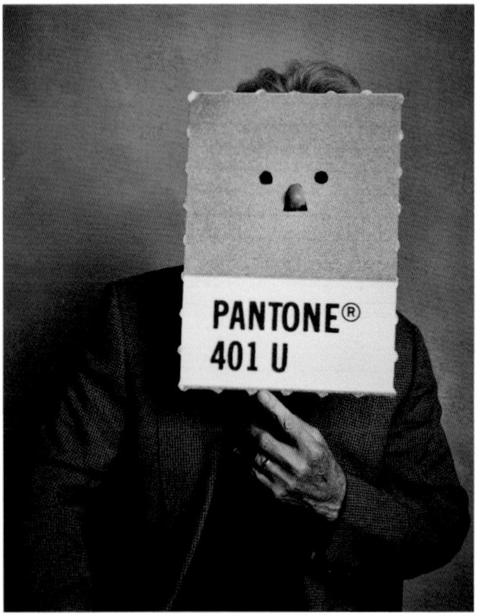

Client assignments crave predictability, yet invention at its best is unpredictable. It's the conundrum of creativity and the design business. At any given moment, you can feel drowned in self-doubt despite your well-trained expectations. This experiment was designed to challenge our confidence and lure us into a state of incertitude. It would be uncomfortable, but there was solace in knowing I wasn't the only Craig squirming.

Unlike a scientific experiment, Project 2 Craigs had no hypothesis; however, we hoped to demonstrate how much a year-long marathon of riddles to "solve" could influence us both. We would either emerge beaten and bruised or reassured that we still had gas in our creative tanks.

How hard could it be? We didn't have a client or a creative brief to answer to. How much pressure could a friendly little project generate? The answer is a lot. It was a masterclass in idea combat, though not with each other, with ourselves. I knew Craig could deliver, but I wasn't sure I could.

I established a couple of rules for myself. Every image had to be created in a 5"x 8" sketchbook. (The only exception was week 42.) I would only use the computer as a means to scan and create files. No manipulating, no repairing mistakes. These limitations would become the first interruption in my regular routine. I would stick to basic mediums—graphite, colored pencils, pen and ink, and cut paper. The minimal size of the sketchbooks and the compressed time frame were a call for speed and brevity. As always, ideas would be paramount.

As a designer, I'm hardwired to communicate clearly —it's the responsibility of the job. However, this supposed strength soon became a hindrance. Right away, I realized that I was approaching this experiment from the wrong angle. Instead of thinking of the weekly words as mandates, I needed to see them as invitations. Signs, not destinations. The objective was to explore and come what may. If I were to accept this as an experiment, I would have to live with the results.

So, I started working differently and let go of my expectations for each finished piece. I accepted the free fall. Rather than execute ideas I was sure would work, I chose ideas I was *not* sure would work. I often made choices simply because the opportunities to render them were irresistible—like the pencil in week 24, the dripping honey in week 46, or the cut-paper domino in week 50. Uncertainty became the name of the game.

It's been easy to digest Craig's images and apply them to my own practice. We share certain design sensibilities. We are both drawn to simplicity without being trite. I am stingy with marks; Craig is spare with light—too much of either overexplains the idea. We leave out as much as we put in, sometimes more. We are compelled to create beautiful and interesting things. Craig's photographs deceptively conceal his struggle; his pursuit of a good idea—the real work behind the work.

Then, there is the collaborative effect of the experiment—something felt rather than measured. My favorite moments came late each week when Craig would suddenly text me his solution. It was like unwrapping a gift. His image and explanation gave me a glimpse into his head. But that was only half of the benefit. Our side-by-side solutions presented a new reality, with our individual images instantly taking on new meaning. Two ideas dancing to the same tune—often in harmony, frequently discordant. Together, they told a different story—one that was more informed and enriched than our individual contributions.

Each piece we made was a cocktail of experience, inspiration, mimicry, ambition, intuition, and luck—and a ticking clock. Project 2 Craigs was an unspoken dialogue, 52 conversations stitched together to tell a bigger story.

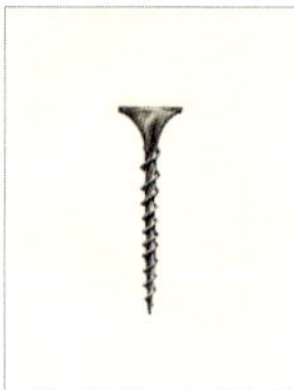
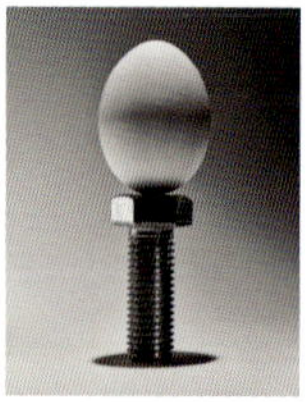
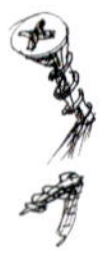
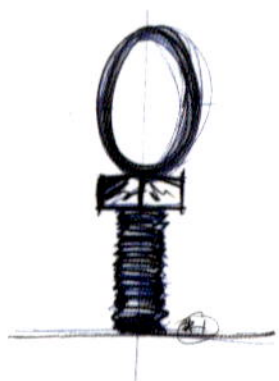
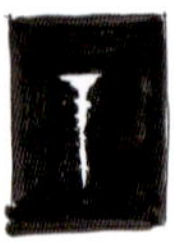

1 Screw

CF I was tempted to be clever, but this is a case in which a faithful depiction of the word/object makes a bold statement. Small objects drawn large take on a heroic presence. A wood screw is a simple, elegant form, perfectly symmetrical with delicate nuances. Graphite is the perfect medium for rendering metal.

CC More often than not, I enjoy concepting and sketching more than taking the photograph. I wanted to start this project with a very heroic image, so I used a bolt to make a podium for the iconically shaped egg, taking creative license to switch the screw for a bolt.

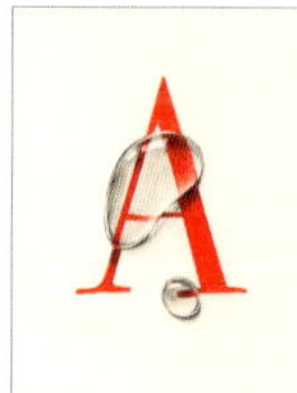
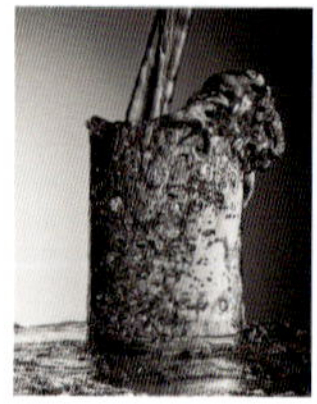
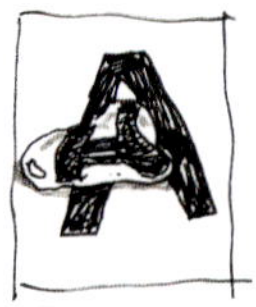
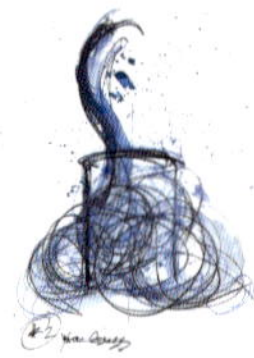
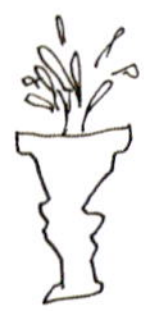

2 Water

CF Liquid is tough to draw because it's difficult to see. What we see through it tells the story. I put a drop of water on a red Bodoni A and challenged myself to draw it with Prismacolor pencils.

CC When you can freeze motion at 1/20,000th of a second, capturing liquid in motion never loses its novelty. This process reveals endless visual surprises that the human eye cannot see.

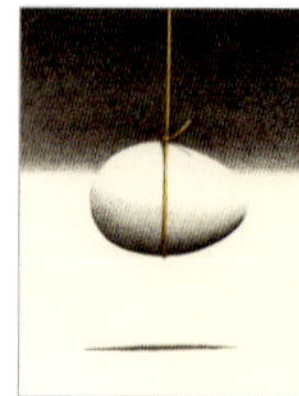
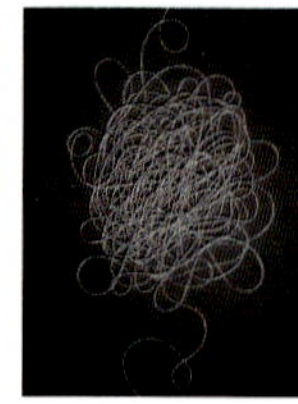
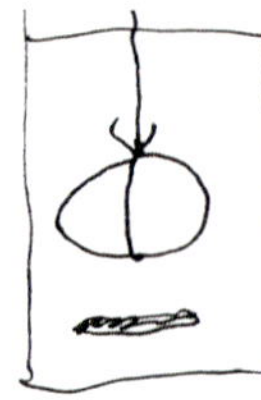
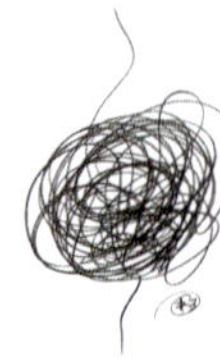

3 String

CF I love the contrast between a line and an object. Craig's egg for 1 (Screw) was the perfect inspiration. Often, I draw from photographs, but this one is out of my head, allowing the egg's edge to be undefined in two places.

CC We were beginning to see if this project would work with each other. For this prompt, I focused less on the photography and more on creating an abstract pattern from a thread. I became cautiously optimistic.

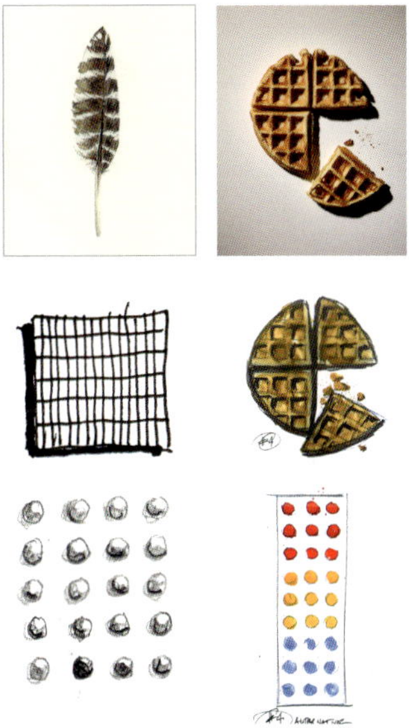

4 Pattern

CF After observing the pattern at breakfast, I initially thought of drawing a Wheat Chex, then basic geometric patterns. I was quickly bored with the perfect repetition and turned to the imperfect patterns in nature, thus the feather.

CC There's nothing more basic than a waffle iron pattern. I made 30 waffles for this shot to get the right color and texture. My hat's off to all the great food stylists—it's not easy! Simple ideas are still my favorite solutions.

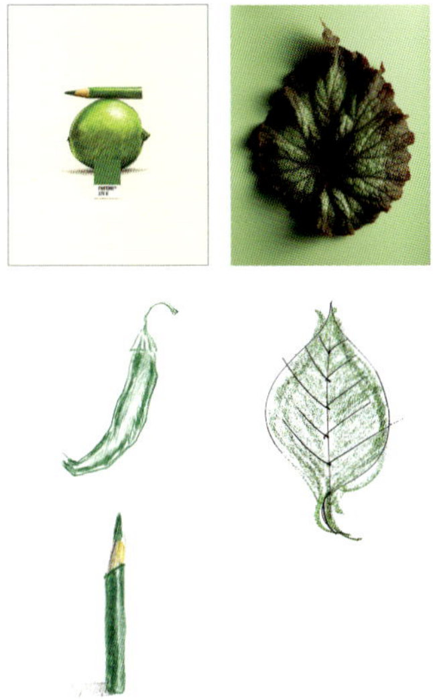

5 Green

CF I couldn't resist nature. I started and quickly abandoned a serrano pepper because it was too limiting. Instead, I drew a green composition of unrelated objects as a testament to the possibilities. I drew the lime and the pencil and stuck down a real PMS chip.

CC I couldn't resist shooting something natural, so I visited my favorite florist a block from my studio. I knew I had found my shot when they cut a beautiful leaf's stem too short. Craig quickly discovered the face cast in the shadow on the left.

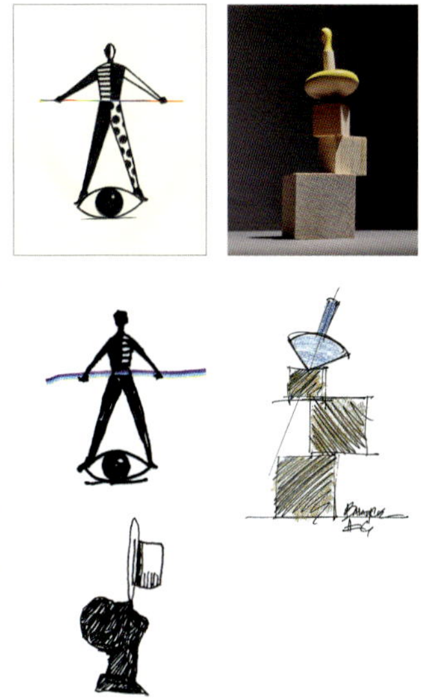

6 Balance

CF Balance afforded a lot of possibilities. In order to appreciate balance, you must see the challenge. I landed on this graphic figure using a multi-color balance pole standing on a rocking eyeball. He's symmetrical and in balance; his outfit isn't.

CC Yes, that was a real spinning top! The toy top came crashing down more times than it stayed spinning. The real balancing act was mine: spinning the top and pulling the shutter before it collapsed. One of the project's best aspects is that it is done without anyone else to help or change your original idea.

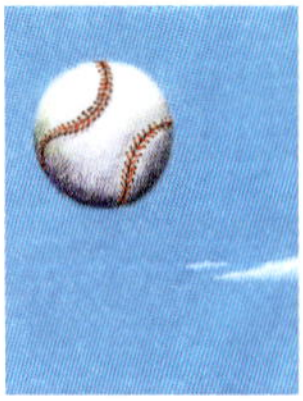
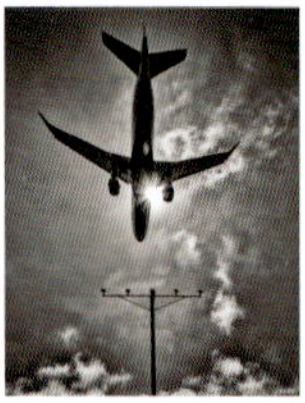
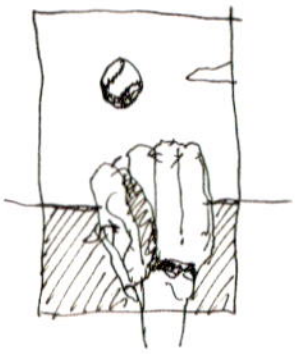
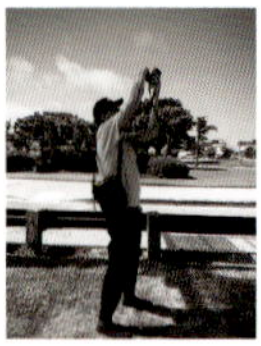
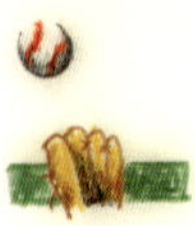

7 Fly

CF A fly ball came to mind because a baseball is so simple to depict. I did a dozen sketches with the outfield fence (a near homer) and even added a glove. That felt like over-telling the story, so I drew the ball from the fielder's viewpoint with a hint of a cloud for scale.

CC After shooting six prompts in the studio, I wanted to get outside. One of LA's most fun and undiscovered locations is this island next to LAX airport, which aligns perfectly with landing planes. I like the juxtaposition of the light tower below the plane.

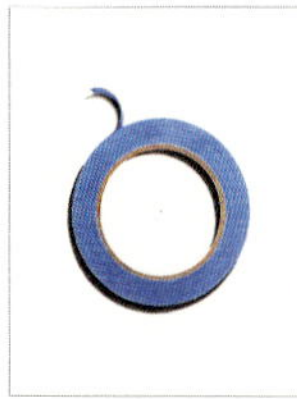
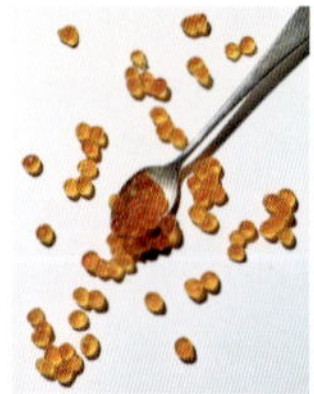
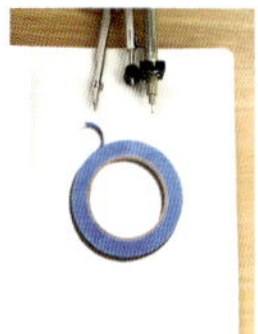
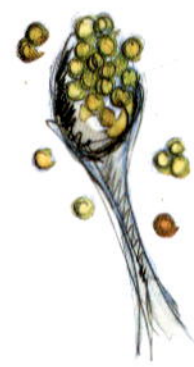
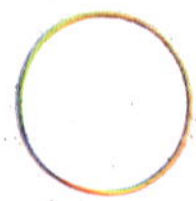

8 Round

CF Everything's round, so a quick look around my studio gave me an idea: a mechanical challenge. Using a colored pencil, I did 25 rotations with a compass holding a blue Micron 01, and done! It's a beautiful object. I left the compass holes for proof.

CC My mind went straight to Irving Penn's amazing caviar photographs for *Vogue* magazine. Circles of caviar with hard shadows were important—I also didn't want it to look or feel retouched. I love a gritty image.

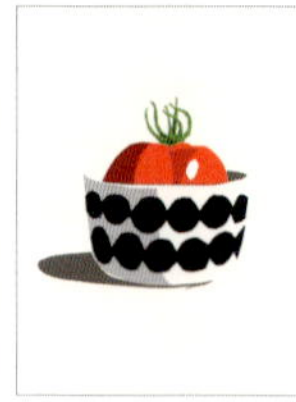
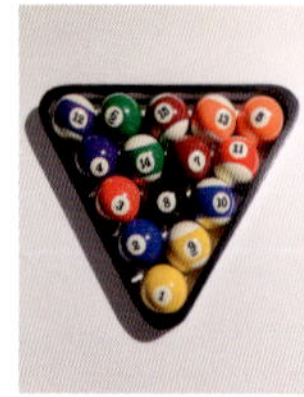
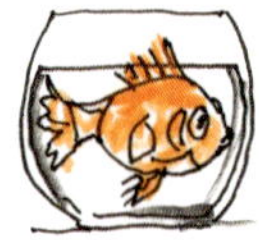
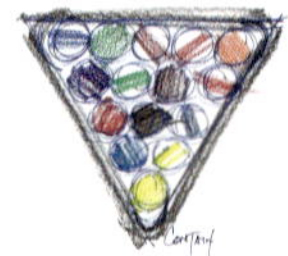
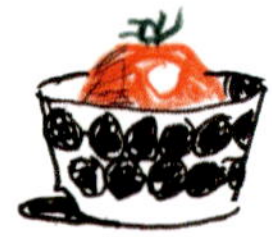

9 Contain

CF I'm challenging myself to make these solutions happen in real time, so I placed a newly harvested tomato in a bowl on the kitchen counter. Instant contained tomato! It was so graphically pleasing—perfect for cutting out of paper, an homage to the Marimekko-designed bowl.

CC My first idea was to photograph a goldfish in a bag, but I couldn't figure out what to do with the fish after the shoot. This led me to my second idea of pool balls—contained typography felt like a good solution.

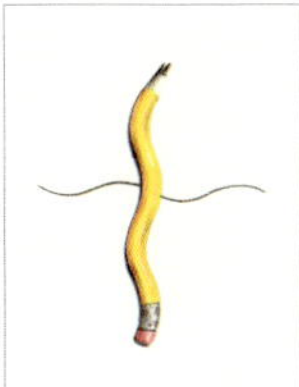
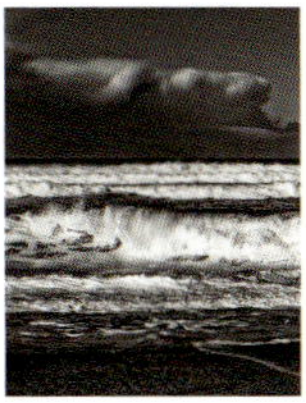
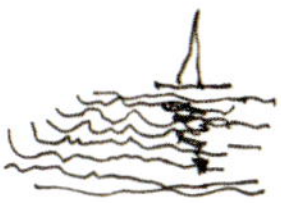
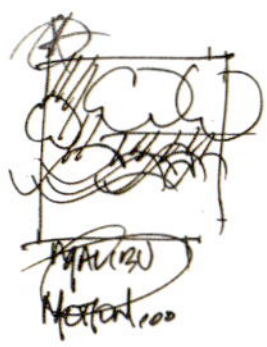
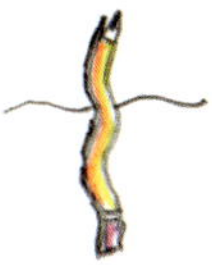

10 Wavy

CF Adjectives are the hardest! I had to resist the ocean, although I pondered it. I elected to describe the irony that a simple wavy line must be drawn with a wavy pencil.

CC One of my favorite places is the northern coast of California. The powerful ocean waves are an enduring subject. What's even more incredible are the sounds of the crashing waves. It is those two senses together that create the perfect moment.

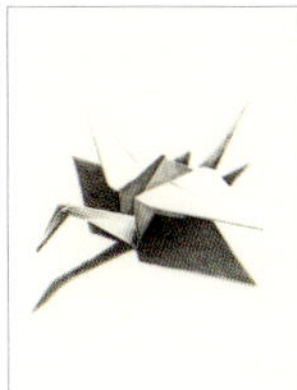
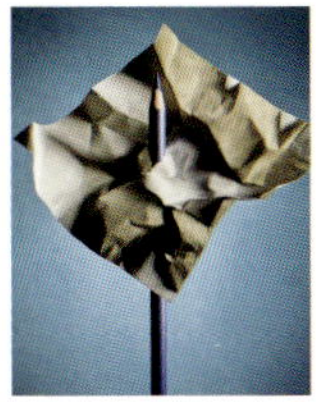
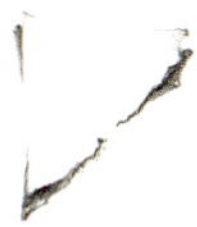
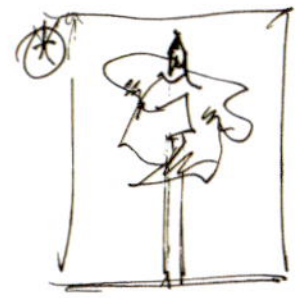
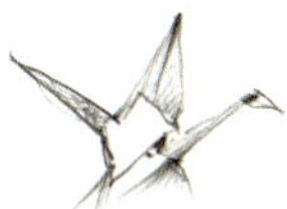

11 Paper

CF How do you make paper interesting? The answer: it's what the paper makes. I constructed a paper crane out of white paper and placed it in front of my sketchbook, lit by my desk lamp. Drawing white paper on a white surface is a classic assignment—defining an object by its shadows.

CC This one could have gone in many directions, but I always visualized a crumpled piece of paper. The pencil became the podium, and the shadows of the paper became a landscape.

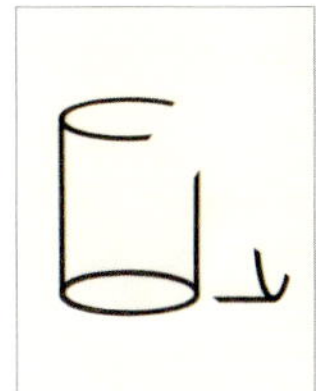
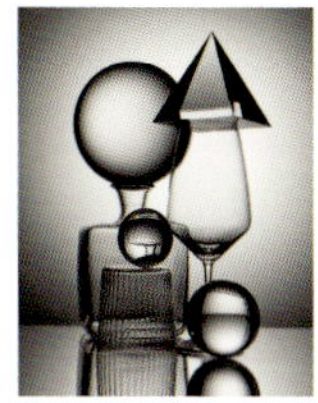
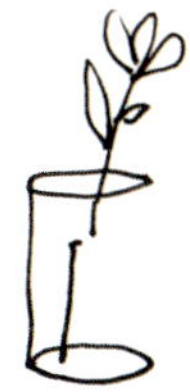
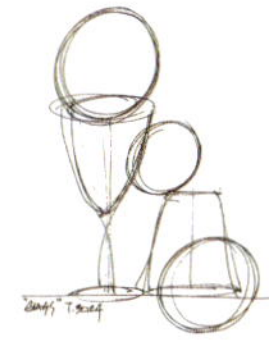
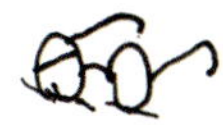

12 Glass

CF I wanted to avoid trying to accurately represent glass because I knew Craig would likely do a sublime glass photograph. My idea came while watching the Brian Eno documentary, as he spoke about simplicity. I used simple graphic language to ask, "What is going on here?"

CC I went with my first idea, which was to create a backlit glass sculpture. I constructed the still life at least ten ways before finally landing on this one. My favorite part was the reflections inside the foreground objects.

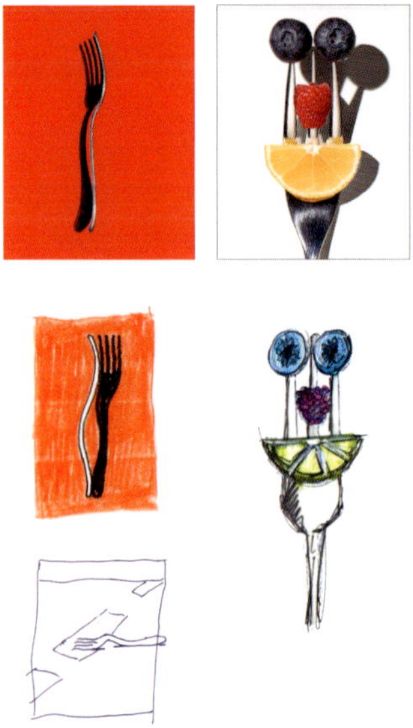

13 Fork

CF My overarching question with these prompts is, "How can I make it interesting?" Sometimes it's as simple as creating an unexpected view. In profile, a fork is virtually unrecognizable; however, its cast shadow renders the answer we seek.

CC I was trying not to take each word too seriously when I came up with this one. The key to making the face was to find a three-pronged fork rather than a four-pronged one.

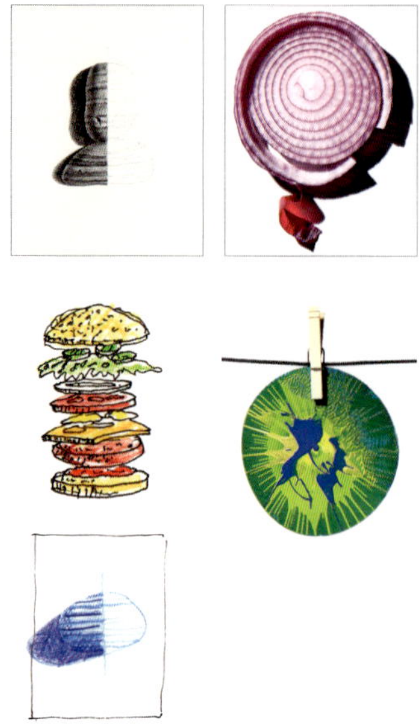

14 Layered

CF I planned to draw the layers of a perfect hamburger until I came across a treasure of a beach stone, presenting the layers of time. The split drawing creates a certain technical quality that I find interesting. In many ways, another layer of time.

CC My first idea went back to my childhood creating layered spin art. That was fun, but it was not good enough for the diptych. The layered onion was my second idea, and it was the perfect solution without trying too hard. Keep it simple.

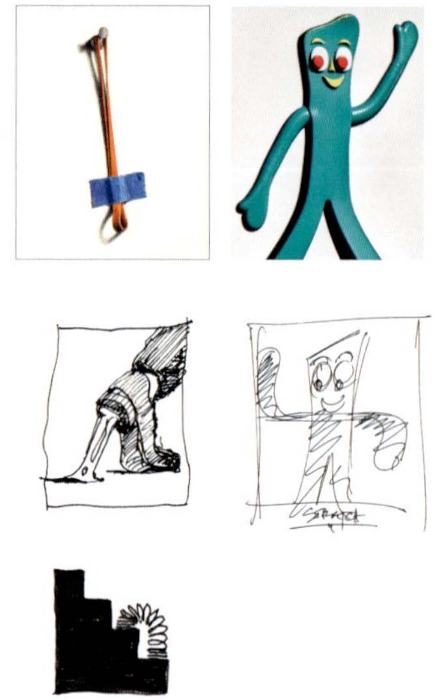

15 Stretch

CF A rubber band is the perfect object of stretch—when it's stretched, that is. I set up a still life with objects on my desk and drew it. I like the challenge of drawing a hyperreal situation on paper. If it's successful, it will tempt you to believe in its reality.

CC I couldn't help myself with another childhood throwback. I like Gumby, damn it! I received a few disturbing stares from passengers on my plane while retouching this image in flight.

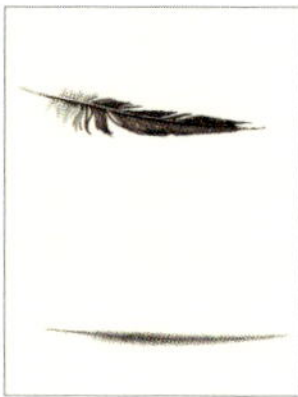
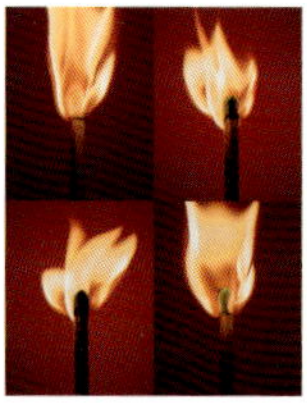
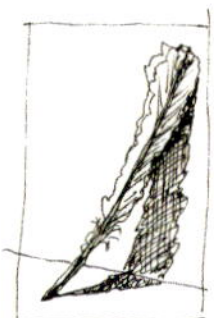
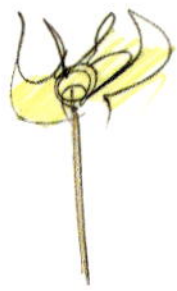
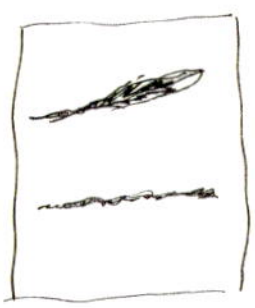
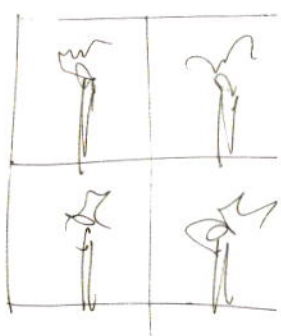
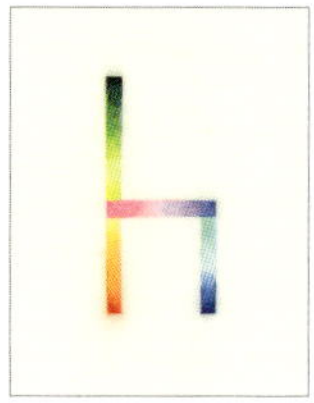
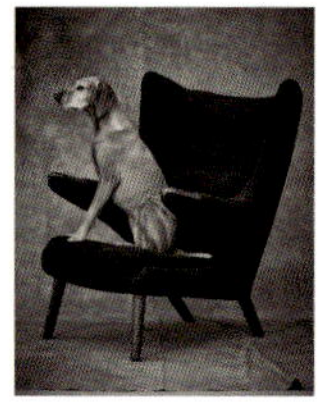
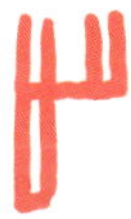
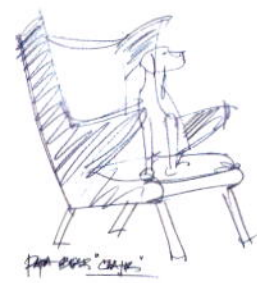
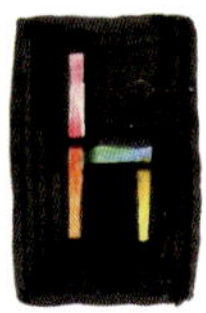
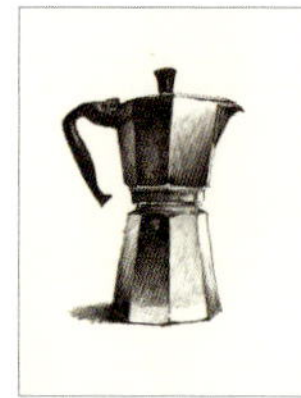
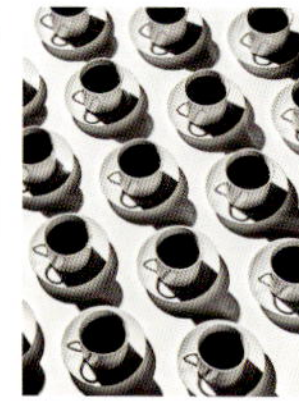
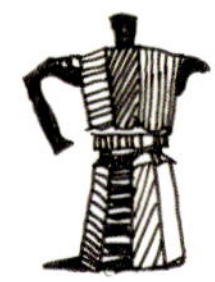
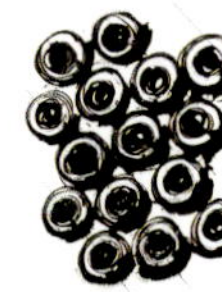
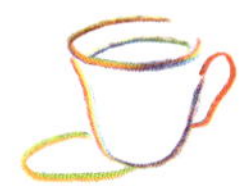
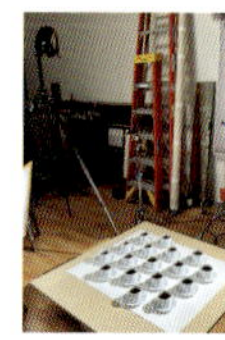

16 Light

CF I chose two meanings of the word. First, the reference to weight—light as a... Second, luminosity, for which shadows are created.

CC No two matches create the same flame pattern when ignited, so a four-panel grid was a great way to show just how unique each flame really was. I used the frame burst mode on my Leica SL2 to capture that split-second moment. The dance of a flame is always exciting.

17 Chair

CF You can draw a chair with three or four lines—the challenge is making the lines interesting.

CC The only thing that could make a Hans Wegner Papa Bear chair look even better would be a Vizsla sitting on it. I shot this in my backyard before the sun came up. The chair is from our living room, and Jo is always ready for a serious portrait.

18 Coffee

CF Of course, I explored the cup. I love drawing a cup! But what says coffee first thing in the morning, besides the smell, is our Bialetti coffee maker. It's a gorgeous object to draw—a perfect graphite subject, with its surfaces and facets—in black and white. The drawing took twenty minutes.

CC One of my favorite books showcases the commercial work of the great Czech photographer Josef Sudek. This work, created between 1920 and 1930, inspired me this week. Added inspiration was a visit to his house and studio in Prague. I wanted to create this in one shot without any image cloning or retouching.

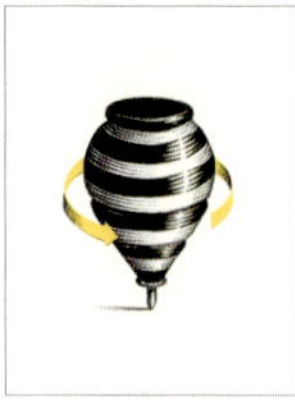
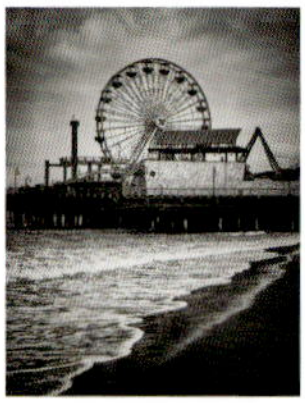
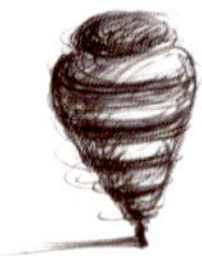
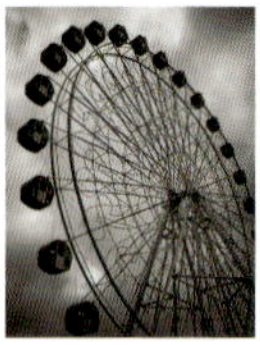
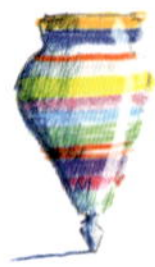
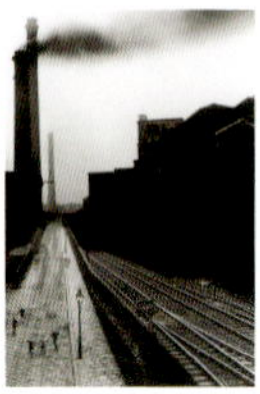

Photo by Bill Brandt

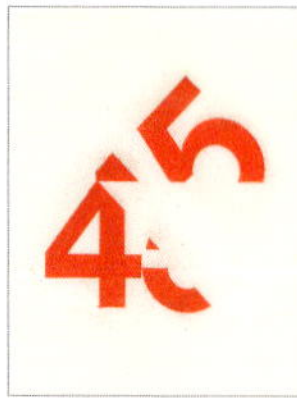
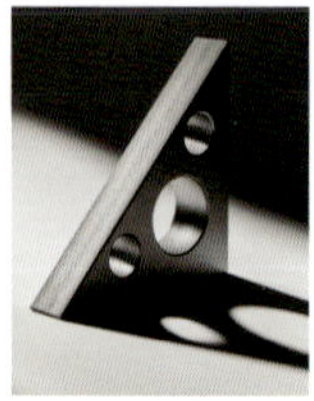
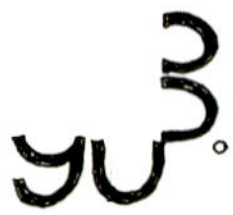
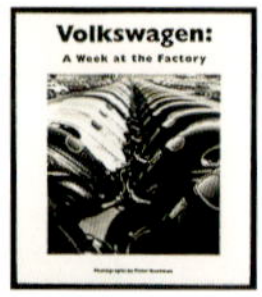

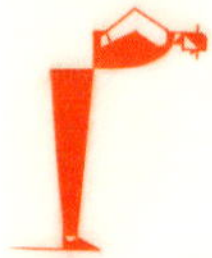
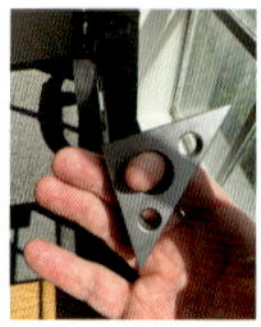
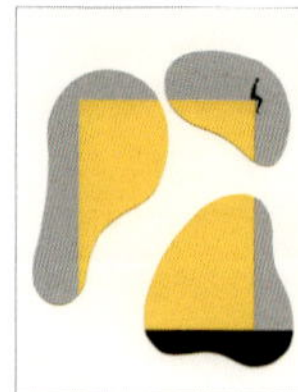
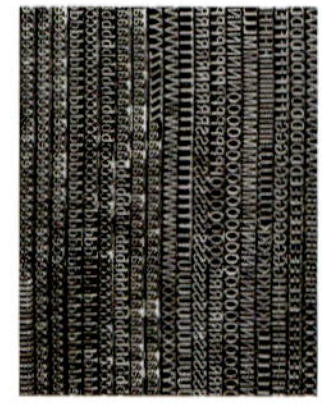
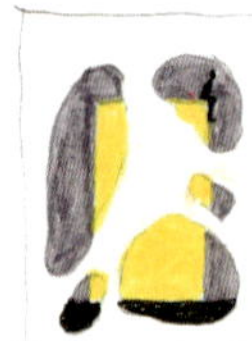
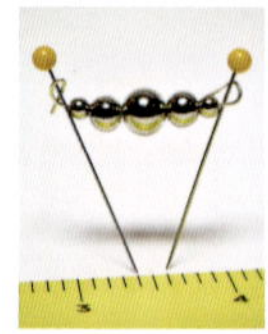
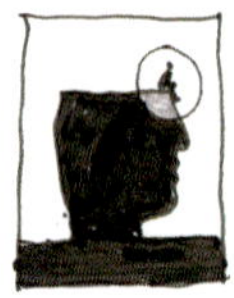
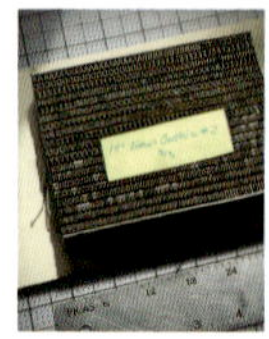

19 Spin

CF I couldn't resist riffing on Craig's spinning top for 6 (Balance). After drawing the little graphic top, I realized it felt static, not quite spinning. So, I made it into a diagram by adding an arrow cut from Pantone paper. I might have over-explained it!

CC I wanted to get out of the studio for this word and I sought a majestic landscape. I scouted this location three times that week, but on that day, the clouds finally came in and I knew it would be a good session. I was thinking about the late great photographer Bill Brandt. Nobody was better at creating an amazing contrasty black and white landscape.

20 Angle

CF I have dozens of 30-, 60-, and 45-degree triangles all over my studio—they are essential tools. The 45 is the most universal and visually perfect. It has a 90 and a 45 angle. I didn't want to draw a triangle; I wanted to draw its purpose. In Helvetica, of course.

CC My inspiration for this week's word came from German photographer Peter Keetman's 1953 book, *Volkswagen: A Week at the Factory.* His photographs of perfectly stacked raw sheet metal still hold up today. My metal triangle photograph was created in honor of his work.

21 Small

CF Something is only small in relation to something larger (scale). So, I needed to create a larger environment for my figure to be small. After I designed the scene, I was bored with it, so I added a mask of jellybean portholes through which to view it.

CC My first idea was to create a tiny sculpture that would be about one inch square. Tiny spheres became my sculpture's focal point, and pins became my flagpoles. I got bored with this idea, and, like a client with too much time, I decided to change directions to a wall of 14-point News Gothic lead type.

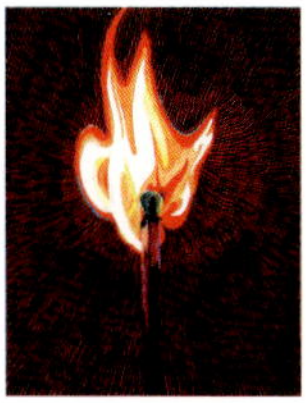
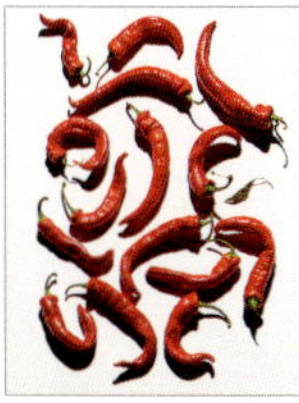
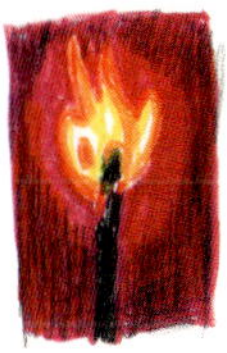
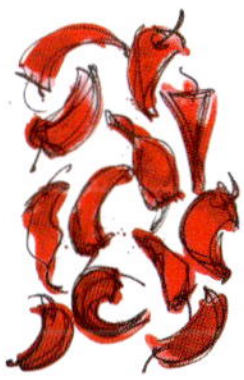
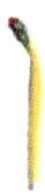

22 Hot

CF The ultimate hot symbol is fire, and since Craig had already photographed burning matches in 16 (Light), I used his photo as a reference for a colored pencil drawing. As a little graphic exercise, I intentionally broke the gradated flame into a few distinct color bands.

CC I started with a hotplate and ended up with red peppers. I am not sure why, but I like intense black shadows and patterns.

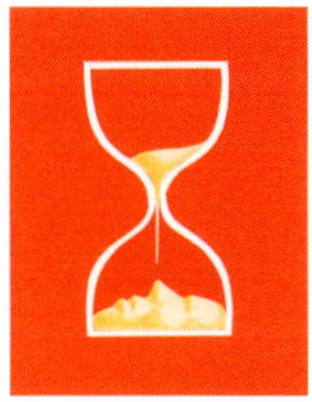
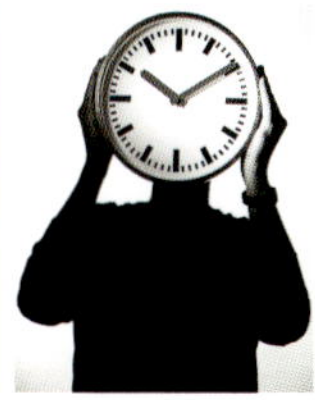
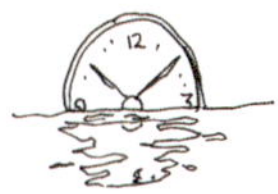
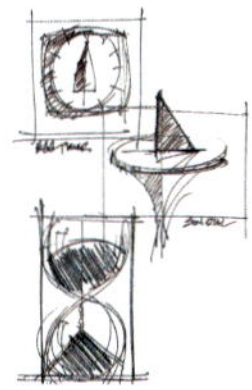
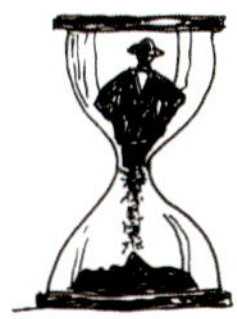
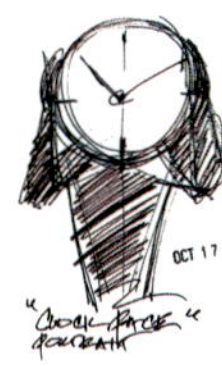

23 Time

CF Time is typically symbolized by timekeepers (watches and clocks). The hourglass is perhaps the most perfect graphic because of its simplicity and opportunity for interpretation. I added a metaphor: time makes us who we are.

CC I had so much fun with this one. I first photographed an hourglass and thought I was finished, but I later came up with the idea of a clock face and couldn't decide which one I liked better. I always tell students to pick a lane and stand by it; this time, I couldn't practice what I preach.

See also runner-up pg. 120

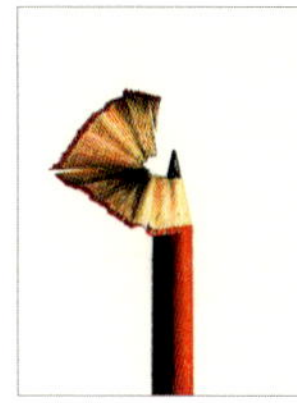
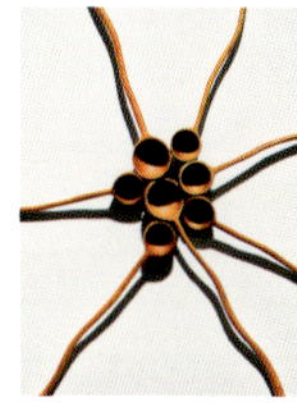
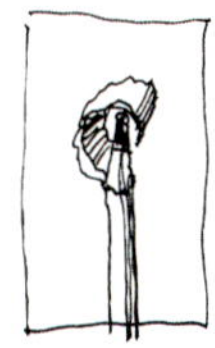
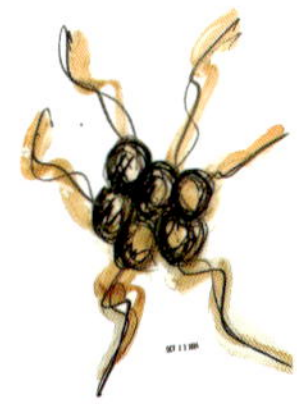
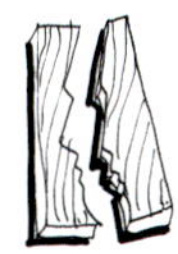

24 Wood

CF Pencils usually get credit for their graphite when they are actually about 75% wood. I love what happens when you sharpen a pencil, especially with an old hand-held sharpener. I decided to pay homage to Craig's pencil in his photograph for 11 (Paper).

CC I didn't want to be too obvious with my selection of wood, so I walked around aimlessly in my neighborhood until I found these spoons at a local shop. I took seven of them and created a pattern. This is essentially design first, wood second.

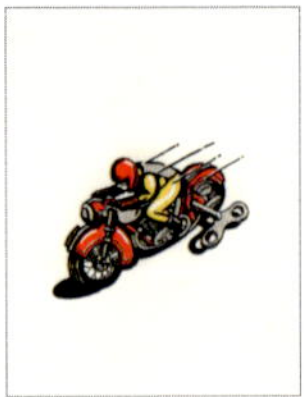
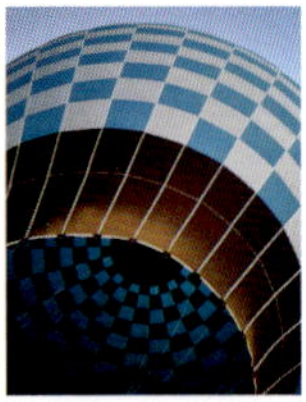
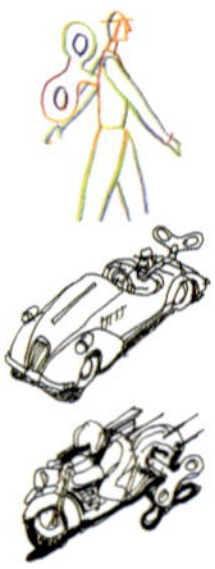
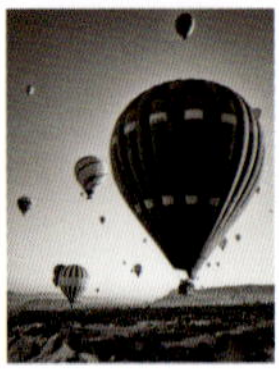

25 Wind

CF I knew blowing wind would be challenging to depict, so I went to the verb. I thought of a wind-up vintage toy. I found a motorcycle and drew it in the style in which it was painted. I added the "whiz lines" and got two for one!

CC While traveling with my wife in Istanbul, I thought it would be easy to find a blowing Turkish flag—but that wasn't meant to be. Seeing a hot air balloon being filled early one morning felt better. A pre-wind moment, so to speak.

See also runner-up pg. 120

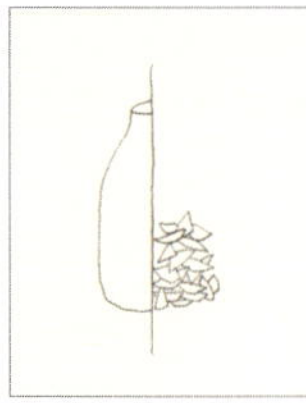
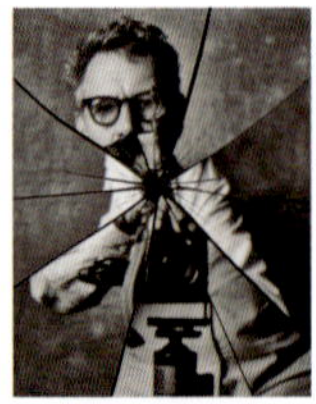
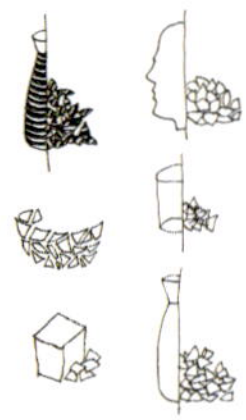
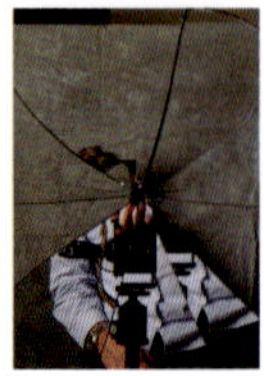

26 Shatter

CF My wife and I were traveling in Japan for this prompt. I saw many sake vessels, and their silhouettes were striking in their simplicity—inspiration supplied. In order to know something is shattered, you must know what it was whole. The simple line drawing honored the simple—but fragile—Japanese aesthetic.

CC Throughout my career, I have shattered everything from light bulbs to glass crystals, but always as a photographic still life. A shattered self-portrait seemed more interesting, so I didn't think twice about smashing a mirror at the studio to capture this one.

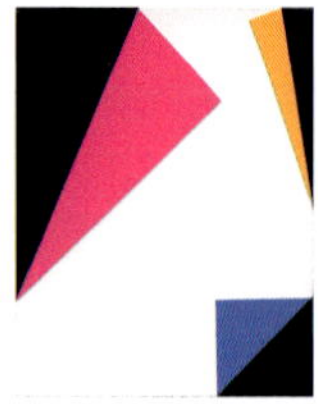
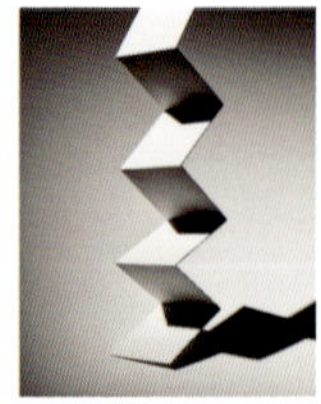
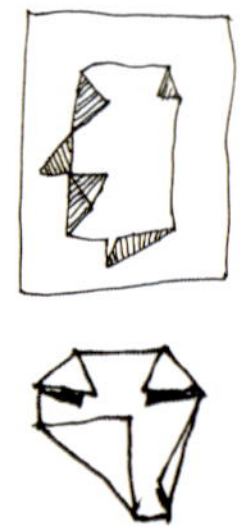
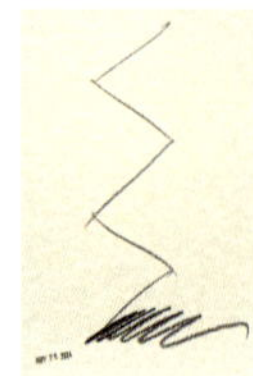

27 Fold

CF My mind inextricably connects folds to paper. I remained under the influence of Japan, and thinking about its utmost simplicity. I made a couple of sketches and a folded model. Then, I cut the segments from PMS colored papers and pasted them into my sketchbook.

CC I like creating images with basic materials. I imagined a photo of a suspended, folded piece of paper. I used one Exacto knife, one piece of watercolor paper, and one straight edge, always cutting half the paper on the outside bend. One more thing: just one light.

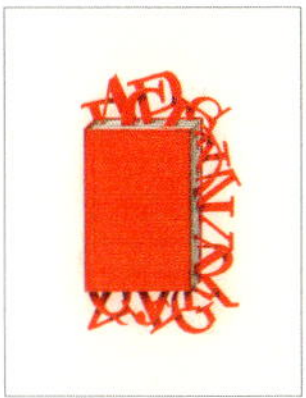
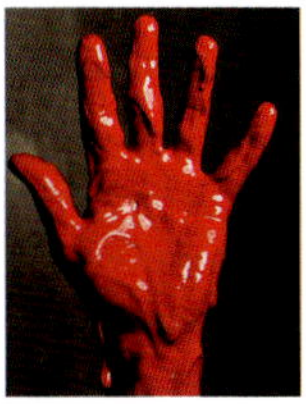
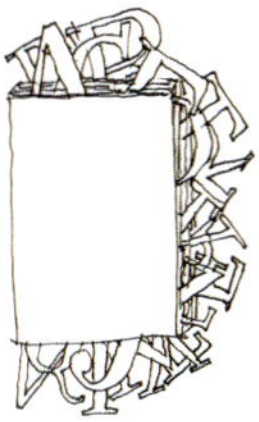
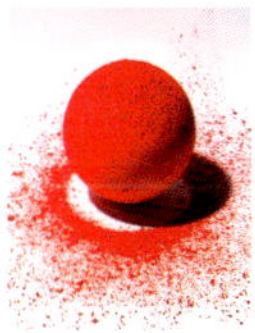
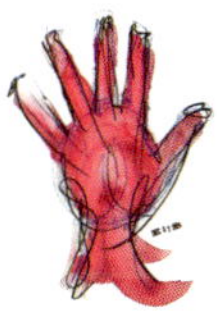

28 Red

CF It's probably the most used color in my design career—possibly the most powerful color. I had just sketched an idea (book and letters), and rather than use multi-colored letters, I solved the problem by coloring it entirely in red. The accidental bonus was the other "read."

CC My original idea was to create a still life covering blocks and spheres with red pastels, but everything changed when I spotted a gallon jug of red acrylic paint at the art store. Dipping my hand into a bucket of paint was the easy part. The hard part was triggering the camera with my other hand.

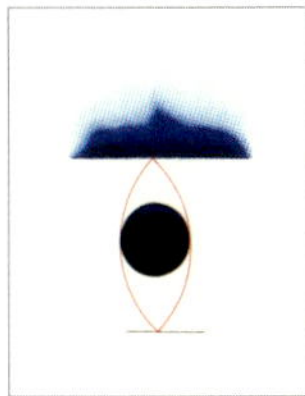
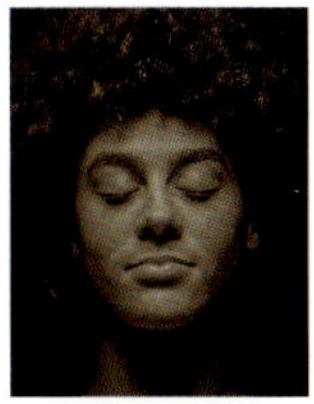
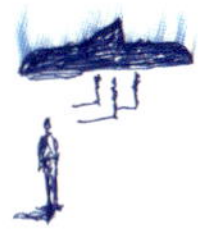
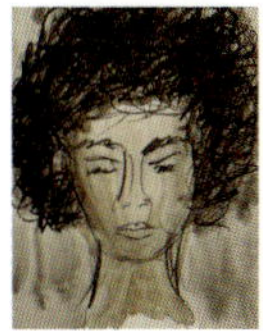
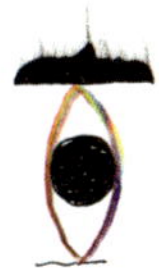

29 Dream

CF Dreams are about seeing in your mind's eye. Our eyes have to be wide open while they are shut. It's a state of being, a place you go. The word asked for an impossible reality. My drawing is inexplicable but very simple.

CC My idea was simple: a dream portrait. I envisioned a woman's face, but very dark. I wanted a portrait as if it were taken from within the mind. The set was silent (even the camera), with very little light. My subject never knew when the picture was taken.

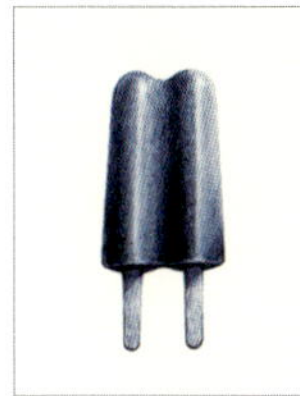
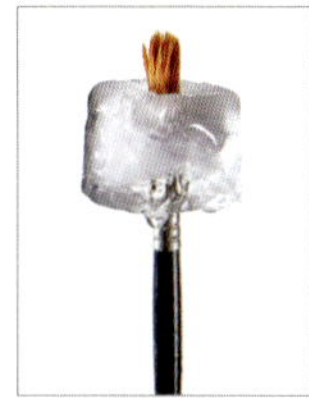
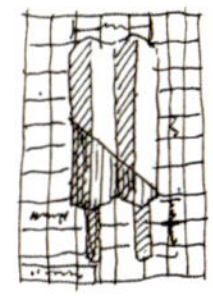
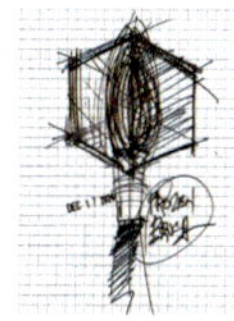
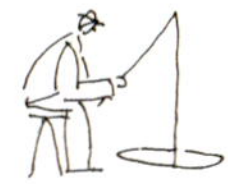
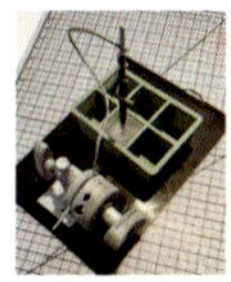

30 Cold

CF There are many possibilities for "cold." I landed on the Twin Pops that were so much a part of my childhood summers, and I thought it would be fun to draw it from memory. As I often do, I drew it a few ways, highly rendered in graphite and a single-line brush drawing. All worked, but ultimately, the graphite drawing felt the coldest.

CC This week was a simple combination formula: Art + Cold = Concept. The paintbrush represented art, and the ice represented cold. Then, it was just a waiting game before the ice melted away to expose the auburn bristles.

See also runner-up pg. 121

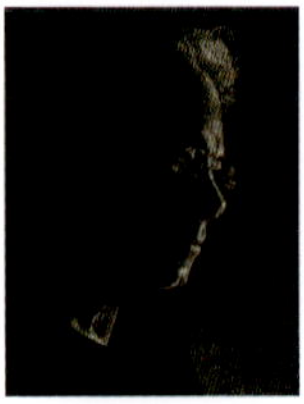
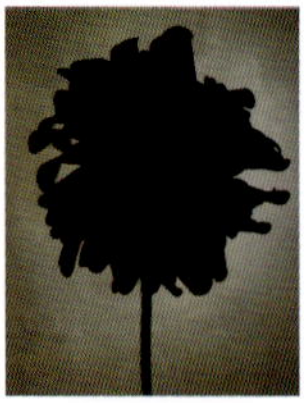
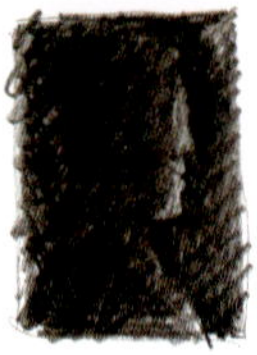
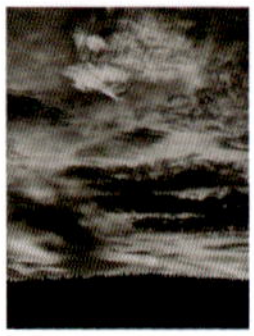

31 Dark

CF Since Craig did a self-portrait for 26 (Shatter), this felt like a good place for me to do one. I took an iPhone photo with a single light and drew it in graphite. I kept darkening the composition until only the essentials remained. The mystery of the shadows presents a certain darkness unto itself.

CC Through my many years of photographic assignments, there would be times when the main light would misfire, resulting in a silhouette of the subject. These accidents create images you never expect and, in many cases, are even better than what you originally planned. This time, I planned it.

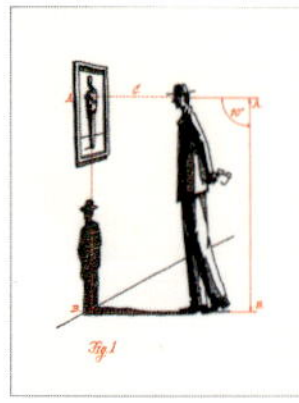
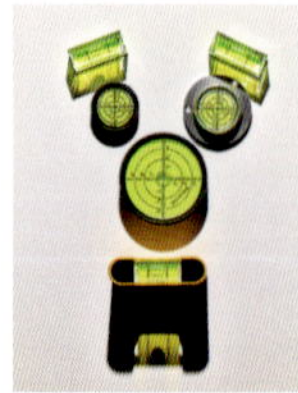
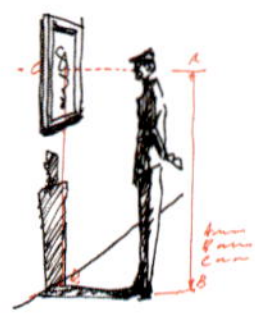
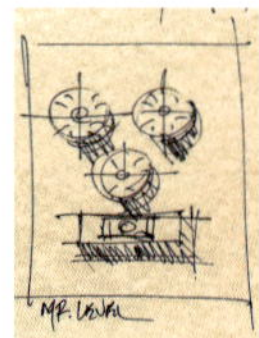
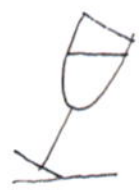
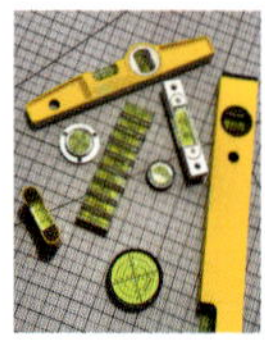

32 Level

CF I like diagrams, particularly scientific explanations. As a concept, level is an absolute fact and lends itself to a diagram. I also love drawing spectators in museums. I had recently photographed a profile of a gentleman in Japan. He became the perfect subject for my "eye-level" diagram.

CC Irving Penn was the master of the still-life face. I used this week's word to pay homage to this great photographer. Photographers are obsessed with keeping things level.

See also runner-up pg. 121

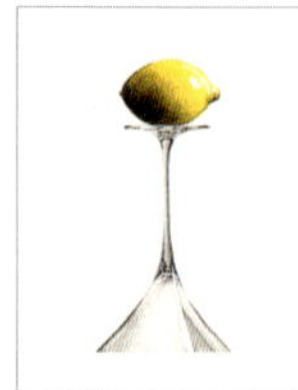
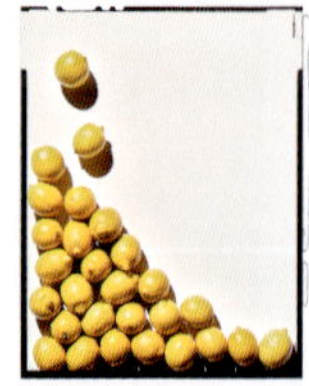
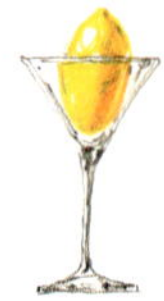
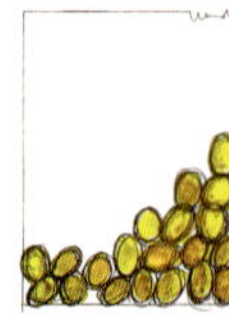
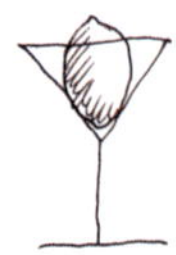
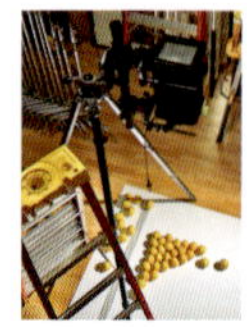

33 Fruit

CF I looked up from my breakfast and spotted a lemon in a bowl. I sketched it inside a martini glass. While photographing my idea, I discovered that the composition was more interesting with the glass inverted. I drew it with graphite and colored pencil—the fruit on a glass pedestal.

CC We agreed on our format at the project's outset: a 4:5 proportion. For most of my career, I've shot with 8x10 and 4x5 view cameras, so I wanted to introduce the camera to the frame. My idea was to use the 4x5 film's edge as a frame for the lemons, which became just as important as the fruit in the image.

See also runner-up pg. 122

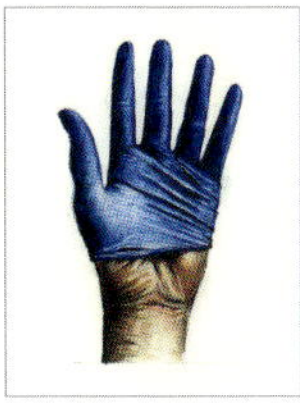
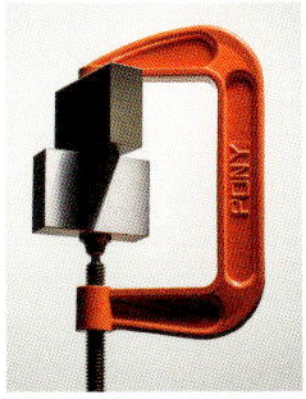

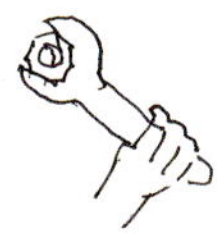
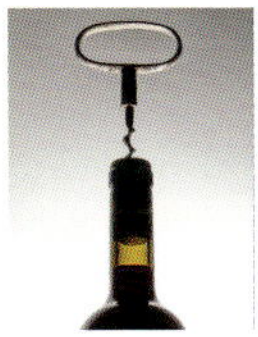
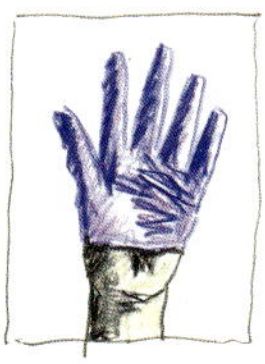

34 Tight

CF Adjectives are the toughest words. I initially thought of a tight situation or tightening a bolt—a kind of mechanical description. Then I pulled on a surgical glove to examine its fit. Sure enough, the unfinished act of putting on the glove exaggerated the tightness. It was fun to draw with colored pencils—a nod to Craig's red hand for 28 (Red).

CC I always found tools to be very inspirational when creating still-life photographs. I wanted to create a Brutalist sculpture using two steel blocks inside a C-clamp. I was also influenced by Walker Evans's black and white photographic series of individual tools taken over a century ago.

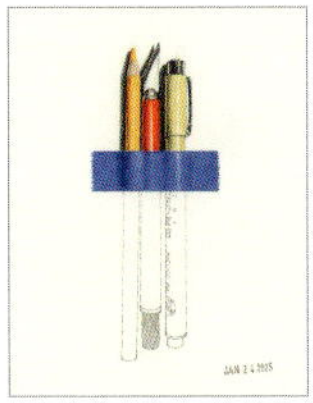
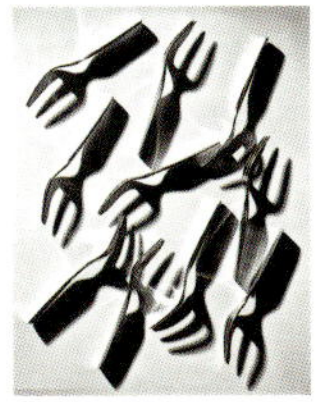
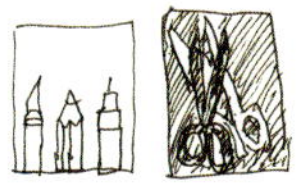
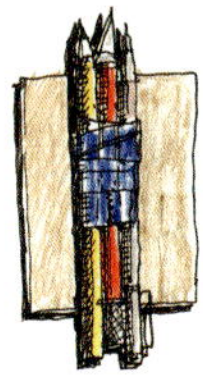
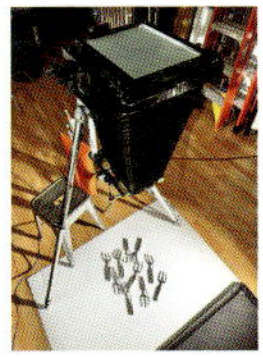
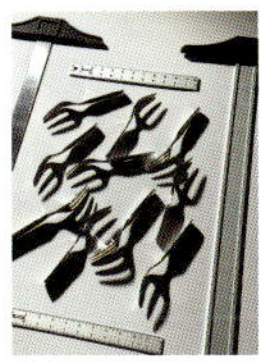

35 Utensils

CF These are the essential hand-held utensils of my job. I draw with a Micron .01 pen and cut with an Exacto Gripster knife with #11 blades. I use colored pencils—my years as a designer gave me an affinity for Prismacolors. I use graphite pencils; in this case, a Berol 2H and a Blackwing. The blue painter's tape in this composition is real. The half-finished drawing showed the utensils at work.

CC The only thing better than shooting with a 4x5 view camera is shooting with an 8x10 view camera. A digital file will never surpass the quality and film grain of an 8x10 Tri-X negative.

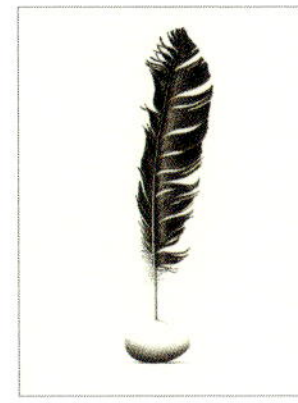
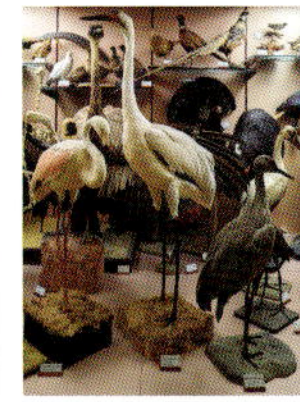
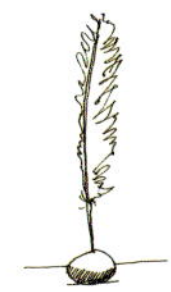
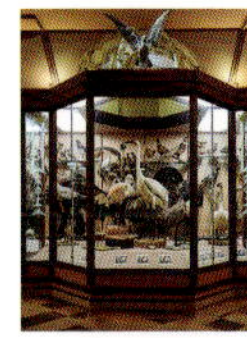
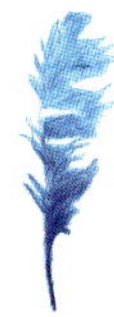
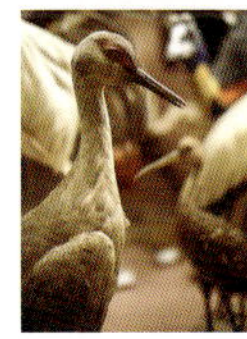

36 Feather

CF A feather is like a piece of calligraphy, so it's hard not to want to draw it in all its beauty. I drew the blue feather, its silhouette with the sky within it. I liked the concept but felt it was missing much of the feather's intrinsic detail, so I drew one more, paying homage to its birthplace.

CC One of my favorite places to explore is the Hall of Birds at the Natural History Museum of LA County. As soon as I got this week's word, I knew that was where I had to be.

Photographs courtesy of the Natural History Museum of Los Angeles County.

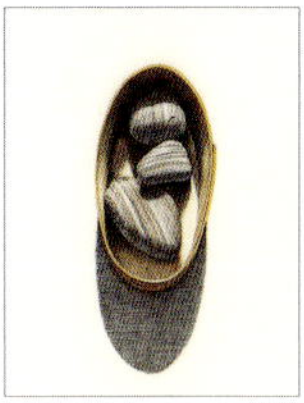
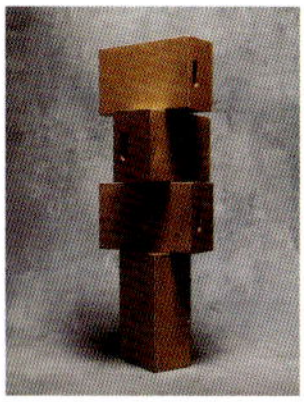
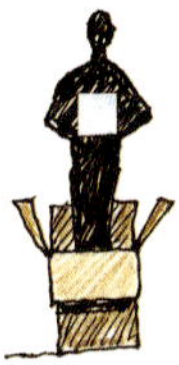

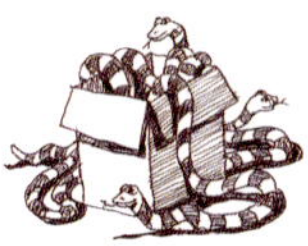

37 Box

CF My first sketches were objects in boxes, a figure and a pile of snakes—neither particularly beautiful. I abandoned the square box for a Shaker box, a gift from my daughter, filled with beach rocks. A literal depiction of “a box of rocks.”

CC The apple box is an essential tool for photo shoots. Every key grip, lead electric, and assistant must know the rules: side one is the shortest, side two is the middle height, and side three is the tallest. This image is more lesson than still life, featuring two out of the three sides. I stacked the four apple boxes and used the natural studio skylight. It was the fastest word to shoot: ten minutes total.

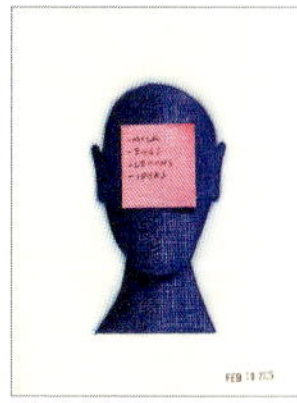
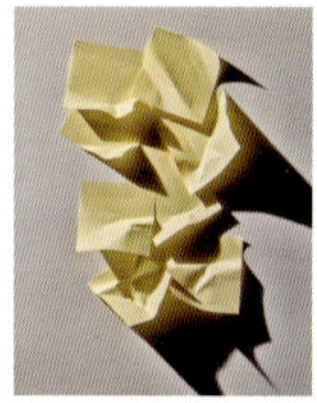
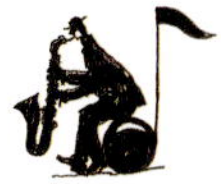
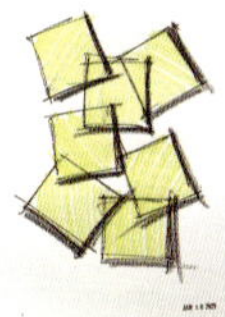
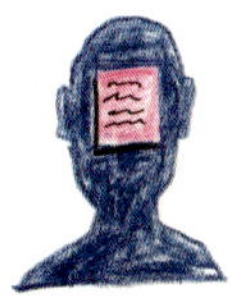

38 Note

CF I live by notes—Post-its, sketchbooks, or a list on scratch paper (which I make daily). They are all designed to free up space in my mind. It seems the more notes, the greater the need for notes! To-dos, shopping lists, and ideas that I don’t want to forget. My biggest problem is remembering where I left that note.

CC My favorite genre is strong concepts with simple solutions. Taking objects out of context to create new ideas, in this case, Post-it Notes. The paper, shapes, and shadows all work together.

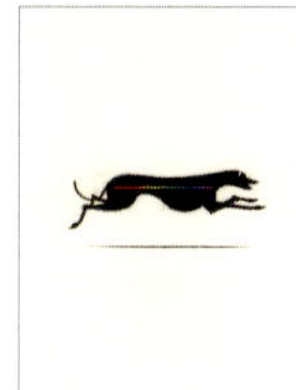
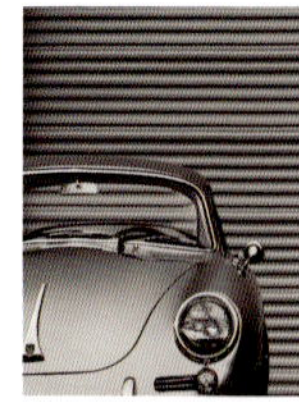
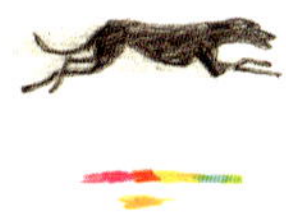
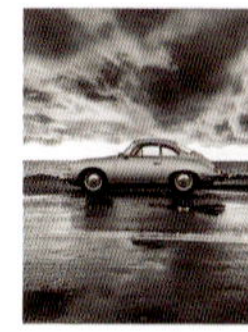
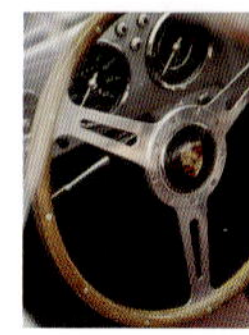

39 Fast

CF We had two whippets, a personification of fast. They had two speeds—38mph and asleep. Their elegant bodies are made to cut the air with their feet only momentarily touching the ground. This is jet-black Tenacity in full race mode.

CC The obvious solution would have been to photograph a scene with some motion blur, but I could not resist photographing my 356 Porsche. It is not really that fast, but it is the fast I like. Obvious solutions are usually predictable and boring, so I went in a different direction. The 356 is a quintessential nod to this week’s word.

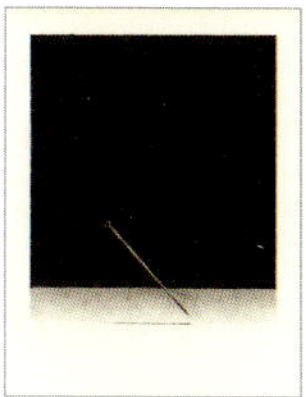
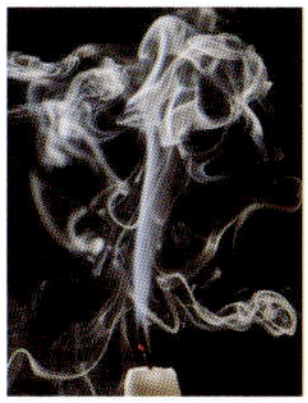
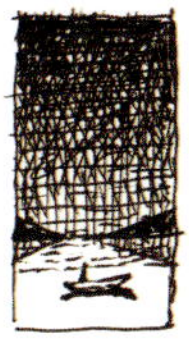
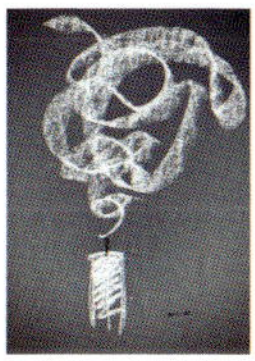
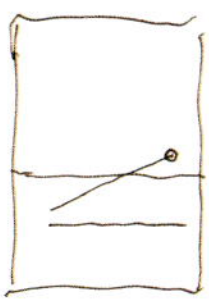

40 Quiet

CF I initially drew a person in a boat quietly floating under moonlight. As often happens, my first attempt freed me to think about the problem differently. Some words come with metaphors we all use to explain them—quiet is one. So quiet, you could… The drawing is of the pin in the last moment of silence.

CC I had flashbacks of being a young altar boy. What I remember most was how quiet the church was once I extinguished the candles on the altar. The movement of the smoke made no sound.

See also runner-up pg. 122

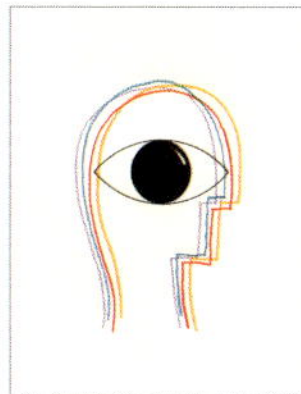
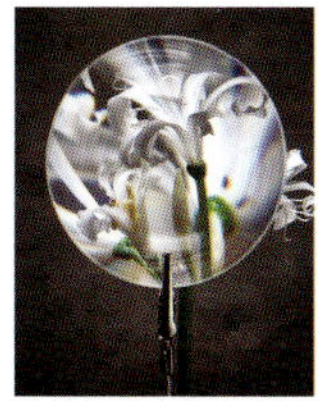
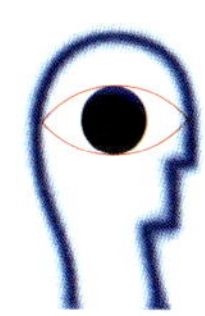
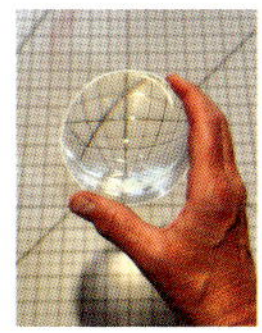
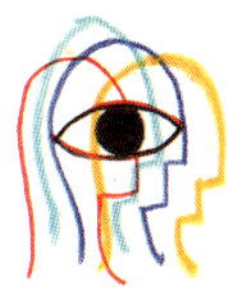

41 Focus

CF Focus is all about visual clarity—things are "in' focus or 'out." I wanted to draw something that represented both. The eye is razor sharp, and the figure appears blurred—a simple visual trick.

CC The direction I chose for this word is playing with Fresnel lenses that magnify your subject, in this case, a flower. It forces you to focus directly through the glass.

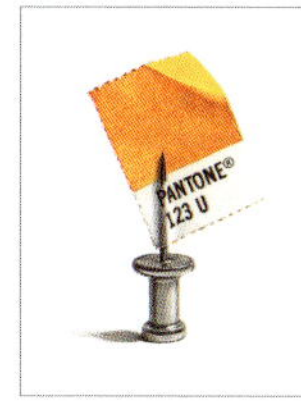

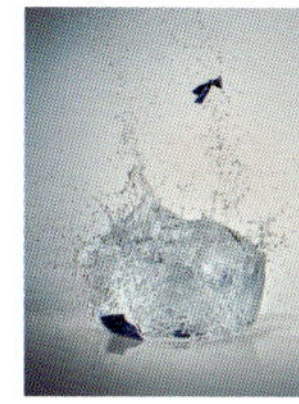
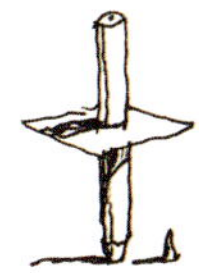
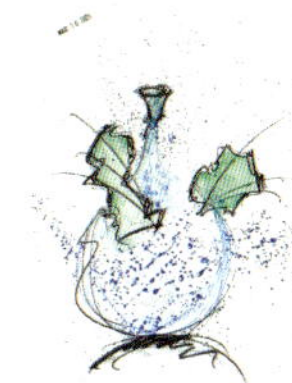
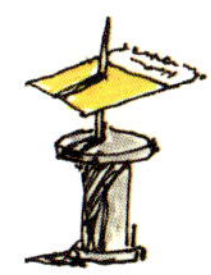

42 Puncture

CF My studio is full of sharp devices—all capable of puncturing something. Pencils, knives, and compasses are good, but the pushpin is sublime. What better object to pierce than a PMS 123 chip. Together, they created a heroic monument to design. Super fun to draw!

CC This was an exercise in perseverance. Puncturing a water balloon and capturing the moment it explodes with a strobe light (with a duration of 1/20,000th of a second) creates the most unexpected images. This captured art only exists in the moment of impact and cannot be seen by the human eye. It is also a lot of fun to do.

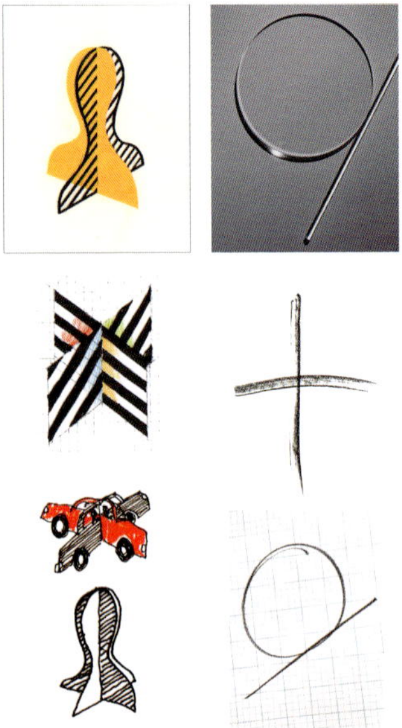

43 Intersection

CF The first thing I drew was the classic form of two colliding planes. It's a beautiful graphic expression, especially with my very '80s aesthetic. The composition seemed thin, so I changed the planes to figures. The intersection became an interaction.

CC One of my all-time favorite classes growing up was geometry. I got to draw all kinds of circles, squares, and triangles. Little did I know that I would carry these skills into my future. This week's photograph represents a line-sphere intersection, and I dedicate this image to my 7th-grade geometry teacher.

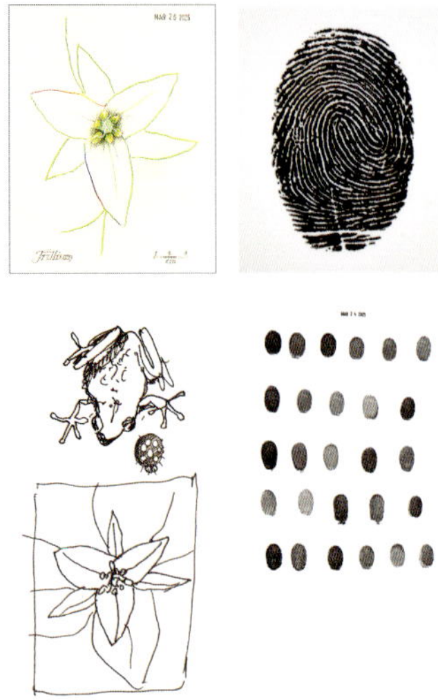

44 Macro

CF I immediately thought of close-up scientific photographs of bugs or frogs! Drawing from nature seemed the right path—maybe a nod to Audubon and the naturalist illustrators. By coincidence, on my morning hike, I had photographed the tiny trillium beginning to open. My drawing is about six times its actual size. I also had Ellsworth Kelly's simple flower drawings in mind—they say so much with so little.

CC The human eye cannot see in macro without an image. The macro lens allows us to see things differently. I like that the thumbprint feels less like a photograph and more like a silkscreen poster.

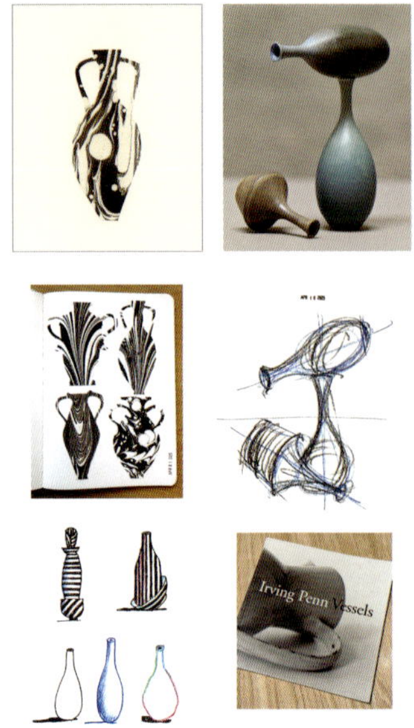

45 Vessel

CF I sketched several simple Japanese vases in pen and ink. Dissatisfied, I looked up ancient Greek and Roman urns to discover their sensuous silhouettes. I cut nine vases from scrap marbleized paper made by my wife, to reference their fluid contents. The resulting discovery is precisely what this project is about.

CC When I saw this week's word, I thought of the great Irving Penn, who created a brilliant show based on vessels at the Pace/MacGill Gallery in 2008. Any attempt to come close to achieving his masterful work on this word lands sufficiently short.

See also runner-up pg. 123

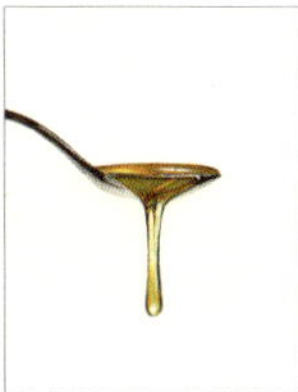
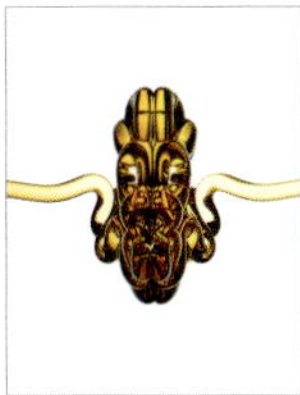
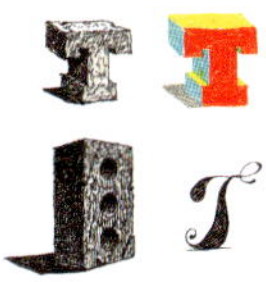
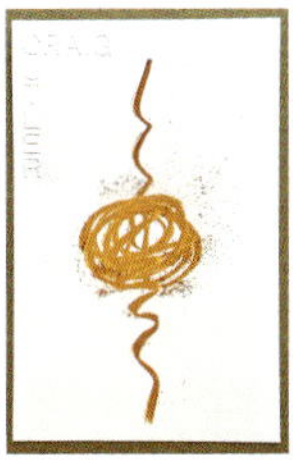
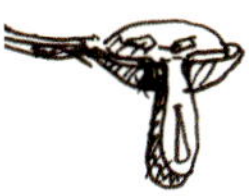

46 Thick

CF It's the boredom of my own ideas that forces me to look around. We have honey bees, and there's something about the slow drip of honey. There's nothing like the viscocity of slow, sticky honey, and how it transmits light. I photographed it and drew it with colored pencils.

CC This week's tools were only a single mirror and a bottle of honey. One hand poured the honey while the other fired the camera. Sometimes, the smallest production creates the best results. What a relief not to have any client feedback! I also like that my image created a face.

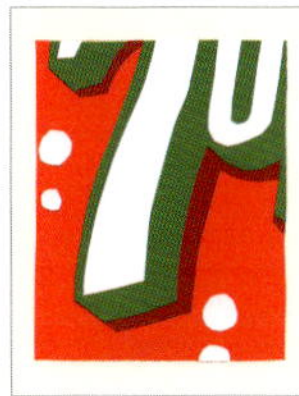
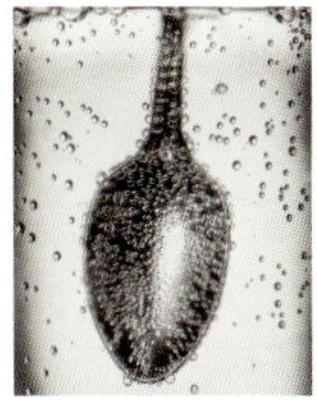
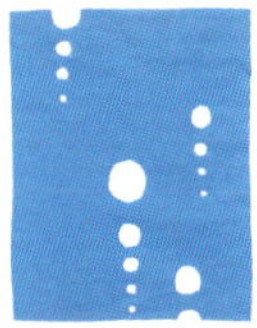
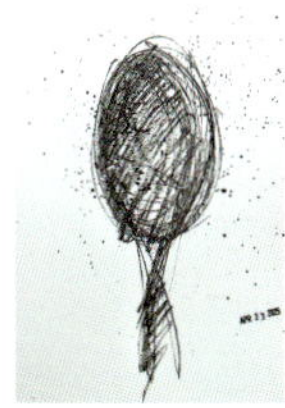
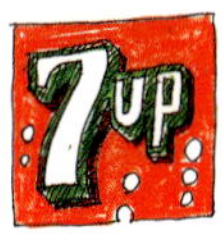

47 Effervescent

CF 7Up came to mind instantly—it's almost sickeningly bubbly. The original bottle design was brilliantly effervescent with its seven ascending bubbles. I paid homage to its brilliance by doing a small crop in cut-paper to show how memorably iconic it is. Simple, smart, elegant.

CC This project is about relearning how to think by creating concepts on your own. I have often spent more time on the idea and less on the execution. It's my favorite aspect of our project. The visual is secondary to the solution. I intended to shoot moving bubbles in a glass, but everything changed once I added a spoon. The spoon became engulfed in bubbles like a jewel.

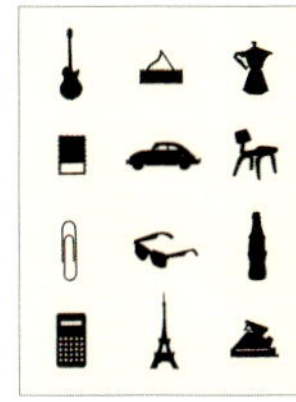
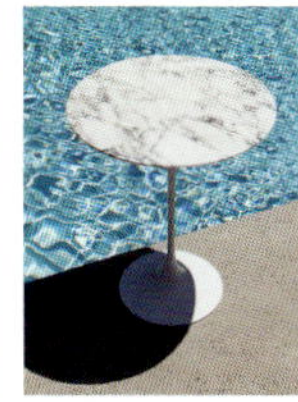
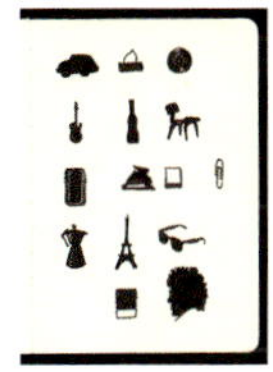
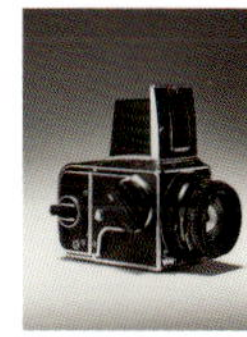
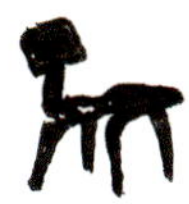
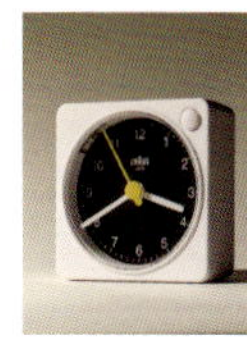

48 Icon

CF Most design icons can be represented in one solid color, with minimal detail—a testament to their classic industrial design. To test my theory, I took a fat brush pen and drew a full page of icons that came to mind. I drew the final twelve with a Micron pen on one sketchbook page.

CC When I hear the word iconic, I think first of timeless pieces in industrial and furniture design. I chose the classic side table designed by Eero Saarinen in 1956. Its iron tulip base creates the perfect shape, complemented by the simple white marble top. I wake up every morning to see this table. Simple design will always remain iconic.

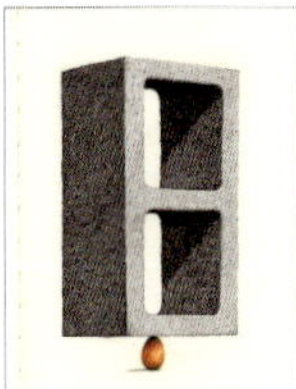
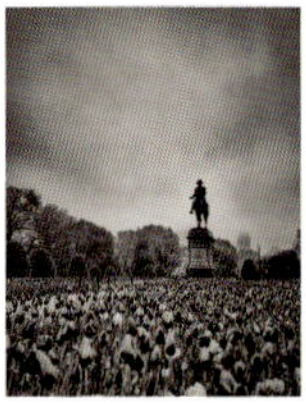
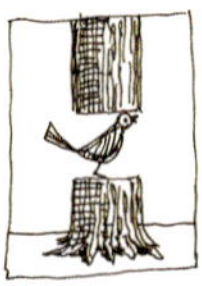
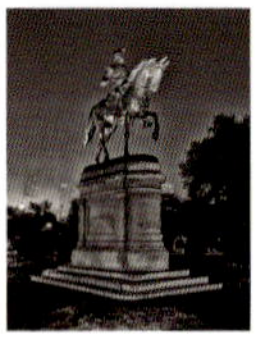
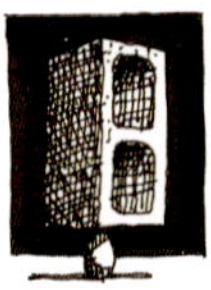

49 Strength

CF In a battle for strength over size, the egg is a champion. Due to the shell's distribution of weight, it has enormous "compressive strength"—the degree to which an object can withstand force before breaking. Vertically, the tiny egg can support 100 to 300 lbs. This was the perfect demo of strength.

CC While visiting my daughter, I saw a statue of George Washington in Boston's Public Gardens. He was under a stormy sky, but very much in command. I loved finding a subject rather than creating a still life for a change. I prefer not to specialize. I was told in a post-college interview that I would never succeed unless I focused on one genre. Why would anyone want to do that?

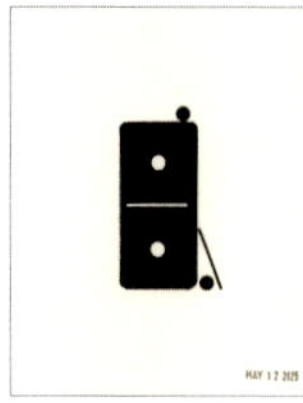
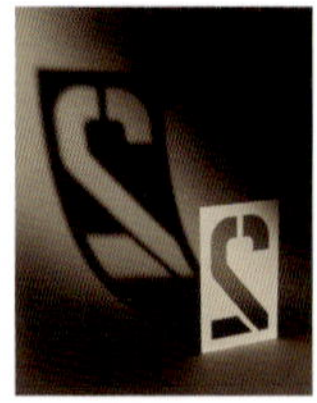
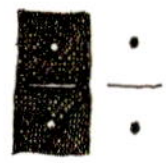
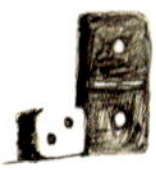
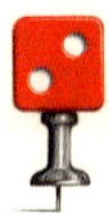
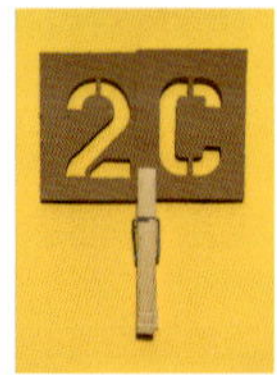

50 Two

CF Dominoes and dice are beautiful counting systems based on a language of dots. Their simple, visual arrangements instantly communicate a value. I chose the domino because it says so much with so little. I cut it out of paper—four pieces in total. By including the line and extracted holes in the composition, we see the domino in an entirely new landscape.

CC I wanted to create an image that could have been done in the 1920s. Something that Man Ray might have imagined. Playing with numbers and projections felt right.

See also runner-up pg. 123

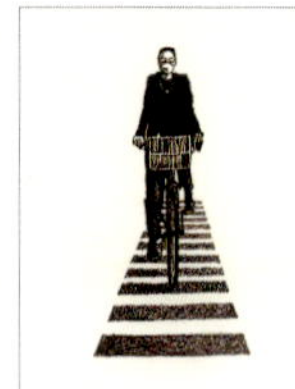
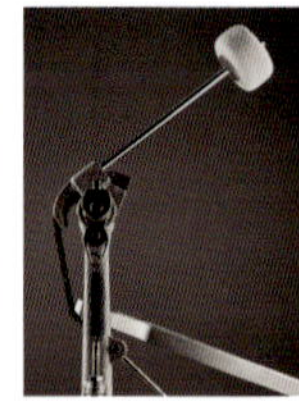
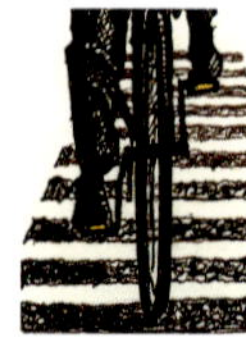
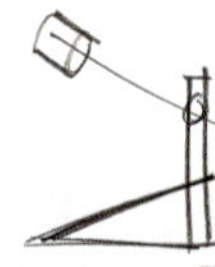
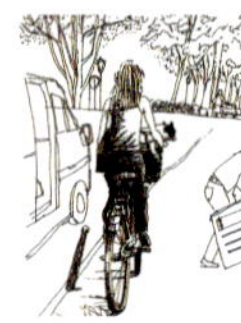

51 Pedal

CF I love photographing cyclists, then sketching them. I drew this cyclist I photographed in Tokyo last year. Dressed entirely in gray and black, she wore a mask and headed straight at me in the crosswalk. Her basket held a bolt of Marimekko fabric, its stripes running perpendicular to the stripes on the crosswalk. There was not a spot of color except for the two orange reflectors on the pedals. She was graphically perfect.

CC A drum pedal's mechanical parts seem so basic. I like all of the angles it creates, from the foot pedal to the felt striker.

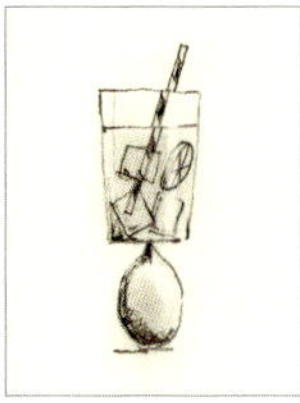
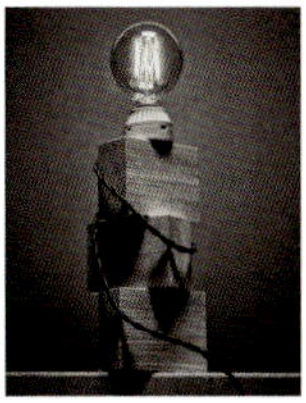
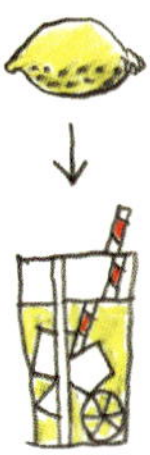
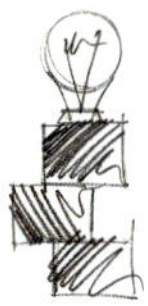
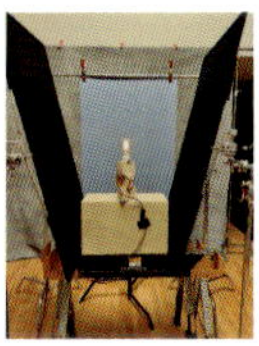

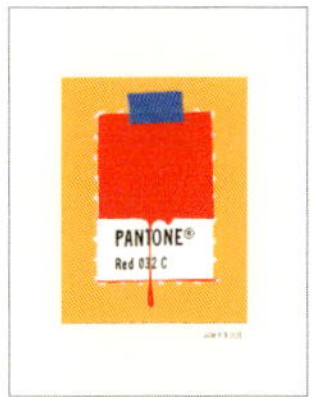

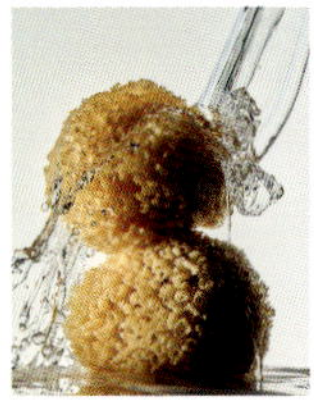
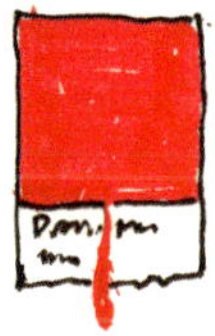
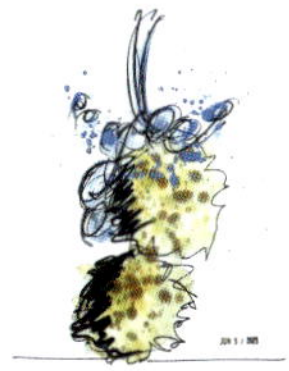

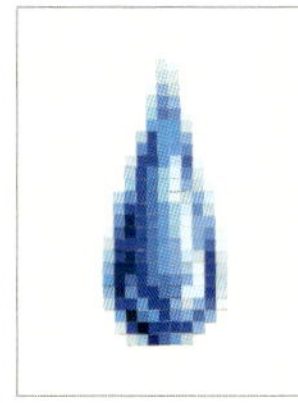
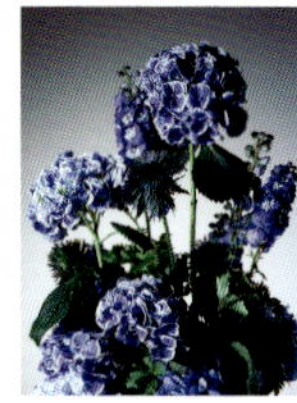
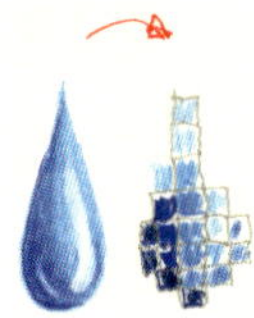
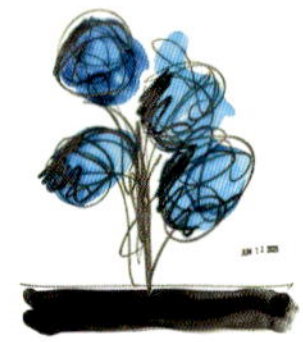

52 Optimistic

CF The saying goes, “If life gives you lemons, make lemonade.” Ideas thrive when working with what you have, not what you don’t have. This includes whatever amount of talent, skill, money, support, or ambition you posess. You have to be optimistic—to believe in endless possibilities.

CC With AI invading every aspect of creativity, I wanted to create a timeless image paying homage to the great photographers of the past. It had to be in black and white, it had to be a studio still-life composition, and it had to have grit. It also had to be an idea I created without any influence from modern technology. Nothing is more rewarding or satisfying than ideas conceived in your own brain.

53 Saturated

CF I love color, especially saturated color. I’m first drawn to red, followed by chrome yellow, then blue. This piece pays homage to the days of print and my favorite PMS color—Red 032. I cut a supersized PMS chip from PMS paper and composed it with the other two primary colors. An over-saturated red!

CC I knew this one had to be a sponge with a water splash. My concept was, “How much water can a sponge hold?” I enjoy creating still lifes with everyday objects presented differently.

54 Blue

CF Blue is a great word because it’s both a color and an emotional state. I sketched a blue tear but I wanted to present it in a more graphically interesting way. So, I pixelated it by building it from 179 quarter-inch blue squares cut from PMS chips. A total value experiment.

CC I chose to go simple. I asked my favorite florist to create an organic arrangement by using only blue flowers that she could find at the famed LA Flower Market.

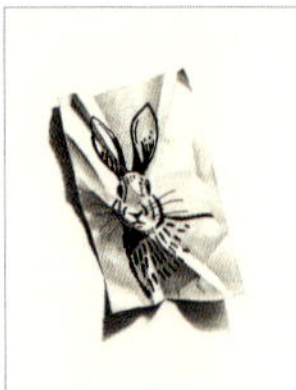

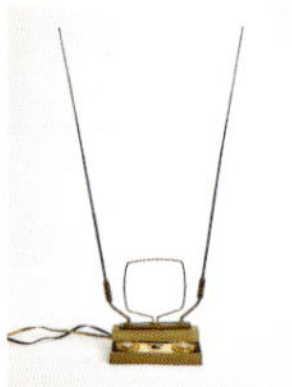

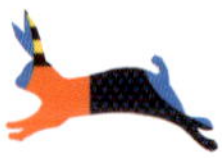

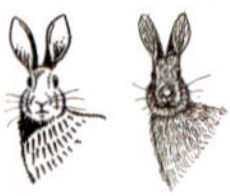

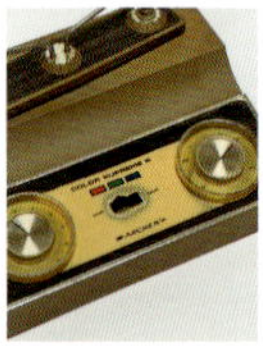

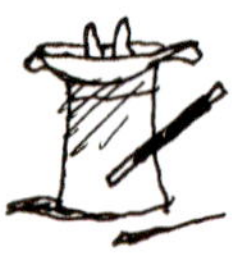

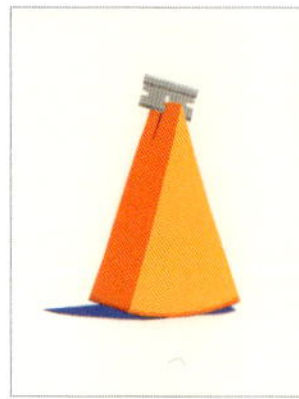

55 Rabbit

CF After a couple failed attempts, I performed a little trompe l'oeil trick to make it more interesting—draw a discarded drawing. A tip of the hat to Craig's crumpled paper in 11 (Paper) and 38 (Note). Ideas are like magic, one moment they're here, next moment they're gone!

CC As a kid growing up in the '70s, there was no cable and every home had one of these on top of their console televisions. We would spin the antenna (nicknamed "rabbit ears") around, trying to achieve a better picture, which was mediocre at best. I didn't try to light the Archer Color Supreme 3 in any way that would bring attention to it. I wanted to document it as a lost artifact from a past generation.

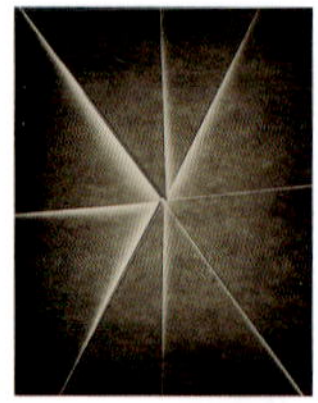

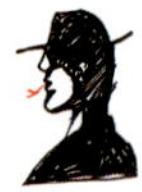

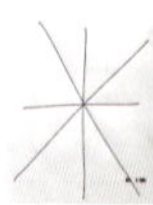

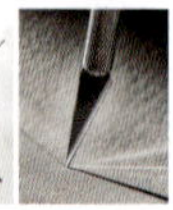

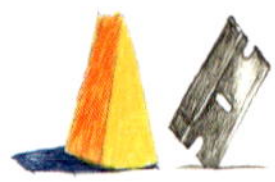

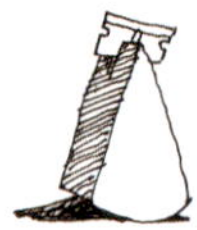

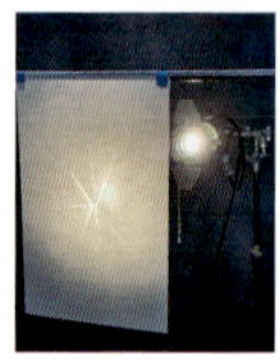

56 Sharp

CF I looked at sharp knives, tongues, and the iconic single-edged razor blade. They all felt too obvious, but sharp cheese didn't. It was sharp in taste and form. However, once I cut the cheese from paper, it fell flat. Fortunately, my earlier razor blade was the perfect foil—metal meets dairy.

CC My first idea came from the hundreds of #11 Exacto blades I went through in art school. The second idea came to me in my sleep: cut a piece of paper with one singular center point and backlight it with one of my favorite lights, the "Mole-Richardson InBetweenie Solarspot." It's a simple Fresnel tungsten light. There is still something very sharp about tungsten light.

Runner-ups

23/2 Time

25/2 Wind

30/2 Cold

32/2 Level

33/2 Fuit

40/2 Quiet

45/2 Vessel

50/2 Two

Craig Cutler

Craig Cutler has operated his photography studio since 1987 to the present. He is commissioned worldwide for editorial, advertising, and corporate assignments. Craig lives and works in Santa Monica, California.

Craig's meticulous combination of craft and style brings an element of art to his work as a director and photographer. Conceptual thinking lays the foundation for his approach as a director and photographer.

At the time of this book's publication, Craig's exhibition titled *Collective Knowledge from Our Changing World* is on view at the Natural History Museum of Los Angeles.

Recent awards include the Cannes Lions Grand Prix, *Graphis* Platinum Photography Award, *Communication Arts* and *American Photography* annuals.

craigcutler.com

Craig Frazier

Craig Frazier has been a designer and illustrator since 1978. His work is recognized internationally for its wit, surprise and simplicity. He is commissioned worldwide for editorial, advertising, and corporate assignments. Craig lives and works in Mill Valley, California.

He is a frequent contributor to *The New York Times* and business publications such as *Harvard Business Review* and *The Wall Street Journal*. He has an extensive roster of corporate clients, including the US Postal Service, for which he has designed seven postage stamps.

Craig published his second monograph, *Drawn* (Goff Books), in January of 2024 following his first monograph, *The Illustrated Voice* (Graphis Press) in 2003. He is also the author and illustrator of twelve children's books.

craigfrazier.com

Acknowledgments

We would like to express our deepest gratitude to the people who have supported and helped bring this project and book to life.

—CC & CF

Liz Bagala. Thank you, Liz, for being the keeper of the secret words and dutifully dealing us our weekly assignment. Thank you also for your assistance in building and maintaining our website (2craigs.com) and our Instagram.

PRINT. Thank you, *PRINT,* and your devoted staff for supporting our project since day one. Thank you Debbie Millman, Amelia Nash, Kim Tidwell, Charlotte Beach, Zachary Petit, Laura Des Enfants, and Deborah Aldrich, for your words, referrals, and promotion of *Project 2 Craigs*.

Joe Morse. Thank you, Joe, for your insightful and articulate analysis of this project. You have lifted the hood on a deeply personal project and identified its relevance to today's creative world.

Kim Tidwell. Thank you, Kim, for your deft editorial skills, appreciation of this project, and knowledge of the subject. Your contribution to the tone and authenticity of our story will ensure its greatest reach.

Gordon Goff. Thank you, Gordon, for your immediate acceptance and support, and for throwing your team behind its speedy publication. You have enabled a meaningful record of *Project 2 Craigs* in design history.

Jake Anderson. Thank you, Jake, for your expertise and steady hand in getting this book off to press and into the hands of the public in short order.

Adrienne Bell. Thank you, Adrienne, for pressing the shutter on my portrait for team Cutler. *-CF*

Goff Books
Novato, California
Published by Goff Books, an Imprint of ORO Editions
Gordon Goff: Publisher

www.goffbooks.com
info@goffbooks.com

Author: Craig Cutler and Craig Frazier
Photographs by Craig Cutler
Illustrations by Craig Frazier
Book design by Craig Frazier
Foreword by Joe Morse
Managing Editor: Jake Anderson
Edited by Kim Tidwell

10 9 8 7 6 5 4 3 2 1 First Edition

ISBN: 978-1-966515-44-9

Color Separations and Printing: ORO Editions Inc.
Printed in China.

Goff Books makes a continuous effort to minimize the overall carbon footprint of its publications. As part of this goal, Goff Books, in association with Global ReLeaf, arranges to plant trees to replace those used in the manufacturing of the paper produced for its books. Global ReLeaf is an international campaign run by American Forests, one of the world's oldest nonprofit conservation organizations. Global ReLeaf is American Forests' education and action program that helps individuals, organizations, agencies, and corporationsimprove the local and global environment by planting and caring for trees.